THE ACTING PERSON AND
CHRISTIAN MORAL LIFE

SELECTED TITLES
from the
MORAL TRADITIONS SERIES
James F. Keenan, SJ, series editor

THE ACTING PERSON AND CHRISTIAN MORAL LIFE

Darlene Fozard Weaver

GEORGETOWN UNIVERSITY PRESS
Washington, DC

Library of Congress Cataloging-in-Publication Data

Weaver, Darlene Fozard.
The acting person and Christian moral life / Darlene Fozard Weaver.
p.   cm. — (Moral traditions series)
Includes bibliographical references and index.
ISBN 978-1-58901-772-6 (pbk. : alk. paper)
1. Christian ethics—Catholic authors. 2. Act (Philosophy) I. Title.
BJ1249.W327 2011
241'.042—dc22
2011003843

∞ This book is printed on acid-free paper meeting the requirements of the American National Standard for Permanence in Paper for Printed Library Materials.

15 14 13 12 11   9 8 7 6 5 4 3 2 First printing
Printed in the United States of America

For
Joseph Daniel Weaver
and
Mary Ann Fozard

CONTENTS

ACKNOWLEDGMENTS

As is often the case in academic life, my work on this book was helped and enriched by so many, even as it was interrupted and delayed by much else. The Louisville Institute awarded me a 2001 summer grant that supported my research and writing on sin; fellow summer-grant recipients provided helpful feedback and a collegial environment for reflection. That work evolved into a paper for the Society of Christian Ethics and an article in the *Journal of Religious Ethics*, "Taking Sin Seriously." I am grateful to the *JRE* for allowing me to draw on that material here in chapter 2. The Wabash Center for Teaching and Learning in Theology and Religion also awarded me a 2003 summer grant that supported early work on chapter 4. I thank the Wabash Center and my workshop cohort for their wisdom, hospitality, and humor. I am grateful to remain in contact with a number of colleagues from our group.

The Center of Theological Inquiry in Princeton, NJ, welcomed me as a member-in-residence during a sabbatical leave from 2004 to 2005. Here, too, I found an intellectually rigorous and warm group of fellow members. The financial and collegial assistance I received allowed me to revise chapters already in progress and to research and draft chapter 5. I am grateful to have found several enduring conversation partners there. The New Wine, New Wineskins group of young moral theologians invited me to write a paper for their inaugural conference years ago, which was subsequently published with other conference papers; I gratefully acknowledge that chapter 3 is a revised and expanded version of that paper, "Intimacy with God and Self-Relation in the World." I thank my fellow moral theologians for their insight and encouragement. I presented portions of chapter 6 at a meeting of the Society of Christian Ethics, where I received valuable feedback and stimulating discussion of the work. I am grateful for the sabbatical leave that Villanova University granted me and for various formal opportunities Villanova afforded to share work in progress. In all these settings and more, so many colleagues—Catholic, Protestant, and Jewish, theologians and philosophers—have offered feedback on work in progress. I give thanks for all their help.

I thank Jim Keenan and Richard Brown for their interest in and support for my project. I appreciate the feedback two anonymous reviewers offered. I have tried to heed their advice. My graduate assistant Siobhan Riley helped with the editing and indexing of the manuscript. I am grateful for the friends whose companionship and conversation enrich my life. Jill Rollet and Brett Wilmot have shared many meals and much laughter with me and my family over the years. Sarah-Vaughan Brakman has shared work, wisdom, and the journey into motherhood with me. Gretchen Bernatowicz is my oldest friend; her loyalty and kindness and long-standing presence in my life are blessings to me. Pia Altieri has been an unfailingly supportive, intellectually stimulating, and wise friend. Special thanks go to Rev. Mark S. Begly and to Sr. Joan Riethmiller, SSJ, for their wisdom and care, which have shaped my thinking and so much more.

I am privileged again to have an opportunity to thank my family. My siblings, in-laws, nieces, and nephews bring such joy to my life. My sister Rachel is also my friend and hero. My husband Sean and our boys Jack, Nathan, and Joseph are the great blessings of my life. I am grateful for their encouragement, their patience, their readiness to play, and their love. I love each of you and I love us all together. I dedicate this book to Joseph, born only one month before I sent the final version of this manuscript to the publisher. I am so very grateful to be mom to this darling boy. He is a gift to us all.

I also dedicate the book to my mother, Mary Ann Fozard. She is truly a remarkable woman. She sets a daily example of faith and courage, kindness and generosity, humor and grace. I wish I were more like her. More than anyone, my mother instilled in me an awareness of God's intimate nearness. A memory from my childhood is a case in point. When I was in elementary school I played on my school's basketball team. My mother faithfully attended my games. She was an ideal fan, such a vocal cheerleader for the whole team, unable to contain her excitement even though athletic competitions among ten-year-olds aren't exactly electrifying. She rang a cowbell during the games and was so recognized and beloved for creating a fun and supportive environment that children from opposing teams would approach her and ask her to ring her bell for them. She always said yes. One game, during what was for me a rare moment of promise playing offense, I dribbled the ball down the court, hoping to get a shot at the basket. As I did so I could hear my mother shouting for me. She didn't yell, "Go, Darlene," or "Shoot! Shoot!" but "God is with you! God is with you!" For all that you are and all you have given, Mom, I am grateful. I love you.

Finally, I gratefully acknowledge permission to use the following material:

Excerpts from *Gilead* by Marilynne Robinson. Copyright © 2004 by Marilynne Robinson. Reprinted by permission of Farrar, Straus and Giroux, LLC, and Virago, an imprint of Little, Brown Book Group. Excerpts from *Silence* by Shusaku Endo. Copyright © 1969 by Monumenta Nipponica. Reprinted by permission of Taplinger Publishing Co., Inc., Peter Owen Ltd., and Chinmoku © 1966, The Heirs of Shusaku Endo.

INTRODUCTION

This book describes the person as a moral agent acting in relation to God. It depicts the acting person within an overarching theological context of sinful estrangement from and gracious reconciliation in God. To describe the way persons negotiate their relationships with God in and through their involvement with others and the world, the book develops its argument under the rubrics of intimacy with God, fidelity to God, and truthfulness before God. It discusses the meaning of intimacy with God with regard to the person's self-relation in order to render the truth that we live, move, and have our being in God. The notion of intimacy helpfully captures and conveys the intrinsic theological significance of our acting. God creates us for and wills our perfection in intimate relation with him.

In our acting we embody and negotiate our free response to God's self-offer. Moral acting is therefore fittingly understood as a matter of fidelity to God. This fidelity (or its opposite) takes shape in the person's involvement with the creaturely goods that God gives for our flourishing in God and with one another. The way we pursue, realize, neglect, or violate these goods—both willingly and unwittingly—impacts us in our multiple relations with God, self, and others. Hence our efforts to name moral actions ought to proceed from and to deepen truthful existence before God. If we are to name our actions truthfully, our naming needs to reflect how they do or do not correspond with the reality of the world under God, including the reality of our created nature, alienated in sin and redeemed in Christ. This means that the truthfulness of our moral descriptions, and of Christian ethics more generally, entails a humble recognition of the integrity of and limits to Christian moral life and ethics. As we learn to speak of sin and grace together, we are drawn into a deeper participation in the reconciliation God accomplishes in Jesus Christ and through the gift of the Spirit.

This argument unfolds as follows. Chapter 1 argues that Christian ethics has largely shifted from an act-centered approach to a person-centered approach. It begins by sketching early Christian moral tradition's roots in penitential practices and the treatment of human actions in manuals of moral theology. Then it identifies general features of recent work in Christian ethics that may justly be considered person centered. Recent trends and debates in Catholic and Protestant ethics either exhibit a standing inattention to moral actions or pay them a curiously nontheological attention. A notable exception to this inattention is a protracted debate in late twentieth-century Catholic moral theology between traditionalists and revisionists regarding moral action. The chapter argues that this debate is preoccupied with issues of moral culpability. Such (in)attention to moral actions courts several problems, including an unfitting agnosticism about the theological significance of human actions and an ironic susceptibility to charges of moral subjectivism.

We then turn to sin, not because sin is the best or most appropriate starting point for theological anthropology, but because the historical relation between moral act analysis and sin continues to influence Christian ethics. Contemporary Christian ethics either neglects the language of sin altogether or tends to construe sin as a power affecting us and the world, or as a basic orientation of the person away from God. A common characteristic of recent theologies of sin is their neglect of sins. This neglect contributes to the unfitting theological agnosticism explored here, undermines the cogency of theologies of sin, and unwittingly permits determinations of moral culpability to govern Christian ethical reflection on persons and moral actions. Chapter 2 argues that the irreducibly theological character of sin permits us to ask after the theological significance of human actions in ways that are not limited to determinations of moral culpability. Such attention alerts us to the historical, particular, and provisional character of human actions.

Chapter 3 explores the connections among particular moral actions, the agent's moral identity, and the significance of those actions for the agent's relationship with God. It argues that, since God creates us for intimacy with him, the person's moral willing and acting involve her in the world of goods that God authors and negotiate her response to God, the origin and end of her freedom. Therefore, particular moral actions merit more attention in Christian ethics than they currently receive. To advance this argument the chapter considers local debates in Roman Catholic ethics regarding fundamental option theory as well as understandings of moral action and personal identity in narrative and virtue ethics.

Chapter 4 forwards an account of human actions in terms of our intentional involvements with creaturely goods. By our moral actions we involve ourselves with material and relational goods in ways that form our wills and contribute to the gain or loss of God in the depths of our self-relation. The moral significance of our actions centrally concerns our fidelity to God. The chapter considers debates between revisionist and traditionalist Catholic ethicists about the object of human choice in moral actions and then explores issues of freedom and responsibility in a world marked by social sin. We thus gain a deeper purchase on the question chapter 3 explored, the import of particular actions for the person's relationship with God.

Chapter 5 explicates the sin of falsehood (as unbelief, self-evasion, and irreverence) and contrasts falsehood with the gift of truthfulness before God. Truthfulness before God enables confession of Christ's lordship and one's sinfulness, gratitude in response to God, and charity toward God's creatures. This account of truthfulness normatively governs the moral practice of naming human actions. If we are to name our actions truthfully, our naming needs to reflect how they do or do not correspond with the reality of the world under God, including the reality of our created nature, corrupted by sin and redeemed in Christ.

Chapter 6 concludes the book's argument with an account of Christian life as our ongoing reconciliation in God. It discusses forgiveness and its relationship to reconciliation. When we forgive we hold someone accountable for her wrongdoing but reframe that wrongdoing so that it no longer determines future relations on terms of alienation, resentment, and the like. Forgiveness makes a new future possible without denying or condoning the past. This new future does not automatically involve reconciliation. Reconciliation encompasses forgiveness but also exceeds it. The chapter turns to the problem of forgiving oneself to explore the import of wrongdoing for the person's moral identity and future relations with God and others. We learn to live as ones forgiven in the church, so the chapter considers ecclesial contexts and then concludes by suggesting the significance of faith in God's reconciling work for Christian ethics. This theology of reconciliation makes our endeavors truthfully to name moral actions a penitent, shared practice in which we come to realize our involvements with sin as we grow in awareness that we are graciously drawn into mutual abiding in God and one another.

CHAPTER ONE

PERSONS AND ACTIONS IN CHRISTIAN ETHICS

Scripture refers to many specific sorts of human actions, often by way of encouraging or forbidding them. The Decalogue, for example, forbids actions like idol worship, murder, adultery, and bearing false witness against one's neighbor. The books of Leviticus and Deuteronomy address a wide variety of human actions, including food preparation, robbery, treatment of boils, and remission of debts. In the letter to the Ephesians Saint Paul writes, "Thieves must give up stealing; rather let them labor and work honestly with their own hands, so as to have something to share with the needy. Let no evil talk come out of your mouths, but only what is useful for building up, as there is need, so that your words may give grace to those who hear" (Eph 4:28–30 [New Revised Standard Version]). He instructs the Romans to "contribute to the needs of the saints; extend hospitality to strangers. Bless those who persecute you; bless and do not curse them. Rejoice with those who rejoice, weep with those who weep. Live in harmony with one another; do not be haughty, but associate with the lowly; do not claim to be wiser than you are. Do not repay anyone evil for evil" (Rom 12:13–17). To the Colossians he says, "Do not lie to one another" (Col 3:9). The Galatians are told, "Now the works of the flesh are obvious: fornication, impurity, licentiousness, idolatry, sorcery, enmities, strife, jealousy, anger, quarrels, dissensions, factions, envy, drunkenness, carousing, and things like these" (Gal 5:19–21).

Are these actions, and the many others treated in the Bible, similarly encouraged or forbidden for us today? It is commonplace to note that we inhabit vastly different historical and social contexts than the ones in which these texts were authored and to conclude—with good reason—that scriptural endorsement or disapproval of specific moral actions does not in every case translate into moral approval or disapproval of those same actions in our time. Granting the difficulties of gleaning practical moral direction from scripture, the point is that God's action on behalf of Israel and in Jesus Christ has normative implications, that some faithful, grateful, fitting response is to be made and cannot be made apart from the way we live, behave, and conduct ourselves.

Of course, scripture not only enjoins and forbids specific moral behaviors; it also—frequently—refers to morality as a matter of interiority. Notice that the verses from Galatians 5 that I quoted above identify more than "actions," understood as discrete behaviors or deeds performed by a human agent. Jealousy, anger, and envy refer to emotions or dispositions to act in particular ways.[1] Impurity, licentiousness, enmities, strife, and factions do not name actions as such but rather qualities of actions, or personal and relational states occasioned by actions. In the Gospel of Mark Jesus distinguishes the command of God from human tradition and reveals the Pharisees' hypocritical preoccupation with external observance of the law. Jesus assures his listeners that evil does not come from outside a person. "For it is from within, from the human heart, that evil intentions come: fornication, theft, murder, adultery, avarice, wickedness, deceit, licentiousness, envy, slander, pride, folly. All these evil things come from within, and they defile a person" (Mk 7:21–23). Hence, anger toward one's brother counts as murder, and lusting after another in one's heart counts as adultery (Mt 5:21–22, 27–28).

What does this interiorization of morality mean when it comes time to evaluate specific sorts of actions? Perhaps we should not begin with or linger over them and devote ourselves instead to the more fundamental and encompassing matter of what sorts of persons and communities God calls us to be. After all, morally good persons and communities can be counted upon to do what is fitting, to conduct themselves well: "No good tree bears bad fruit, nor again does a bad tree bear good fruit; for each tree is known by its own fruit. Figs are not gathered from thorns, nor are grapes picked from a bramble bush. The good person out of the good treasure of the heart produces good, and the evil person out of evil treasure produces evil; for it is out of the abundance of the heart that the mouth speaks" (Lk 6:43–45). It would seem that character is of primary moral importance and that consideration of particular moral actions or moral norms should be a derivative task for Christian ethics.

Looking to scripture to understand the relative importance of actions in the moral life, we cannot help but note that the New Testament also proclaims our freedom from the law and does so in a way that muddles the religious significance of moral actions. Jesus, to the consternation of the Pharisees, did not rebuke his disciples for collecting and eating grain on the Sabbath, and he healed on the Sabbath (Lk 6:1–10). Importantly, Jesus prefaces his healing with a rhetorical question aimed at the Pharisees—is it better to do good or evil on the Sabbath? To save life or destroy it? Freedom from the law is not freedom from moral obligation. Clearly we are obliged by God. We must answer his gracious initiative, and this answer is one we give with our lives. This answer does not correlate neatly with observance of human moral laws. What God asks of us evidently sometimes violates

(Lk 6:1–10), sometimes exceeds (Mt 5:21–22), and sometimes means keeping (1 Cor 8:1–13) human moral laws. Consider Saint Paul's discussion of circumcision in Romans 2:13–29. If the Gentiles, who do not have the law, nevertheless do what the law requires, they are really members of God's chosen people, and their spiritual circumcision is worth more than a literal circumcision. The Christian's freedom from the law is in fact a summons to act in faithful response to God, who is the source of morality.

Notwithstanding the moral importance of our interior lives and the complex relation of moral obligation and moral laws, scripture undoubtedly regards the way we treat others as a barometer for our relationship with God. The concept of *sedaqah* is central to the Hebrew scriptures or First Testament. It means justice; the particular character of this justice is determined historically by God's action on behalf of Israel. Because God delivered Israel from oppression, a just response forbids them from oppressing aliens and enjoins them to care for those who are vulnerable (Ex 22:21–23). Our actions toward others directly bear on our relationship with God. Indeed, as Matthew 25:31–46 puts it, when we feed the hungry and clothe the naked and visit prisoners we do these things to Christ himself. This is not a matter of works righteousness, the mistaken belief that we earn our salvation by our good works. It is a matter of fidelity and truthfulness. To confess that Christ is Lord while willfully persisting in a manner of life at odds with the gospel is to betray the Lord one confesses, to live as a liar. "If a brother or sister is naked and lacks daily food, and one of you says to them, 'Go in peace; keep warm and eat your fill,' and yet you do not supply their bodily needs, what is the good of that? So faith by itself, if it has no works, is dead" (Jas 2:15–17). Our actions are the sign and sacrament of our knowledge of and love for God so that "by this we may be sure that we know him, if we obey his commandments" (1 Jn 2:3).

Given all this one might reasonably expect that the work of Christian ethics includes making thoughtful and resolutely *theological* moral judgments about particular sorts of human actions. Yet this is not the case for much of contemporary Christian ethics. In some quarters ethicists intentionally eschew analysis of moral actions even when addressing practical moral issues. Rather than morally evaluate particular sorts of sexual acts, for example, ethicists will point to qualities of morally good sexual relations. There are good reasons to do so, morally and theologically, but costs as well. In other quarters ethicists may analyze specific moral actions very closely but quite apart from sustained theological reflection. In these cases theology becomes mere window dressing to what are essentially natural law arguments. Still others ponder moral action by referring it to the person's inner self-determination or fundamental orientation (as in prominent strands of Roman Catholic ethics) and/or narrative and virtue-based accounts of human agency

7

(as in prominent strands of Protestant ethics and a growing number of Catholic ethics).

These approaches helpfully resist reducing ethics to the resolution of moral quandaries or the formulation of moral prohibitions. They also ward off premature moral judgments about persons on the basis of their acts. But for a variety of reasons these approaches display an undue agnosticism about the import of particular actions for the person's relationship with God. Consequently, they do not adequately understand the acting person as one who, by virtue of God's prior offer of grace and the reflexive character of her moral acting, comes into or avoids greater intimacy with God and willingly (if sometimes unwittingly) involves herself with social and material goods so as to qualify her relationship with God in terms of fidelity or betrayal. Too much focus on the person's inner self-determination or on virtues can also undermine our capacities to describe and name moral actions in ways that refer them to the acting person and to the world God has made and continues to act within. Living truthfully before God includes learning to speak truthfully about moral actions, which in turn requires us to learn how to acknowledge both the gravity of sin and the gratuity of grace.

This book attempts to forward a robustly theological account of how persons simultaneously work out their identities, involve themselves with the fellow creatures and goods this world has to offer, and negotiate their relationship with God, in whom they live and move and have their being. Human beings are made to know and love God. Our acceptance or rejection of God's love for us is a decision we work out over the course of our lives. It is not reducible to our particular actions, but it cannot be separated from them. By our actions we affect ourselves, others, and the world in quite powerful ways. We can make and unmake, build up and destroy, liberate and oppress, heal and wound one another. As we do so we encounter and respond to a God who is intimately near to us and who wishes us to grow into a deeper, more conscious intimacy with him. This requires both our interior transformation and increasing integrity in the way our actions manifest and contribute to this transformation. Fidelity and truthfulness are therefore key to thinking about how we fashion ourselves through our actions in relation to God and neighbor. Christian life is a matter of our ongoing reconciliation in God. So we finally must refer all moral actions to God's redeeming and sanctifying work in Jesus Christ and the Holy Spirit and to the church, where we learn to abide in God and in one another.

This chapter will examine how prominent strands of Christian tradition have construed the relation between persons and their actions and present an overview of the argument that later chapters develop.

CHRISTIAN MORAL TRADITION AS ACT CENTERED

We can better appreciate how contemporary Christian ethics treats (or neglects) moral actions by first considering how earlier Christian, particularly Catholic, moral tradition centered around the moral analysis of acts. Indeed, contemporary Catholic ethics is sometimes referred to as "personalistic" or "person-centered" in contrast to centuries of "act-centered" Catholic moral theology prior to the Second Vatican Council (1962–65).[2] The distinction oversimplifies earlier Catholic moral tradition. Still, it provides a helpful orientation.

John Mahoney's important and influential work *The Making of Moral Theology* traces the tradition's long-standing focus on moral action, and more specifically sins, back to the emergence of auricular confession. Before the sixth century, the sacrament of confession typically occurred publicly and only once in a lifetime. That began to change in Irish monasteries during the sixth century, where younger monks were receiving spiritual direction from their older brethren. These relationships afforded a context of pastoral care so that the discussion of sins was part of a larger commitment to spiritual growth and healing. In this context, private and repeated confessions began to occur. As the monks ministered to people in local villages, the practice of private and more frequent confessions spread among the laity. Handbooks developed, perhaps under the aegis of the Welsh synod, to help priests administer the sacrament.[3] They included questions for the priest to ask a penitent and suggested appropriate penances for specific sins. Consider this excerpt from the *Penitential of Cummean*:

> 18. He who eats the skin of his own body, that is, a scab, or the vermin which are called lice, and also he who eats or drinks his own excreta—with imposition of hands of his bishop he shall do penance for an entire year on bread and water.
>
> 19. One who instead of baptism blesses a little infant shall do penance for a year apart from the number or atone with bread and water. 20. If, however, the infant dies having had such blessing only, that homicide shall do penance according to the judgement of a council.
>
> 21. Small boys who strike one another shall do penance for seven days; but if (they are) older, for twenty days; if (they are) adolescents, they shall do penance for forty days.[4]

The monks eventually brought the handbooks with them to the European continent, and the practice of private and more frequent confession spread there as well.

Penitential handbooks proliferated. While they generated some real opposition among members of the Church's hierarchy, their pastoral success and their practical usefulness in helping to train a woefully uneducated priesthood led various synods to standardize and authorize summaries as regular confession became the general rule.[5]

Mahoney articulates a now-standard set of complaints about the penitentials, criticisms that apply to preconciliar Catholic act analysis in general.[6] To begin, preconciliar moral theology implies an atomic picture of the moral life. That is, rather than treat the totality of the person and her moral life, it focuses on the moral (de)merit of individual acts, particularly in relation to divine law.[7] Moreover, as Mahoney charges, correlating sins with punishments that are doled out and supervised by the Church makes it difficult for sinners to take responsibility for their own moral lives. Further, the line of questioning made the priest into an expert, thereby fostering in the sinner a sense that she could not trust herself to know what she was really doing and why. Presumably, the questions that penitential handbooks suggested the priest ask a penitent were to foster in the sinner an awareness of her interior life. But, because this examination of conscience was undertaken within a situation that focused on objective actions and their correction, the transformation of the penitent's passions and intentions was left aside in favor of a more behavioral approach. This act-centered approach encouraged scrupulosity and moral rigorism. Says Mahoney, "It was the Church's growing tradition of moral theology which was itself heavily responsible for increasing men's weakness and moral apprehension, with the strong sense of sin and guilt which it so thoroughly strove to inculcate or reinforce, and the humiliations and punishments with which it drove its message home."[8]

Further, Mahoney claims that moral theology prior to Vatican II "has invested numerous actions with an inherent capacity for moral self-commitment which they could not bear, and has become fascinated by concepts often in a complete divorce from reality. It has, indeed, almost domesticated and trivialized sin.... And in its attaching the element of sin so readily in the past to positive Church laws on frequently trivial matters as a sanction to their observance, it has only helped to devalue the currency, and done little to engender and foster a healthy respect for real sin."[9] Preconciliar moral theology inflates the significance of particular actions for the person's identity and relationship with God and in doing so trivializes the meaning of sin. The penitential handbooks encouraged a preoccupation with sins, which ironically deflected penitents from growing in a real understanding of sin, forgiveness, and personal moral responsibility.[10]

This preoccupation with sins continued throughout Catholic moral tradition prior to Vatican II. Certain periods do display a more expansive, scripturally based, and positive approach to the moral life, including the Scholasticism that developed in the early Middle Ages. Scholastic theology developed in university contexts, and as James Keenan notes this theology was more attentive to scripture and more teleological than the theological perspective of the penitentials. Scholastic "moral theology specifically studied humanity as responding lovingly to the initiative of God."[11] In the university context theology no longer originated out of nor aimed primarily at pastoral concerns; it developed as an academic discipline, differentiated from other fields of study and governed by its own principles, yet in conversation with other, including secular, disciplines and cultural institutions. In this context Thomas Aquinas wrote his *Summa theologiae*, which treats, among other things, the human person in relation to God as his final end, the nature of human action, law, and virtue. Aquinas treats morality within a larger theological framework of *exitus et reditus*; given that humans are creatures made by and meant for God, morality concerns the way our free acts are ordered or disordered in relation to our proximate end of human flourishing and our final end, God.

During the Middle Ages various factors led to moral theological literature that was increasingly under the control of the magisterium, increasingly systematic, and increasingly juridical.[12] One factor was the rise of papal power, thanks to Pope Gregory VII's assertion of papal superiority over the Church and in secular matters. Another factor was the emergence of jurisprudence. To be sure, moral theology's indebtedness to forensic rubrics has roots in the biblical use of legal categories to describe God's dealing with humanity, as well as the apostolic authority to bind and loose (Mt 16:19, 18:18).[13] But prior to Gregory VII's declaration of papal supremacy there were no professional judges or lawyers and no hierarchical court system; law was principally local in character and was embedded in customs and social structures. Papal rule more or less rested on the Justinian Code (529–34) and a large number of disparate decrees issued over the centuries. These decrees were collected and systematized before and during Gregory VII's papacy and constituted the beginning of canon law. Another factor was the creation of the Easter duty, the duty to confess sins and receive Eucharist at least once a year, issued by the Fourth Lateran Council (1215). The Dominican and Franciscan orders developed manuals of moral theology to assist clergy in hearing confessions and assigning penance for sins. "Thus, despite the integrated theology of the scholastics, those involved in the moral lives of ordinary Christians were almost entirely concerned with matters of sin."[14]

Moral theology migrated again, from universities to the newly emerging seminary system that developed in the late sixteenth century as part of the Counter-Reformation. The aim of training priests to administer the sacraments continued to affect the substance and tone of moral theology. As seminary textbooks, manuals of moral theology yoked moral theology firmly to ecclesiastical authority and over the centuries increasingly to papal authority. They remained preoccupied with law, whether in their defense of the tradition during the Counter-Reformation, or in the throes of the probabilism debates (a protracted controversy concerning when laws and theological opinions bound conscience and when they did not), or following the 1918 revision of canon law.[15] After Pope Leo XIII published his encyclical *Aeterni patris* in 1879, the manuals became part of the neo-scholasticism and neo-Thomism Leo encouraged by urging renewed study of Thomas Aquinas.

Manualist moral theology dominated Catholic moral reflection until the time of Vatican II. Over these four centuries the manuals did evolve, but as John Gallagher notes, certain structural and substantive features remained constant.[16] Structurally, the manuals treated general moral theology (the nature of the human act, conscience, law, sin), special moral theology (particular sins, identified either as violations of the Decalogue or as acts contrary to the virtues), and canon law requirements regarding the sacraments.[17] Substantively, the manuals were deeply indebted to the theology of Thomas Aquinas, yet their theological scope was more narrowly concerned with what was relevant for assisting priests in resolving cases of conscience. Hence, although their moral theology is undeniably teleological— the moral life concerns the person's relation to her natural and supernatural ends—the focus falls on conduct and actions contrary to these ends, that is, sins. Says Charles Curran, the manuals "never considered the important role of grace in the moral life."[18]

Of course, Catholic moral tradition is much broader than the successive literary genres stretching from the penitentials to the manuals. Monastic and mystical traditions enriched Catholic moral understanding in a variety of ways. J. Philip Wogaman describes the moral "paradoxes" of these traditions.[19] They blend a concern for humility with ideals of perfectionism and spiritual progress. They exhibit spiritual-ethical elitism even as they embody and express service to the whole church. Monasticism and mysticism cast discipleship as a way of life rather than a moral code, and yet they deeply value works of spiritual discipline and devotion. Solitude and renunciation of self and world make up one set of values, even as community, love for neighbor, and engagement with the world count as other values one can discern among monastics and mystics.

Catholic moral tradition also includes other forms of disseminating church teaching, from papal encyclicals to homilies offered in local parishes, along with a wide variety of practices that express, instantiate, and cultivate Catholic values— for example, devotions, spiritual reading—as well as artistic expressions of Catholic moral vision and commitments, and the many forms of service and social activism conducted by the institutional Church and the Catholic faithful. Nonetheless, there is a great deal of truth in the going story about Vatican II and moral theology. It suggests that moral theology essentially developed as a discipline done by priests and for priests, that it was focused more on sinful actions than on the whole person as a recipient of divine grace, and, moreover, that sin was understood largely in legal terms and with a view to determining how culpable of sin a penitent might be. In the years leading up to Vatican II, a number of alternative approaches to moral theology began to emerge.[20] For instance, Bernard Häring's three-volume *Law of Christ* was thoroughly a Christocentric study that construed the moral life in terms of the person's encounter with Christ. It emphasized the moral centrality of love, the person's awareness of values, and the priority of grace over the law.[21] The characteristics of works like Häring's—their attention to scripture, their broader focus on the person, their emphasis on love and the virtues rather than sin and the law— signal the moral reorientation that Vatican II both called for and itself enacted.

Vatican II called for a renewal of theology in general and made special mention of moral theology. The "Decree on Priestly Training" (*Optatum totius*) urges a "perfecting of moral theology" by means of scriptural nourishment and by integrating theological disciplines more fully.[22] Moral theology, animated by the personalism that characterizes the council's theology, was to illuminate the loftiness of the faithful's calling and their obligation to bear fruit in charity for the life of the world.[23] It is worth noting that this renewal, while taking for granted that the discipline of moral theology is yoked to a seminary context and priestly formation, ultimately aims at assisting all the faithful. Moreover, rather than fix on determining the moral status of particular actions so as to avoid sin, moral theology has a more positive task, to show the nobility of their call. Following chapter 5 of *Lumen gentium* (the Dogmatic Constitution on the Church) we may say that this call is to nothing short of holiness.[24] Finally, moral theology was to show the moral life as principally a matter of positive obligations, the duty to do good, to bear fruit, to build up the world in the work of love.

Moral theologians responded enthusiastically. Post–Vatican II Catholic ethics exhibits considerable vitality and diverse responses to the council's mandate. Much of this work markedly contrasts the earlier tradition's preoccupation with sins and moral act analysis (though as we will see revisionist and traditionalist ethicists engaged in significant debates regarding moral acts). Postconciliar theology rethinks the aims of ethics and the character of moral life by placing the person front and center. If moral theology is to be adequate it needs to do justice to the person as a whole. This commitment is warranted theologically and philosophically. Theologically it fits the Church's emphasis on Christian life as a response to the call to discipleship. Philosophically it fits growing appreciation for the historical, socially situated, and dynamic character of human life.

Before turning to examples of person-centered ethics, it is important to note that Protestant ethics has never been act-centered in the way that Catholic moral theology has. Neither has it been monolithic, which means that generalizations are inevitably just that. While the focus on moral acts in Catholic ethics has been linked closely to a preoccupation with sins in a way that reduces or trivializes sin, Protestant ethics typically displays an awareness of sin as a power or force that affects people radically. James Gustafson argues that Catholic moral theology's ecclesiastical function in relation to confession, along with its magisterial context and underlying exitus et reditus framework, account for the tradition's focus on moral act analysis. By contrast, Protestant ethics "has been more pedagogical than juridical."[25] The difference strikes deeper than matters of ecclesiastical function or magisterial context. Granting the theological diversity of Protestant ethics, Gustafson nevertheless argues that an alternative paradigm underlies and informs its pedagogical character.

Whereas the exitus et reditus framework underlying Catholic moral theology encouraged attention to specific deviations from the proper end of human life, the Reformers interpreted the human relation to God in terms of trust or its absence. Sin is more basic than sins; it consists in unbelief, contempt of God, a fundamental hostility or refusal to trust in and love God. Sin is thus construed primarily as a religious and not a moral problem, requiring a religious and not a moral answer. Sins are the manifestations or moral fruits of this basic religious problem. Accordingly, for the Reformers "grace was strongly perceived to be mercy, and not so much the rectification, redirection, and fulfillment of nature."[26] The corrective for sin is to change the relationship between God and humanity. The paradigm of trust/distrust versus orientation/disorientation changes the theological context for moral reflection and downgrades the theological or religious seriousness of morality. Moral misconduct does not itself detract from or impede salvation. In the context of trust/distrust, ethics "becomes a matter of describing the motives and the dispositions that faith and grace induce, and the pattern (love of neighbor) in which they issue."[27]

Although Protestant theologians eschew the sort of act analysis that has characterized so much of Catholic ethics, they do, of course, describe the practical relevance of Christian faith and offer moral analyses of and guidance concerning practical moral problems. Martin Luther, whose insistence that we are justified by faith alone proved so momentous for the church, also insisted that Christian faith would issue in good works of love for one's neighbors.[28] According to Luther our works flow from and enact gratitude toward God for God's gracious justification of us. Dietrich Bonhoeffer, concerned that Luther's sola fide was providing cover for complacent Christians, decried a "cheap grace" that assured salvation while ignoring the costs of discipleship and promised Easter without having first to undergo Good Friday.[29] In the late nineteenth and early twentieth centuries the social gospel movement expressed the practical relevance of Christian faith in terms of the Christian responsibility to resolve social ills.[30] Later theologians like Karl Barth, Reinhold Niebuhr, and Paul Tillich would criticize the social gospel movement for its optimism about human capacities and political life and its insufficient attention to sin. Barth in particular criticized the tendency to fit the gospel to liberal Protestantism's perception of the demands of the day. All of these theological perspectives, remarkably different in method and content, nevertheless share the conviction that, though good works do not justify us, Christian faith makes a difference that matters for us as agents.

CONTEMPORARY CHRISTIAN ETHICS AS PERSON CENTERED

While the distinction between act-centered and person-centered ethics is typically applied to describe Catholic moral theology, it is fair to say that contemporary Christian ethics in general is person-centered. Recent work in sexual ethics and virtue ethics shows a wide moral regard for the person as a historically situated, culturally shaped, irreducibly social, dynamic, and embodied moral agent. Regard for the person not only contextualizes but limits what Christian ethicists believe they can say about particular moral actions, especially regarding their religious or theological significance.

Sexual Ethics

Sexual ethics received a great deal of attention in earlier Christian moral tradition, and Christian ambivalence about bodies, pleasure, and sexual relations is well known. Traditional Christian sexual ethics centers moral analysis around the act of heterosexual coitus. This act is taken to be *the* sexual act and is understood to have both procreative and unitive dimensions. The official teaching of the Catholic magisterium is (1) that these two meanings are properly morally realized only within the exclusive and permanent bond of marriage and (2) that it is always morally wrong deliberately to separate these dimensions of the sexual act.[31] Particular sexual and reproductive practices are evaluated with reference to the conjugal act thus understood. Masturbation, artificial contraception, and in vitro fertilization, for example, are judged morally wrong because each involves the intentional separation of those dimensions. Other sorts of arguments attend Catholic moral analyses of particular sexual acts and relationships. *Humanae vitae*, for instance,

not only argues that contraception is intrinsically wrong by virtue of its separation
of the procreative and unitive dimensions of conjugal love, the encyclical argues
against contraception on consequentialist grounds as well, predicting a "general
lowering of morality," men's loss of "respect for the woman," and the danger of
state-coerced contraception.[32]

Criticisms of traditional Christian sexual ethics abound. This ethics primarily is criticized for centering around the act of heterosexual marital coitus. The
tendency to reduce sexual ethics to the investigation of which acts are morally
permissible or not, coupled with the tendency to make those determinations by
assessing them in relation to the conjugal act, courts a physicalism that reduces
the complexity of human sexuality to biological structures and/or discrete physical events. Traditional Christian sexual ethics, critics continue, employs a static
account of human nature (often indebted to scientific claims that are no longer
credible, not to mention misogynist), naively treats the normative significance of
natural givens, and distracts moral attention away from the social and structural
dimensions of moral problems and larger cultural values and meanings. Christine
Gudorf notes that "such a focus implicitly teaches sexual moral minimalism, i.e.,
that virtue in sexuality consists of avoiding these specific sexual acts. This moral
minimalism gives no guidance in or opportunities for reflection on sexual virtue
as the process of constructing sexual relations, genital and non-genital, which are
just, loving, and promotive of individual and social growth."[33] For these and other
reasons, Lisa Cahill reports, "I am not as interested in demarcating specific offenses
against sexual virtue as I am in finding the directions in which sexual value and
happiness generally lie."[34]

Recent work in Christian sexual ethics does of course engage practical moral
issues like cohabitation, divorce and remarriage, contraception, artificial reproductive technologies, and homosexual relations. The person-centered way these
issues are investigated typically involves normative reference points other than or
in addition to the conjugal act.[35] Margaret Farley's *Just Love*, for instance, begins
her investigation of sexual ethics with an account of human sexuality.[36] This involves her asking and answering larger questions about the moral significance of
the body, gender socialization, and the diversity of sexual desire and experience.
For Farley sexual practices and relations are evaluated not with primary and exclusive reference to the act of heterosexual coitus, but in relation to an idea of human
flourishing. The moral question to ask of particular sexual acts is whether they
instantiate a love that does justice to the concrete reality of both the lover and the
beloved.

Farley identifies several norms that help to specify the qualities of just and loving
sex: nonmaleficence, free consent, mutuality, equality, commitment, fruitfulness,

and social justice. Along the way Farley considers the Christian ethical legacy that has shaped the church's thinking about human sexuality, marriage, procreation, and particular sexual practices. She explicitly engages scripture, tradition, secular disciplines, and experience as sources for Christian sexual ethics. While Farley's account of sexuality and her normative framework are conversant with Christian resources, neither is substantively theological. That is, Farley does not provide explicitly theological reasons or warrants for her practical conclusions. The book's overall argument is that many sexual activities and relationships are compatible with human flourishing and capable of instantiating just love. Accordingly, they would fit within a Christian sexual ethic redeemed of its patriarchal and hierarchical tendencies and more engaged with the findings of secular disciplines regarding human sexuality. Presumably, Farley would regard such actions and relations as compatible with growth in personal relation with God, but the book does not consider such questions.[37]

Marvin Ellison argues that heterosexuality and marriage should not provide the framework for sexual ethics. Rather, sexual ethics should be centered around justice. Here, too, his concern is not to evaluate particular sexual behaviors but to provide a larger framework for thinking about the well-being of humans as social and sexual creatures. "Justice includes the moral obligation to promote one another's common decency and to honor our need for intimacy and affection."[38] Justice rules out from the beginning any action or relationship that is abusive or exploitative. "From a justice perspective, it is entirely fitting not to grant special status or moral privilege to heterosexual marriage, but rather to celebrate *all* sexual relations of moral substance whenever they deepen human intimacy and love."[39]

The theological warrants for Ellison's argument are rather general and underdeveloped. He writes, "Loyalty to the God 'of the grace of glory' is the basis of the church's theological and ethical mandate to seek justice passionately, including sexual justice. In accepting this mandate, the church agrees to become a gracious place—a place of hospitality and safety, a kind of 'unoccupied territory' where persons can experience and delight in loving and being loved." Ellison goes on to say, "The moral challenge before the church, then, is this: It must choose between perpetuating a patriarchal ethic of sexual control and gender oppression or pledging its commitment to an ethics of gender justice, of mutuality between women and men, and of respect for sexual diversity." Ellison understands this choice morally to warrant same-sex relationships as well as heterosexual marriages open to additional sexual partners. "Although justice requires relational fidelity—honoring and responding fairly to the demands of a relationship—the precise requirements for maintaining faithfulness cannot be predetermined in any formal fashion."[40] Ellison does not support these practical conclusions, particularly the last, with sustained arguments that follow from his theological premise. Like Farley's larger work, Ellison's argument enlists theology to provide a general moral orientation, but the moral arguments themselves are not substantively theological.

When particular moral practices are analyzed in contemporary Christian sexual ethics, the tendency (except in official Catholic sexual ethics) is not only to consider them in reference to normative relational qualities but also in relation to social contexts. To return to the example of contraception, Amy Laura Hall situates her moral analysis of it in a larger study of American culture and Protestant religious life. In her volume *Conceiving Parenthood: American Protestantism and the Spirit of Reproduction*, Hall links contraception historically to eugenics and larger cultural attitudes regarding domesticity and progress.[41] Theologically she looks to doctrines of creation, salvation, and eschatology rather than an account of the conjugal act. Situating contraception and other moral practices in a larger social framework illumines moral dimensions of contraception and connects it to experiences of kinship, domesticity, parenthood, sex, and family planning that simply go unnoticed or are merely alluded to in slippery-slope warnings of the traditional act-based analysis. Hall's volume is only one example of Christian ethical attempts to refer particular sorts of moral actions to their larger moral contexts.[42]

These person-centered and more socially engaged approaches to sexual ethics are generally widely welcomed, even as significant disagreements about some practical questions continue. Advocates of traditional Christian sexual ethics also make the case for the adequacy of their approaches to the person and characterize this ethics as a countercultural alternative to problematic sexual attitudes, institutions, and practices. Often they fault more revisionist or progressive approaches for failing to reckon with the moral significance of human embodiment as sexually differentiated and human sexuality as having an inherent procreative telos.[43] As we will see in following chapters, these divergent approaches often crystallize in debates wherein each side argues that the other side fails to do justice to the person as an agent and subject by somehow distancing her from her concrete actions.

Virtue Ethics

Virtue ethics is making quite a comeback in Western philosophical and Christian ethics.[44] Rather than ask after the rightness or wrongness of particular actions, virtue ethics asks, "What kind of person ought I to become?" Virtue ethics focuses on character formation, the cultivation of dispositions and habits that dispose one to discern wisely and act well. While much ancient and medieval moral thought in the West dealt with virtue, the modern focus on reason and moral foundations eclipsed issues of character, affect, and communal habit-forming practices in favor of deontological approaches like Kant's and consequentialist approaches like utilitarianism. Philosophers like G. E. M. Anscombe began expressing dissatisfaction with deontological and consequentialist moral theories in the 1950s.[45] In the 1970s and '80s Alasdair MacIntyre helped fan this dissatisfaction and revive virtue ethics. He criticized modern moral philosophy for detaching ethical principles from the communal contexts, traditions, narratives, and practices necessary for them to be intelligible and integrated. According to MacIntyre, moral rules depend upon some more fundamental idea of the human good. This idea is embedded and sustained in the operation of tradition and narrative.[46] Virtue ethics thus has a teleological orientation. It entails some idea of human excellence (*arete*) that is conducive to human flourishing or happiness (*eudaimonia*), which we seek to realize through the exercise of practical wisdom (*phronesis*).

A healthy number of Christian ethicists are among those reviving virtue ethics. The work of Joseph Kotva is one example.[47] According to Kotva, scriptural perspectives on morality share with virtue ethics a focus on interiority versus external actions, personal formation in relation to God and neighbors, imitation of moral models, and growth in understanding one's own life and community in light of God's gracious action in Jesus Christ. Not everyone agrees with Kotva that Christian and virtue ethics are so naturally and self-evidently compatible.[48] Some read scripture as advocating obedience to God's will, or see a tension between virtue ethics' emphasis on human flourishing and excellence and the place of self-sacrifice in Christian life. Nevertheless, a number of prominent Christian thinkers take up virtue ethics as a deliberate alternative to a focus on moral actions.

James Keenan's work on virtue ethics illustrates this sort of turn. Virtue ethicists, says Keenan, "are not primarily interested in particular actions. We do not ask 'Is this action right?' 'What are the circumstances around an action?' or 'What are the consequences of an action?' We are simply interested in persons." Keenan goes on to say that virtue ethics instead asks three related questions: "'Who am I?' 'Who ought I to become?' 'How am I to get there?'"[49] Keenan rightly notes that virtue ethics asks more fundamental and enduring questions than one finds in ethics that focus on moral dilemmas or quandaries like abortion, euthanasia, and capital punishment. This is not to say that virtue ethics isn't practical. To answer truthfully the question "Who am I?" we must consider our behavior. The question "Who ought I to become?" involves developing a vision of who we ought to be and striving to attain it. The third question, "How do I get there?" is a matter of prudence. Prudence is the virtue that determines and directs the other virtues. The cultivation of prudence is a lifelong task. It requires setting realistic goals for ourselves and regularly asking whether we are behaving in ways that habituate ourselves in the virtues. Keenan thus describes virtue ethics in a way that highlights its consideration of human agency, yet contrasts it to approaches that reduce ethics to the analysis of quandaries or actions isolated from the questions virtue ethics poses.

Stanley Hauerwas emphasizes the importance of vision and narrative for human agency and the virtues. "Being a Christian involves more than just making certain decisions; it is a way of attending to the world. It is learning 'to see' the world under the mode of the divine. . . . A Christian does not simply 'believe' certain propositions about God; he learns to attend to reality through them." Moreover, "the claim of the Christian is that his language actually envisages the world as it is."[50] Hauerwas, influenced by MacIntyre, argues that a person's moral vision is produced by the narratives or stories that structure her self-understanding and action. The Christian is one who learns to attend to reality through the story of God's saving action in Jesus Christ. These stories disclose to her the truth about the world and her own existence. As her own life is inscribed into the larger Christian narrative, she comes to see herself both as a sinner in need of forgiveness and as one receiving forgiveness through no merit of her own. For Hauerwas we grow in the virtues not by a "constant effort to reach an ideal but by discovery, as we look back on our lives and, by God's forgiveness, claim them as our own. Character, in other words, names the continuity of our lives, the recognition of which is made possible by the retrospective affirmation that our lives are not just the sum of what we have done but rather are constituted by what God has done for us."[51]

Feminist theologians, philosophers, and social scientists have been important catalysts in and contributors to the revival of virtue ethics. The work of Carol Gilligan and Nel Noddings sparked a significant body of research on gendered forms of moral reasoning and the so-called ethics of care. Gilligan's volume In a Different Voice criticizes the work of moral psychologist Lawrence Kohlberg for privileging a principle-based approach to morality and, in light of that, concluding that girls reached comparatively lower levels of moral development than boys.[52] Gilligan contends that girls exhibit styles of moral reasoning that are more focused on relationships than abstract principles. Noddings similarly contrasts an ethics of care and an ethics centered on justice or principles, even as she argues that, properly speaking, caring is ethical when the one caring acknowledges that care is obliged.[53] Christian feminists draw on Trinitarian theology and Jesus's evident concern for marginalized persons to argue for a normative standard of right relationship.[54] This replaces juridical approaches to ethics and challenges dualistic moral frameworks and hierarchical moral communities. Feminist virtue ethics highlights our freedom of conscience even as it binds us to ask after and to cultivate a morally fitting response to the particular situation, relationship, and person that demands our care.[55] Some feminists have criticized the essentialism of approaches like those of Gilligan and Noddings and insist upon the social construction of gender and the contextual character of morality.[56] In all, feminists have contributed to greater moral concern for relationships, the virtues that characterize morally worthy relationships among persons, and social analysis that situates moral reflection and critically analyzes the structures that undermine right relationship.

Like any ethical approach, virtue ethics is subject to criticism. Some thinkers argue that virtues are culturally relative. For example, qualities prized in one culture—say, independence or self-sufficiency—might not evoke the same endorsement in other, more communitarian contexts. What counts as modesty in one culture differs in another. Who even merits consideration in the exercise of justice differs cross-culturally and historically. For MacIntyre cultural variation with regard to specific virtues is to be expected, since virtues are necessarily grounded in the particular narratives and practices that structure a community's moral ethos. The notion that moral ideals must be detached from particular communities or traditions is one of the Enlightenment pretensions MacIntyre criticizes. Others can address this criticism by looking to basic, cross-cultural human capacities, experiences, and needs.[57] Some idea of justice—rendering to others their due—is discernible in all human communities, for example. The task is then to navigate ways of understanding, respecting, and critically engaging the particular interpretations and practice of such virtues.

Other authors criticize virtue ethics for an inability to address situations in which virtues might conflict. The reply that such conflicts only *seem* to be conflicts fails to satisfy. Lisa Cahill instead writes of "adverse virtues," "which can characterize choices which represent human attempts to act with integrity in the midst of unavoidable conflict and adversity."[58] Such choices are not virtuous in the usual sense of fulfilling human potential or being reasonable. Neither are they essentially sinful, since they are courageous and worthy efforts to discern the best course of action in an impossible situation. Lisa Tessman argues that conditions of oppression make moral goodness more difficult for the oppressed; moreover, the character traits or "burdened virtues" requisite for resisting oppression also undermine the agent's goodness. Burdened virtues "include all those traits that make a contribution to human flourishing—if they succeed in doing so at all—*only* because they enable survival of or resistance to oppression (it is in this that their nobility lies), while in other ways they detract from their bearer's well-being, in some cases so deeply that their bearer may be said to lead a wretched life."[59]

The principal criticism of virtue ethics concerns the relations between specific virtues and concrete actions. If virtue ethics focuses on the development of character traits or moral habituation, what help does that offer when an agent confronts a practical moral dilemma? Ought I to support my local government's plans to develop a retail area in a particular neighborhood or not? Should we proceed with plans to adopt a baby we now know is at risk for Down syndrome? Do I vote for a candidate whose economic policies I support but whose foreign policy approach I oppose? The lack of clear action guidance also makes moral formation or education more muddled. My husband and I want our sons to learn that being part of a family means pitching in with the household work. We also want them to learn to be good stewards of their resources, to develop early the habits of saving and donating some of their money. And of course we want them to experience the security of knowing that we will love and support them unconditionally. To do all this, should we pay them an allowance only when they do their chores or regardless of whether they help around the house? We can be clear about the virtues we would like to inculcate in ourselves, our children, and our communities but be unsure just how to go about this. Moral exemplars can help, but I am skeptical as to how much help the question "What would [insert moral exemplar] do?" provides. The point is that insofar as virtues do not correlate clearly with concrete actions, virtue ethics appears incomplete.

This is not to say that virtues are disconnected from actions. Quite the contrary. Virtues dispose us to act well. The natural virtues (versus what Aquinas called the theological virtues) are acquired through action. We habituate ourselves through practice. Virtues are, however, open-ended in the sense that a variety of actions might express or instantiate them. Courage for one situation or for one agent might involve fighting, and for another it might involve walking away or peaceable resistance. The fact that virtues are open-ended in this way is not necessarily a problem and, as Jean Porter argues, may well be a strength.[60] The virtuous person is one who does what is fitting in the concrete circumstances. The action guidance required to discern what that fitting deed might be is supplied by the virtue of prudence or practical wisdom. Nonetheless, it is true that virtue ethics tells us about agents but not enough about particular actions or the world in which we act; to understand the acting person adequately Christian ethics must locate her in creation, the field of human action.

Here we have only glimpsed aspects of the broad, diverse, and dynamic field of Western Christian moral inquiry. Recalling my earlier caution that neatly dividing Christian moral tradition into act-centered and person-centered approaches is generally a Catholic—and at that a narrow—way of understanding the tradition, it is nevertheless possible and valuable to note some contrasts. Whereas Catholic moral theology prior to Vatican II was atomic—parceling morality into discrete acts—Protestant and post–Vatican II Catholic ethics are generally more attentive to moral relations, social contexts, and the person's moral life as a whole. Whereas the bulk of pre-Reformation and Catholic manualist moral theology was preoccupied with sins, Protestant and postconciliar Catholic ethics endeavor both to take sin more seriously and to frame ethics positively in terms of the virtues, relational qualities, and social conditions that reflect fittingly God's gracious introduction of his Kingdom and personal call to discipleship. Accordingly, contemporary Christian ethics is less juridical and behavioral. Consider how the authors discussed above frame sexual ethics in terms of normative qualities that individuals and couples are to strive to inculcate, or the way virtue ethics directs moral focus to our dispositions and affections.

Whereas penitential and manualist moral theology made confessors into moral experts and eroded lay moral responsibility thereby, much of contemporary Christian ethics, as Gerald McKenny notes, assumes that a great deal of morality is "up to us." He makes this point in an essay on responsibility. McKenny argues that the concept of responsibility developed along with modernity's secularization; in keeping with "the modern withdrawal of God from the world" human responsibility for determining what is morally good and obligatory grew.[61] Whereas the penitential and manualist focus on sins encouraged scrupulosity and anxiety, much of contemporary Christian ethics emphasizes God's profligate mercy and loving desire for us to flourish and be saved. Finally, penitential and manualist moral theology inflated the significance of particular actions for the person's identity and relationship with God. As we will see in chapter 3, revisionists make a similar charge against Pope John Paul II's treatment of intrinsically evil acts and the fundamental option. Contemporary Christian ethics instead tends to emphasize that particular actions are only limited expressions of the person and therefore could not determine one's moral identity and religious relationship with God. Unfortunately, an understandable reticence to morally presume the state of a person's relationship with God simply on the basis of an action we can attribute to her too often leads Christian ethicists to conclude that there is very little we can say about the religious significance of particular actions.

CONTEMPORARY CATHOLIC DEBATES ABOUT MORAL ACTS

A significant body of literature in Catholic ethics from the 1960s onward does bear directly on moral action. Much of this literature originally developed around the issue of contraception. The publication of Pope Paul VI's encyclical *Humanae vitae* (1968) created considerable controversy. It is well known that the commission originally formed to study the question of birth control produced a majority report that concluded that recourse to artificial contraception is morally legitimate under some circumstances. Paul VI's decision to uphold Church teaching against contraception met with vigorous responses, including significant public dissent. As theologians argued about contraception, another argument developed and took on a life of its own, a debate that developed between scholars who in the debate's heyday were often called "proportionalists" and "basic goods theorists."[62] This debate centers around moral norms but entails theories of human action. The disagreement can be difficult to sketch neatly for several reasons. The position often labeled "proportionalism" is not uniform, is sometimes attributed to thinkers who reject the term, and is persistently misrepresented as a form of consequentialism that holds that it is acceptable to do what is wrong for the sake of some good end. The version of natural law that was often called basic goods theory in the debate's heyday clusters around the work of Germain Grisez, Joseph M. Boyle, and John Finnis. The "basic goods theory" moniker has fallen out of use. Finnis and Robert P. George have developed in its stead a form of jurisprudence that they identify as the "new natural law" theory.

Recent magisterial documents, particularly the 1993 papal encyclical *Veritatis splendor*, show affinities with basic goods theory, yet offer a different version of natural law than that developed by Grisez and company. The debate initially focused on the principle of double effect but came to encompass the closely related questions whether there are any intrinsically evil acts or any absolute negative norms. To complicate matters further, in *Veritatis splendor* John Paul II links the matter of intrinsically evil acts to the idea of a fundamental option for or against God. He claims that there are intrinsically evil acts—for example, adultery—and that a person can resolve his or her fundamental option in a single act; this means that a fundamental option "is revoked when man engages his freedom in conscious decisions to the contrary, with regard to morally grave matter."[63] I will refer to the whole set of disagreements in terms of revisionist and traditionalist debates.

Peter Knauer's 1967 essay "The Hermeneutic Function of the Principle of Double Effect" was key to early debates about contraception and the larger disagreements that ensued. The principle of double effect assists ethicists in analyzing actions in morally ambiguous situations. As scholarly consideration of the principle developed in the decades after *Humanae vitae*, some revisionist moral theologians began to argue that all moral actions are morally ambiguous—they all have good and bad features, at least given the limitations of finitude. These good and bad features are in themselves premoral values and disvalues. Moreover,

> causing certain disvalues (nonmoral, pre-moral evils such as sterilization, deception in speech, wounding and violence) in our conduct does not by that

very fact make the action morally wrong, as certain traditional formulations supposed. These evils or disvalues are said to be premoral when considered abstractly, that is, in isolation from their morally relevant circumstances. But they are evils. Thus theologians sometimes say that they are morally relevant, but not morally decisive. They are morally relevant because they ought to be avoided as far as possible. The action in which they occur becomes morally wrong when, all things considered, there is not proportionate reason in the act justifying the disvalue.[64]

Revisionists like Richard McCormick argued that the decisive moral criterion is proportionate reason: whether the premoral value that is at stake in my decision justifies the premoral disvalues that attend a particular course of action. If the value at stake is not proportional to or greater than the disvalues my acting will incur, the moral act is morally wrong. Revisionists note that a premoral disvalue cannot be directly intended for its own sake; that is, it cannot be the end sought when we act. Given proportionate reason, premoral disvalues may be directly or indirectly intended in order to avoid some greater evil or tolerated as a regrettable effect of seeking the value that is at stake through this particular course of action.[65] A premoral value may also be sacrificed for the sake of some equal or greater value.

Basic goods theorists argue that what they call proportionalism implies a standard against which values and disvalues are measured when in fact there can be no such standard. This is because the goods we encounter in the world are incommensurable. Sometimes basic goods theorists make this point in mathematical language: goods like friendship, authenticity, knowledge, and health share no common denominator that permits their comparison.[66] What makes them "basic" goods is that one reasonably may act for their sake alone.[67] Grisez and company understand morality in terms of the way persons determine themselves in relation to these goods through their choices and commitments. Grisez builds his interpretation of natural law out of an account of practical reason. He suggests that the principle Thomas Aquinas identified as the first precept of practical reason ("seek good and avoid evil") is not itself a moral precept but founds moral precepts. Given this foundation, human action must be ordered to human flourishing to be intelligible—that is, to be truly a human act. Of course, actions can be more and less intelligible in this regard, but given this Grisez articulates the first principle of morality as follows: "In voluntarily acting for human goods and avoiding what is opposed to them, one ought to choose and otherwise will those and only those possibilities whose willing is compatible with a will toward integral human fulfillment."[68]

This fulfillment only comes through the attainment of basic goods. Grisez identifies eight basic goods of three types: reflexive goods of self-integration, practical reasonableness and authenticity, justice and friendship, and religion; substantive goods of life (which includes health and procreation), knowledge of truth and aesthetic appreciation, and skillful activities in work and play; and finally marriage, which is a distinct good.[69] These goods are self-evident, but the movement from the first principle of morality to the attainment of any of these goods is mediated through intermediate principles, which Grisez terms "modes of responsibility." For example, "One should not be moved by a stronger desire for one instance of an intelligible good to act for it by choosing to destroy, damage, or impede some other instance of an intelligible good."[70] This means it is wrong to attack any of the basic goods or to sacrifice one for another. Granted, we cannot act for all of the goods at once, but Grisez claims that we can remain open to those we are not pursuing at a present time.

Both revisionists and traditionalists provide theories of human action in the course of considering moral norms. They approach particular moral actions in ways that concern the person's intentionality or will in relation to human values or goods. Revisionists generally picture this relationship as one in which persons by their actions bring about or cause values and disvalues, goods and evils. The morality of particular actions is determined by the presence or absence of proportionate reason, which itself concerns what the person intends (directly or indirectly) in the particular circumstances in which she acts. One important implication of this, say revisionists, is that we cannot determine in advance the moral value of "acts abstractly considered." As we will see in later chapters, the notion of acts abstractly considered figures prominently in their arguments against traditionalists. Because the moral meaning of any particular action is crucially determined by the particular agent's intentions in her given circumstances, another implication is that we cannot presume to know the religious significance of her action, what it expresses or brings about for her relationship with God.

For their part, traditionalists begin with practical reason and emphasize human choices regarding goods that contribute to human flourishing. Goods and evils aren't so much caused by human actions, as though they were products, effects, or consequences of our actions, as they are aspects of human fulfillment that constitute the field of human action. Morality is a matter of the position the will takes in relation to these goods. Traditionalists argue that some actions—those that involve direct attacks on basic human goods—can be identified as always wrong. As we noted above, Pope John Paul II argues that when such intrinsically wrong acts involve grave matter they constitute a negative fundamental option—that is, a religiously decisive rejection of God.

CONCLUSION

We began by noting various scriptural perspectives on the importance of moral actions in Christian life. Actions are sometimes subordinated to moral interiority, and sometimes emphasized as barometers for and mediums by which we negotiate our relationship with God. Christians experience themselves as called to respond to God's gracious initiative. God has acted on our behalf in Jesus, "in whom we have redemption, the forgiveness of sins" (Col 1:14). This good news is efficacious. It changes things, changes us, in ways that sharpen and relativize the import of our moral actions. We are to "lead lives worthy of the Lord, fully pleasing to him, as [we] bear fruit in every good work and as [we] grow in the knowledge of God" (Col 1:10). For "whoever says, 'I abide in him,' ought to walk just as he walked" (1 Jn 2:6). And yet Christians lament with Saint Paul that the good we wish to do is not what we do (Rom 7:19) and find in our weakness cause to rejoice with him that Christ's grace is sufficient (2 Cor 12:9).

How, in the light of Christian faith, should we understand the import of particular actions for the person's moral and religious identity? Is it possible to speak of moral actions impacting one's relationship with God—positively or negatively—without succumbing to a Pelagian works righteousness? What do the sufficiency of grace and the unfinished character of human freedom mean for moral reflection on concrete behaviors and relationships? Can Christian ethics be adequate if it deliberately eschews reflection on the sorts of actions or behaviors contrary to virtue, regardless of whether there are good pastoral, philosophical, and theological reasons for that reticence? In the next two chapters I will argue that the worthy concern to avoid premature judgments about persons on the basis of their actions is amounting to an unfitting agnosticism in Christian ethics regarding the religious significance of particular sorts of actions. Alternatively, can Christian ethics be adequate if its treatment of moral actions fixes on disputes about how to determine moral culpability? Moral actions have religious depths and theological significance that exceeds such determinations. Preoccupation with moral culpability signals theological misunderstandings of human agency.

Much of contemporary Christian ethics distances moral actions from God, from the self who acts, and from the world. Virtue ethics, for example, traffics in moral descriptions of persons, and while these are significant for the person's actions they are not finally about those actions, nor do they tell us about the world in which we act in response to God. Recent Catholic debates regarding moral actions tend to be theoretically overdetermined and remain preoccupied with moral culpability in ways that echo penitential and manualist moral theology. The difference, however, is that the general conviction of contemporary Christian ethics is that there is very little we can say about the theological significance of particular actions. This reticence is clearly on display in recent theologies of sin, to which we now turn.

NOTES

1. Colossians 3:9, cited above, is preceded by an admonition that focuses mostly on dispositions: "But now you must get rid of such things—anger, wrath, malice, slander, and abusive language" (Col. 3:8).
2. See Curran, *Catholic Moral Theology*, 144–46. See also Wojtyla, *Acting Person*.
3. Mahoney, *Making of Moral Theology*, 5.
4. Bieler, *Irish Penitentials*, 129.
5. Mahoney, *Making of Moral Theology*, 15.
6. See also chapter 7, "The Confessional," in Wogaman, *Christian Ethics*.
7. See Mahoney, *Making of Moral Theology*, 225–27; Gallagher, *Time Past, Time Future*, 85.
8. Mahoney, *Making of Moral Theology*, 28.
9. Ibid., 32.
10. The next chapter will consider theologies of sin that were developed to supplant a focus on sins.
11. Harrington and Keenan, *Jesus and Virtue Ethics*, 4.
12. We can distinguish the *magisterium cathedrae pastoralis*, the juridical power of the church's hierarchical officeholders, from the *magisterium cathedrae magistralis*, the scholarly authority of theologians. See Mannion et al., *Readings in Church Authority*; Congar, "Theologians and the Magisterium."
13. Mahoney, *Making of Moral Theology*, 35.
14. Harrington and Keenan, *Jesus and Virtue Ethics*, 5.
15. See Blaise Pascal's scathing criticism of probabilism in *Provincial Letters*; see also Fleming, *Defending Probabilism*.
16. Gallagher, *Time Past, Time Future*.
17. Ibid., 30.
18. Curran, *Catholic Moral Theology*, 9.
19. See Wogaman, *Christian Ethics*, 65. The following draws from chapter 6 of Wogaman's book.
20. Curran, *Catholic Moral Theology*, chap. 2.
21. See Häring, *Law of Christ*. See also Lottin, *Principes de morale*; Gilleman, *Primacy of Charity in Moral Theology*.
22. In Flannery, *Vatican Council II*, no. 16.
23. Ibid.
24. See *Lumen gentium*, chap. 5, in Flannery, *Vatican Council II*.
25. Gustafson, *Protestant and Roman Catholic Ethics*, 3.
26. Ibid., 9.
27. Ibid., 15.

28. See Luther, "Freedom of a Christian." See also McKim, *Cambridge Companion to Martin Luther.*

29. Bonhoeffer, *Cost of Discipleship.*

30. Rauschenbusch, *Theology for the Social Gospel.*

31. See Pope Paul VI, *Humanae vitae* (1968), Vatican website, www.vatican.va/holy_father/ paul_vi/encyclicals/documents/hf_p-vi_enc_25071968_humanae-vitae_en.html. See also Congregation for the Doctrine of the Faith, *Donum vitae* (1987), available online as "Instruction on Respect for Human Life in Its Origin and on the Dignity of Procreation," Vatican website, www.vatican.va/roman_curia/congregations/cfaith/documents/rc_con_cfaith _doc_19870222_respect-for-human-life_en.html.

32. *Humanae vitae*, no. 17.

33. Gudorf, *Body, Sex, and Pleasure*, 15.

34. Cahill, *Sex, Gender and Christian Ethics*, 117.

35. See, e.g., Salzman and Lawler, *Sexual Person*; Gudorf, *Body, Sex, and Pleasure*. For an examination of the rhetoric in Christian arguments about sexual morality, see Monti, *Arguing about Sex.*

36. Farley, *Just Love.*

37. Some more constructive theological reflection on sexual morality can be found in Salzman and Lawler, *Sexual Person*; Roberts, *Creation and Covenant*; Alison, *Faith beyond Resentment*; Rogers, *Sexuality and the Christian Body*; Rudy, *Sex and the Church.*

38. Ellison, "Common Decency," 238. See also Nelson, "Love, Power, and Justice."

39. Ellison, "Common Decency," 238.

40. Ibid., 237, 238, 239.

41. Hall, *Conceiving Parenthood.*

42. See, e.g., Brakman and Weaver, *Ethics of Embryo Adoption*; Ryan, *Ethics and Economics of Assisted Reproduction.*

43. See, e.g., Althaus, "Human Embryo Transfer and the Theology of the Body."

44. See, e.g., Hursthouse, *On Virtue Ethics*; Crisp, *How Should One Live?*; Annas, *Morality of Happiness.*

45. Anscombe, "Modern Moral Philosophy." Philippa Foot was also influential; see her *Virtues and Vices.*

46. See MacIntyre, *After Virtue.* See also his *Three Rival Versions.*

47. Kotva, *Christian Case for Virtue Ethics.* See also James Keenan's discussion of Kotva's work in Harrington and Keenan, *Jesus and Virtue Ethics*, 67–71.

48. Jean Porter makes this point in her essay "Virtue."

49. Keenan, "Virtue Ethics," 84.

50. Hauerwas, *Vision and Virtue*, 46.

51. Hauerwas and Pinches, *Christians among the Virtues*, 124–25.

52. Gilligan, *In a Different Voice.*

53. Noddings, *Caring.*

54. See, e.g., Johnson, *She Who Is*; LaCugna, "God in Communion with Us"; and Parsons, *Cambridge Companion to Feminist Theology*, to name a few.

55. Farley's *Just Love*, e.g., argues that love is just when it befits the concrete reality of both the lover and the beloved (200). See also Patrick, *Liberating Conscience*, 76–80.

56. See, e.g., the chapters on essentialism in Parsons, *Feminism and Christian Ethics*.

57. Consider the "capability approach" developed by Martha Nussbaum and Amartya Sen in *Quality of Life*. See also Nussbaum's *Women and Human Development* and *Frontiers of Justice*. Nussbaum is not a virtue ethicist as such, but like the virtue ethicists mentioned here she finds an Aristotelian ethics hospitable for moral reflection on human well-being or flourishing.

58. Cahill, *Theological Bioethics*, 119.

59. Tessman, *Burdened Virtues*, 95.

60. Porter, "Virtue."

61. McKenny, "Responsibility," 237.

62. There is a vast literature surrounding this debate. Interest was primarily in parts of Europe and in the United States and has subsided in recent years. As I indicate here, new natural law theory continues work initiated during the debate's heyday. Aline Kalbian argues that proportionalism's contributions to Christian ethics endure in virtue ethics, feminist ethics, and casuistry. See Kalbian, "Where Have All the Proportionalists Gone?"

63. John Paul II, *Veritatis splendor*, no. 67.

64. McCormick, "Killing the Patient," 17.

65. For discussion of directly versus indirectly intending evil, see Schüller, "Direct/Indirect Killing"; McCormick, "Commentary on the Commentaries"; Connery, "Morality of Consequences"; Porter, "'Direct' and 'Indirect.'"

66. Proprotionalist Edward Vacek finds fault with this analogy; see his "Proportionalism."

67. Grisez, *Christian Moral Principles*, 181.

68. Ibid., 184. The cited work is volume 1 of Grisez's multivolume systematic moral theology, *The Way of the Lord Jesus*. Grisez continues to write this system. Those seeking a summary of his theory should consult Grisez and Shaw, *Fulfillment in Christ*. See also the recent Festschrift for Grisez: George, *Natural Law and Moral Inquiry*.

69. Finnis provides the same list, excepting marriage, in *Fundamentals of Ethics*, 51.

70. Grisez, *Christian Moral Principles*, 226.

CHAPTER TWO

DISRUPTION OF PROPER RELATION WITH GOD AND OTHERS: SIN AND SINS

The previous chapter described a shift in contemporary Christian ethics from a focus on actions to a focus on persons. It identified certain problems and deficiencies that result from either an insufficient or a mistaken sort of attention to the moral and theological significance of particular actions. A prompt turn to a chapter on sin may seem an inauspicious start if we are to respond to these problems. As we saw, much pre-Reformation Christian moral thinking and most of Catholic ethics up until Vatican II were not only act centered but preoccupied by sins (indeed, the acts at the center of moral analysis were chiefly of the sinful sort).[1] Protestant ethics displays a long-standing worry that focusing on sins signals a failure to take sin seriously as a force that affects us profoundly.[2] Moreover, it can also fuel legalism, scrupulosity, and works righteousness and thereby hinder rather than help an understanding of sin as above all the "disruption of proper relation to God," to use Alistair McFadyen's term. Contemporary Catholic ethics is reluctant to attend to sins and explicitly counters earlier Catholic moral tradition. The attempt to overcome pre–Vatican II preoccupation with sins is part of a broad and welcome shift in central moral categories. Catholic ethics generally no longer centers on the analysis of discrete right and wrong actions to get at the reality of sin; rather, it centers on the person and her relations to God, neighbor, self, and world.

Protestants and Catholics alike recognize that a preoccupation with particular sins deflects moral attention from one's dispositions and intentions; the moral life then concerns the avoidance of sinful acts rather than growth in virtues like love, justice, and wisdom. It also breaks the moral life into discrete moments rather than casting it as an organic whole or an ongoing narrative.[3] Moreover, focusing on sins eclipses the systemic and institutional forms sin takes.[4] So widespread contemporary Christian ethical neglect of sins is part of salutary efforts to craft richer and more adequate understandings of the person as a relational creature situated in complex sociohistorical situations. Significant strands of Roman Catholic ethics, for example, take sin seriously not by confining it to sins, but by developing theologies of sin.[5]

Nevertheless, there are good reasons to reject the discourse of sin altogether. It seems too allied to anachronistic and faithless views of God as wrathful and punitive and to excessively juridical accounts of atonement and salvation. Reinforcing these theological difficulties is sin's operation as a peculiar rhetoric deployed by particular Christian communities to serve equally troubling social and political agendas. Even if sin talk could capture something true about our existence in relation to God and others, it seems too prone to scapegoating and self-righteousness. Its value as a conceptual resource is undermined by its destructive effects as a rhetorical device. Perhaps if we are to speak of sin we need to disconnect it from its theological grounds and convert it into a moral or therapeutic psychological category. Then again, why do we bother to speak of sin at all? What reasons do we have to resurrect sin when the experiences, struggles, failings, and horrors to which it might refer can be adequately and perhaps more compellingly described by nonreligious (e.g., psychological and ethical) resources that are friendlier to public discourse and to modern rationality?

McFadyen argues that because sin is the disruption of our proper relation to God, "it is of the essence of sin-talk . . . that it should function as a *theological* language, and this is the source of its distinctiveness from and irreducibility to other languages through which the pathological may be discerned and described."[6] Thus, reticence to speak of sin or attempts to evacuate its theological referent collude with "the general retreat of God-talk from public life and discourse. Losing our ability to speak of the world's pathologies in relation to God represents a serious, concrete form of the loss of God that is a general characteristic of contemporary, Western culture." McFadyen is particularly troubled by "the reductive reading of the language of sin in moral categories."[7] Modern moral discourse presupposes autonomy as a condition for moral acting and accountability; it converts sin into a language of blame devoid of reference to God and ignorant of the way sin preconditions freedom as an inheritance of guilt for something we have not done.

Whether they construe sin in terms of a radical decision of the self or in terms of social processes and structures that situate the self, contemporary Christian treatments of sin tend to posit an inner or transcendental core to the person that is not corrupted by sin; this is evident in the sorts of distinctions they draw between sin as a power or situation in which one participates and sinning by personal acts. "It is only personal acts for which one is said to be responsible; only through them that one may incur guilt. . . . It is, after all, only sin in the sphere of the personal (which, despite the overall affirmation of the social as a dimension of the personal, is nonetheless construed in individualistic terms when it comes to the issue of accountability, responsibility and guilt) for which I am responsible and which therefore holds real seriousness for my personal being."[8]

In short, such accounts of sin, Catholic and Protestant, continue to underplay sin as a power or force that affects the person and mistakenly persist in construing sin through the prism of moral culpability. This is all the more curious a problem for contemporary Catholic theologies of sin, since they seek to counter the tradition's earlier tendencies to bind sin too tightly to sins—that is, personal acts—and to moral culpability. Catholic efforts to construct a theology of sin insist rightly that acts are limited expressions of the person and as such do not disclose or determine the whole story about her before God. However, such theologies of sin prompt attention to moral acts (as, e.g., always involving premoral values and disvalues) that too often proceeds apace and apart from decidedly theological attention to them.

The challenge theologians face, says McFadyen, is not to make sin more amenable to secular or pretheological descriptions of pathology, but to identify its distinctive theological referent and show its explanatory power. If sin talk yields a distinctive contribution to our understanding of pathology, then strictly secular descriptions of pathology are incomplete and inadequate. In other words, the distinctively theological character of sin talk proves to be the sine qua non for a truthful understanding of the many ways proper relation to God has been and is disrupted.

I believe that McFadyen is largely correct, except that in his concern to resist tendencies to translate sin into a moral category indebted to a distinctively modern understanding of autonomy, responsibility, and culpability, his attempts to display the explanatory power of sin neglect the importance of particular sins. A Christian theology of sin, be it Protestant or Catholic, becomes abstract and thin apart from recognition of the sorts of sins that give it content and allow it to sink talons into the moral life. Inattention to sins also creates theological difficulties because it obscures the fact that God is the source of freedom and value: since God is this, the acting subject negotiates her relation with God as she freely disposes herself toward and against the objective goods and values that constitute her moral life with others before God. Therefore, inattention to sins poses ethical problems as well. By distancing sin from its expression in particular acts we may take sin more seriously as an existential condition, and we may express the faith and hope that God's mercy rightly evokes. Then again, this distancing may neglect the power of acts in a person's history to make and unmake, to build up and to destroy.

My overall aim is to account better for the relation between persons and their moral actions so as to provide a more robustly theological understanding of our acting in relation to God and in the world. Given the importance of Christian thinking about sin and sins as a contributing factor to the problems I described in chapter 1, and given the importance of sin and sins for human being and acting, we need first to examine how contemporary theologies of sin go wrong. I am not calling for lists of sin acts or a revival of Catholic manualist moral theology but arguing, minimally, that a theology of sin ought to include attention to sins. Such a project is rightly undertaken over against the kind of attention earlier Catholic ethics paid to sins, one that reduced sin to sins and identified sins on the basis of external acts and through determinations of moral culpability. But an adequate counter to this attention is not a standing inattention. Theological insights under-lie the Christian ethical shift from acts to persons, but this shift can be reactive, amounting to an overcorrection that itself requires correction. By entering the thicket of some Catholic efforts to construct a theology of sin, we can see they do not yet do justice to the concern that Catholics now share with Protestants to take sin seriously as a power or force. We will also see difficulties that vex their attempts to rehabilitate an understanding of personal sin by replacing earlier Catholic tradi-tion's preoccupation with sins with a view of personal sin as a basic orientation.

My larger argument goes well beyond the need to include attention to particu-lar sins as a component of doctrines of sin. Sin is the disruption of proper relation with God issuing in and resulting from the disruption of proper relation to our-selves, others, and the world. It includes but is not reducible to morally culpable wrongdoing. I argue that the theologies of sin I consider try to distinguish sin and moral culpability by distancing (though not separating) sin and concrete ac-tions.[9] These efforts allow determinations of moral culpability to constrict what we may say about the theological significance of acts. Such theologies of sin thereby undermine the theological referent of sin as a discourse that concerns more than moral culpability and encounter ethical problems. We would better acknowl-edge that sin is not reducible to moral culpability if we reconnected sin to moral acts.

I argue that the theological referent and analogical character of sin and sins enable us to recover earlier Catholic tradition's concern to determine what kinds of actions count as sinful, but now without confining our attention to external acts or moral culpability. Asking after the presence or absence of sin in personal acts only makes sense in light of sin as a force and orientation, even as accounts of sin as a force and orientation are abstract apart from consideration of the sorts of acts that express and sustain that force and that fashion such an orientation. Moreover, this inquiry contextualizes questions of moral culpability in light of the historicity, particularity, and provisionality of sinful acts, thereby positioning us better to ac-count for the relation of persons and their moral actions in light of intimacy with, fidelity to, truthfulness before, and reconciliation in God.

RECENT CATHOLIC THEOLOGIES OF SIN

Charles Curran has argued, with others, that Catholic moral tradition underplays the importance of sin.[10] Curran identifies three historical reasons to support his claim. First, Catholic ethical reliance on natural law grants reason a supremacy that neglects sin as a theological category and exhibits an optimism that neglects the effects sin has on human reason and human nature. Second, the antiecumenism of Catholic tradition prompts theologians to downplay sin in their attempts to distinguish Catholic theology from Protestant approaches.[11] Finally, Catholic pre-occupation with particular sins signals a failure to take sin seriously inasmuch as sin is perceived "as *only* an act, not as a power or force that deeply affect[s] the individual person or the world" (39). Curran goes on to say, "If sin is only an act [versus a power or force], it does not have much influence and can easily be eradicated" (ibid.). As we noted in chapter 1, John Mahoney argues that a preoccupation with sins like that exhibited by the Celtic penitentials ironically "domesticates" and "trivializes" sin. It isolates and exaggerates one aspect of the moral life. This "devalues the currency" of sin by investing acts "with an inherent capacity for moral self-commitment which they [can]not bear."[12] The Celtic penitentials and the manuals of moral theology understood and classified sins according to the choice of particular objects, like lying; this method implies that sin is itself an object of choice, rather than a force or power. Moreover, in the "gloomy gestalt" of this preoccupation, moral theology developed in growing isolation from the rest of theology and as an extension of canon law.[13]

Postponing for a moment the question whether contemporary Catholic moral theology yet takes sin seriously enough, we can explore the more serious attention it has given to sin. For Curran, due recognition of sin is part of adopting an adequate theological stance. He proposes one that includes the fivefold mysteries of creation, sin, incarnation, redemption, and resurrection destiny (33). This stance influences our use of sources for moral reflection (scripture, tradition, reason, and experience). Our stance and sources are also influenced by the ethical model we employ. Curran favors a relational-responsibility approach like H. Richard Niebuhr's.[14] This model does not view the person primarily as one who lives under the law, as deontological models do, or as a maker who acts for certain ends, as teleological models do. It sees the person as situated in relations with God, neighbor, self, and world. Scripture attests to the importance of these relations. Theological doctrines like the Trinity and grace require a relational understanding of the person, as does philosophical insight into the historicity, contingency, and diversity of human existence.

Accordingly, Curran understands sin in terms of the person's multiple relations. It is "basically alienation from God and others" that takes personal and structural forms (45–46). Curran's commitment to a relational-responsibility model clarifies his call to take sin more seriously and establishes what doing so, on his count, does and does not require. So it is important to attend to his understanding of the person.

According to Curran, "the person is a perduring reality. Actions come and go but the person continues and remains" (87). Catholic theology recognizes this by affirming what Curran calls an intrinsic account of salvation. It is not an extrinsic justification that God imputes to the person. Rather, because grace affects and changes the total person, salvation refers to God's gracious self-gift and the person's acceptance of it. Because it effects an ontological and real change in the person, and because the person is situated in multiple relations, salvation involves a basic orientation or commitment of the person that touches all of her relations. This orientation, says Curran, manifests itself in virtues that dispose an agent to particular acts that in turn affect her relations. Curran's emphasis on the primacy and perduring character of the person is representative of the general personalism of contemporary Catholic moral theology. With respect to sin, we see it in attempts to replace the tradition's earlier understanding of personal sin in terms of discrete acts with a more relational and dispositional account that centers on the person's relation to God. The basic point is that if salvation involves an orientation toward God, sin likewise involves an orientation, one by which the person rejects God.

A number of moral theologians describe the person's basic orientation in terms of the fundamental option (something discussed at length in the next chapter), the "freedom to dispose of oneself" in a decision "which is actualized in a free and absolute 'yes' or 'no' to that term and source of transcendence which we call 'God.'"[15] Curran and others criticize fundamental option theory for downplaying the social and historical dimensions of human existence. Though he expresses "some hesitations" about the theory, Curran endorses the significance of the person's basic relational orientation for Christian ethics, and his approach to sin is legitimately understood as situating sins in the broader context of transcendental freedom (98).[16] Such an understanding of the person means that taking sin seriously requires due recognition of sin as a power or force that affects the person, her multiple relations, and the world, and as a basic orientation away from God. It does not require us to return to a focus on sinful acts.

There are three ways this recognition of sin expresses itself in Curran's ethics. First, it informs his sense of the possibilities and limits of natural law. "The presence and influence of sin results in a more chastened natural law approach. Sin does not destroy or annul the created and the natural but definitely affects both human reason and human nature" (38). Of course, the finitude, contingency, and complexity of persons and the world chasten natural law as well. Coupling a natural law methodology with a relational-responsibility model provides a historically conscious and inductive approach to moral reflection that "recognizes the difficulty of arriving at certitude on specific moral principles and norms. By its very nature such an approach is tentative and more open to revision in light of change and development" (152). Reason and experience can discover and verify general and specific human goods and values. But as practical reason considers specific norms and situations, it encounters more contingent circumstances and more possibility of "exceptions in moral truth and obligation"—that is, exceptions to the specific principles of natural law (151). Since finitude and contingency are not sin, the indeterminacy of moral reason and the possibility of erroneous judgments are not the same as the "weakness" of reason due to sin (39).

Moreover, the goodness of creation, redemption, and our resurrection destiny all theologically warrant a certain optimism about moral reason. Nevertheless, if we are to recognize the power and force of sin, we require more clarification of the difference and relation between finitude and sin. Presumably, sin weakens reason by distorting it—say, through egoism, self-deception, and so forth. Curran does discuss the importance of forming one's conscience and of virtues like honesty and a self-critical attitude, but sin does not figure heavily in these passages, nor does Curran explicate the experience of sin's effects on reason through examples of particular sins.

This brings us to the second way Curran's recognition of sin informs his ethics. He says, "Severe conflict situations can always arise in a sinful world that is not yet at the fullness of God's reign" (42–43). This means that "sometimes the presence of sin in the world forces us to do what we would not do if sin were not present. Yes, we must struggle against sin, but we may also have to live with sin's consequences. . . . At times the presence of sin will justify some compromises in what should be done" (44). There is, Curran recognizes, a danger of caving in too readily to the presence of sin; yet "the presence of sin in the world can at times influence the proper moral response" (45). Moreover, "an individual might be existentially incapable of fulfilling the requirements of objective morality at a particular time in certain circumstances. In doing all that one existentially can do and in remaining open to a greater fullness, the person's act is actually formally good despite the material evil involved" (193).[17] Curran makes this point with reference to an invincibly erroneous conscience by drawing distinctions between the tasks of pastoral counseling and moral theology. He is expanding the invincibility of such a conscience (which is sincere but not culpably ignorant) beyond a lack of knowledge to a psychological condition (173–74, 193).[18] Presumably, sin as a force compounds the limits of reason and "influences the proper moral response." The appeal to formal goodness wards off claims of guilt in anything beyond moral terms—moral wrongdoing may characterize the act, but sin does not.[19]

Curran's main point is a long-standing one in Catholic moral tradition: The person must act according to her conscience, even though it may be erroneous (194). I have no quarrel with this claim or the distinction it implies between the objective wrongness of an act and the person's subjective moral culpability. However, I want to press its implications for endeavors to take sin more seriously as a power or force and as a matter of one's orientation to God. We can do this if we consider the third way Curran's attention to sin influences his ethics, particularly his understanding of the relations among persons, particular moral acts, and our moral designations of them. Curran argues, "In every moral act I contribute to making myself the kind of person I am, but I also do a particular act that affects myself, others, and the world in which we live. . . . In every act I must be properly related to myself as the moral person who is subject and agent, and also properly related to the reality of the objective situation itself" (172). In other words, human existence has subjective and objective poles. "The subject pole concerns the human person and involves one's basic orientation and the virtues or attitudes that characterize each one. The object pole considers the world, the communities, and the relationships in which people live and the values and principles that direct them in these areas" (83). As we might expect, Curran's relational-responsibility approach leads him to stress the subjective. Says Curran, "By my actions I make myself the person I am; and by my actions I do things for good or for ill in this world. I am both subject and agent" (88). Even so, "the moral person and the person's character and virtues are more significant for morality than the individual particular act" (87). Virtues mediate the person's basic orientation and dispose her to particular actions.

Nevertheless, because there is an objective pole of human existence, Curran also considers the proper place of moral principles and norms that guide human actions. Understanding how we arrive at moral principles returns us to Curran's chastened natural law and to the reality of conflict. Reason does not simply apply general principles to particular cases but moves inductively from experience and practice to moral judgments. Natural law involves a two-way street between principles and specific situations. Reflection on moral experience can refine particular principles and determine when there might be conflicts that constitute exceptions to them.

The reality of conflict, says Curran, is both ordinary and severe. Ordinary conflicts occur among the goods and values that constitute human existence. Curran is open to, though also critical of, positions advanced by those Roman Catholic ethicists sometimes called proportionalists. At present we need only note that Curran suggests that goods and values can conflict and therefore are best understood as premoral. Bodily integrity, for example, is a premoral good. It can conflict with other related goods like physical health. For instance, when a limb becomes gangrenous, a properly moral decision involves determining whether the good of bodily integrity may be sacrificed for the sake of physical health—that is, whether there is a proportionate reason to act against the good of bodily integrity by, say, amputating the gangrenous limb. A proportionate reason in this case justifies the physical act of mutilation.

This is not to say that a good intention justifies a morally wrong act. The physical act of mutilation could be a means to secure the good of physical health, or it could be intended as an end—that is, as torture. This difference highlights why, for Curran, we cannot adequately understand acts in terms of their external or physical structure alone. The crucial task is to discern the moral object or species of the act, and this requires deliberation and judgment that are attentive to circumstances and intention. As we will consider more fully in the next chapter, all of this bears importantly on debates about absolute moral norms and intrinsically evil acts. The point that concerns us here is simply that, for Curran, "the moral value of human actions is derived primarily from the subjective side—the mental and moral condition of the agent that others can know only in a very imperfect way" (192). Given that ordinary conflict is this important for understanding and evaluating particular acts, how much more complicated and imperfect will these tasks be in cases of severe conflict?

Thus far we have seen that the presence of sin in the world as a power or force affecting the person (1) weakens reason and (2) sometimes creates severe conflict situations that "influence the proper moral response" and "will justify some compromises." If these facts are part of what existentially limits the person, must we conclude that sin as a power or force, along with social sin, helps to create nonculpable ignorance and thereby mitigates personal or actual sin? I expect that some would offer the rejoinder that the person strives to do the best she can, that she acts with a good motive and therefore does not sin. This means that sin is not coterminous with moral culpability, and in such a case moral culpability is also limited to the objective wrongness of her act, while the person and her act remain subjectively good.

Now, if sin is not coterminous with moral culpability (a claim I do not dispute), but is instead a power that affects the person and, most properly, an orientation away from God, where does sin go in the case at hand? By the terms of the example, one cannot find it in the person's orientation. Is the point that original and social sin help to create the moral arena and possibilities within which the person exercises her freedom? That they operate *around* and *on* but not *in* her? Is it that the language of sin, in this instance, characterizes her *situation*, but will

39

only characterize her *orientation* if she activates her relation to sin through a free decision? Do we, ironically, lose a sense of sin here as a force affecting her radically, by implying some reservoir of freedom or agency untouched by it? The problem is how to understand the presence or absence of sin in the person's act given a tension between understanding sin as a power or force affecting the person and as a free, personal orientation.

Within contemporary Catholic theologies of sin, the moral determination of culpability does not settle (and indeed cannot and ought not settle) the question of sin's presence or absence (192). Nevertheless, it should not displace this question, nor should it set the terms for answering it. Because the question of sin's presence or absence is a *theological* ethical and spiritual one, it rightly muddles and reaches beyond our moral conceptual distinctions. Recall that Curran is distinguishing the tasks of pastoral counseling and moral theology. Note, too, that James Keenan argues that if the person is doing all she existentially can do and remains open to a greater fullness, she may require advice about how to order her actions rightly, but she does not require exhortation. If she is not striving to do the best she can, to love as much as possible, she may require exhortation as well as advice.[20] These distinctions are valid, but they do not clarify how personal sin relates to sin as a force that affects the person radically. Moreover, as Keenan knows, even if the person is doing all she existentially can do, God is always calling her into deeper intimacy, into an ongoing conversion. Since sin is not coterminous with moral culpability, sin talk need not obviate this point; it could stress it.[21] Furthermore, sin talk could, as I will suggest later, foster self-critical reflection and cultural criticism of the kind that might broaden the existential capacities of the person.

The tension between sin as a force and as a personal orientation becomes a problem for a theology of sin that neglects sin's expression in moral acts, because, at the very least, it is unclear how moral acts fit in this tension. Do they connect these two dimensions of sin? If so, sin as a force becomes less serious than the acts through which the person activates her relation to it. Sin as an orientation privileges acts in relation to sin as a force—acts graft an agent into the economy of sin— and this sustains the link between sins and moral culpability even as it implies that the force of sin mitigates culpability. Sin as an orientation also downplays those acts; they are partial expressions of the person, such that whatever culpability we might assign them, we cannot, and ought not, infer sin's presence or absence in the act on the basis of that assignation. As we will see, attention to acts takes the form of a moral analysis that is resolutely agnostic about their theological import. Such agnosticism risks making sin as an orientation abstract apart from consideration of the sorts of sinful actions that forge and incarnate it and yields a thinly theological analysis of moral acts. Such attempts to tease apart sin and culpability begin to divest us of the explanatory power of sin talk as a means for locating and understanding the act in the person's fundamental God relation.

How does Curran's argument about persons, acts, and our moral designations of them fit with his theology of sin? He argues that

> one should not refer to external acts as sinful or not, but as right or wrong. At best one could use "sin" analogously to describe the external act alone, but because of past distortions in the Catholic tradition, it is much better to describe the objective act in itself as "right" or "wrong." On the basis of the external act alone, one cannot determine whether or not sin exists. In light of the relational-responsibility model, sin is seen in terms of multiple relationships. Mortal sin is the breaking of our relationships with God and others while venial sin weakens these fundamental relationships. On the basis of the external act alone, one can never know whether the relationship with God and others has been severed or not (192).[22]

What is the upshot of this more serious attention to sin? On the one hand, sins become less important. Sin, most properly, consists in a rejection of God, an aversion or disorientation. Many sins, the so-called venial sins, do not amount to such a radical decision; they are sins only analogously. We cannot know whether a particular act is a mortal sin, a decisive rejection of God, simply by observing the act and its departure from the moral law. As Keenan puts it, "The fact that one performs disordered actions only indicates the degree to which one lacks personal freedom or suffers disorders in various dimensions of one's personality. These actions do not indicate that one fails to strive to love as much as one can."[23] Moreover, if sin consists primarily in a radical rejection of or orientation away from God, it may well be rare, especially if we take seriously God's universal saving will and human freedom's internal orientation toward God (an implication that may undermine the effort to take sin seriously as a force). "The ground and ultimate aim" of the person's freedom, says Franz Böckle, is God, "with the result that, even where [the person] does wrong he can only do this subjectively because of his restless search for the good, at which he aims under the mask of a temporary pseudogood. In other words, he is always bound in his orientation toward good and his freedom is always inwardly qualified."[24] Mortal sin requires a "complete expenditure" of freedom in a decision against God.[25] And because freedom is open-ended, categorical choices are partial and revisable.[26] Thus, contemporary Roman Catholic theologies of sin exhibit a certain disinterest and agnosticism about sins. This clears the way for a moral analysis of acts in terms of a distinction between rightness and goodness, intention and motive, premoral values and disvalues, and so forth.[27]

41

On the other hand, even if actions by themselves, to use Keenan's words, "do not indicate that one fails to strive to love as much as one can," and thus are less important than one's basic orientation and less important than the virtues that modify that orientation, nevertheless, actions *might* indicate this failure in striving. Böckle argues, "This means that the question of venial sin takes on new emphasis. An apparently harmless lack of love of one's neighbor may, when it is seen in this light, be a reflection of fundamental selfishness. This selfish attitude may not perhaps be expressed in the form of horrifying acts violating the middle-class moral code, but it may well be what we mean by mortal sin."[28] This point, in and of itself, warrants more reflection on sins than contemporary Catholic ethics gives. Reluctance to pay this kind of attention arises from dissatisfaction with the kind of attention manualists paid to sins, chiefly one that downplayed the force of sin, reduced sin to particular acts by overlooking its primary constitution in an orientation, and was too quick to impute sin on the basis of external acts.[29] The remainder of this chapter will show why a better kind of attention to sins is possible and why it is compatible with a theology of sin that stresses the person's orientation and the power of sin as a force that affects her and her multiple relations.

First, however, we can press our inquiry into the argumentative scaffolding that supports contemporary Catholic theologies of sin, especially their tendency to distance sin from its expression in moral acts. Let us return to the claim that an act may be formally good despite the material evil it involves. It helpfully illustrates how deliberate attempts to tease apart sin and moral culpability in some Catholic theologies of sin nevertheless allow determinations of the latter to constrict reflection on the theological significance of particular acts. This undermines the very attempt to acknowledge that sin is not reducible to moral culpability. The distinction between formal goodness and material evil rests on at least two important insights that have emerged already. First, sin cannot be identified necessarily and exclusively with violations of the moral law. Curran and others who make this claim are noting the possibility of a gap between particular moral principles and the objective moral goods and values to which they point. Second, sin cannot be identified necessarily and exclusively with particular external acts; that is, snapshots of an act do not convey the agent's intention or motive. The person is always more than her acts. These two points mean that one can be good yet do something that violates a moral principle, that one can act in conformity with moral principles but with a bad or malicious motive, and that wrong and/or bad acts, where they do exist, may be uncharacteristic or misrepresentative of the person's basic orientation toward God.

All of these points are, I think, correct. The agnosticism about acts that they prompt is warranted to a significant degree. The distancing of sin from moral acts, however, presents some difficulties inasmuch as the theology of sin that underlies it ironically prompts a thinly theological moral analysis of acts.[30] This thinly theological analysis of acts becomes clear when we see what it neglects about God and the person and how it is driven by concerns to counter Catholic tradition's earlier reduction of sin to external acts and questions of moral culpability.

The discourse of sin affirms God as the source of freedom and value. As the source of our freedom, God is our highest good, the authentic end of all our aspirations. We have already seen why recognizing God as the source of freedom calls for an appropriate agnosticism about acts. God is also the source of value; God gives us as gifts the various goods and values that constitute our existence in the world. They are opportunities to encounter God by delighting in and cocreating what God has made. They are also markers of proper relation to God, others, and the world. A theology of sin requires a sustained recognition of the person acting in the world and with others before God. She is always working out her relation to God in her acting. Theologies of sin that neglect sins may lose sight of the fact that in our moral acts we take up relations to these objective goods and values that constitute our lives with others and before God. The fact that God is the source of freedom and value corresponds to a fact about the person as an acting subject who reflexively fashions herself in and through her free involvements with the goods God gives. Her bearings to and against them redound; she is always also transacting a relationship with a living God who is the author of these goods and the origin and end of her freedom.

Sin mars the world in which we act, weakens our moral reflection, and lurks in our hearts. Sin is a fact, force, and disorientation. But what is unclear in some Catholic theologies of sin is how, in our subjective relation to goods and values, we freely negotiate our relation with God in the acts we perform. Put differently, the distancing of sin and moral acts trivializes our acting in the world, denuding its religious import and its real and powerful effects on ourselves, others, and the divine. I agree with Curran's insistence that "by my actions I make myself the person I am; and by my actions I do things for good or for ill in this world" (88) and that "in every act I must be properly related to myself as the moral person who is subject and agent, and also properly related to the reality of the objective situation itself" (172); however, I think the sorts of theologies of sin considered here, and revisionist Catholic ethics more generally, tend to undercut the reflexive character of our acting.

I think this is true of fundamental option theory, too. Though I am sympathetic to the theory, contemporary Catholic uses of it explicitly recognize but do not adequately play out the claim that transcendental freedom is only actualized in categorical freedom. This makes them vulnerable to criticisms like those of Pope

John Paul II. After all, if we do a wrong act with a good motive, the act may well elude subjective moral culpability; but the wrongness of the act may express the alienating force of sin. Moreover, because our acting is reflexive—that is, because we make ourselves the persons we are by our acts—a wrong but good act may nevertheless affect our freedom and desire, debilitate us, and dispose us toward future wrong action. It may also undermine or weaken the social conditions that situate and shape freedom and desire, that constitute possibilities for relating fittingly to God, others, and the world. The person's orientation, while not reducible to her acts, is shaped by and through her acts, which may bear the effects of and sustain sin as an alienation from God and others in ways that reach beyond determinations of moral culpability.

Curran and others would not deny this, but they lack the theological conceptual wherewithal concretely to affirm it. Contemporary Catholic theologies of sin, ironically, replace the naive theological legalism of the tradition's earlier equation of sins and acts with an attention to acts that is less theological than it should be, because they fail to appreciate the theological moral correspondence between God as the source of freedom and value and the person's subjective self-determination in and through her free involvements with the objective goods God gives. Consider, for instance, the way in which discussions of premoral values are also strangely pretheological. Freedom's orientation to and operation vis-à-vis these goods is not extended to or grounded in the divine.

Curran's ethics, for example, yokes the objective pole of ethics more to principles than to theological claims about God as the source of freedom and value. The problem is not that Curran and others insist that the subjective pole of morality is primary, but that they insufficiently render the theological grounds of morality's objective pole and undercut the reflexive or self-constituting character of personal activity. The former mistake underplays the moral realism of theological claims. It fuels a reading of such Catholic ethics wherein due recognition of the importance of intention, conflict among goods and values, and the imperfect formulation of moral principles become fodder for charges of moral subjectivism.[31] The latter mistake neglects the theocentric implications of the person's involvement with the goods and values of creaturely life, such that Curran's widely shared concern to ward off claims of moral culpability forestalls not only premature moral judgments about persons on the basis of acts, but also theological and spiritual inquiry into how the alienation of sin expresses itself in and is sustained by personal acts. Agnosticism about acts ("on the basis of the external act alone, one cannot determine whether or not sin exists" [192]) distances sin from moral acts and leaves sin to the mystery of intention and orientation. If sin is not only an orientation but a force, and if sin is not coterminous with moral culpability, there is a good deal more we can say about particular acts as they may express and sustain the alienation of sin without confining our attention to external acts alone.

Contemporary Catholic theologies of sin have several merits. They refer moral acts to the person's relation with God, described as her basic orientation, and her multiple relations with her self, others, and the world. They offer moral descriptions chastened by due recognition of the person's particularity and openness before God and the presence of sin as a power or force in the world. They urge and exhibit spiritual and pastoral sensitivity. Keenan ends his study of goodness and rightness, for example, by suggesting that if we offer God only the rightness of our acts, "then perhaps we have not yet begun to encounter the fullness of that union which we seek, and more important, into which we have been invited. Broken as we are, we offer God our entire selves, willing that there be no limit in our striving."[32] Nevertheless, I wonder if we yet take sin seriously enough without attending to sins. In what follows I suggest how we may do so in a way that is faithful to these merits.

SPEAKING OF SIN AND SINS

A series of distressing stories from the state of Nebraska emerged over the summer of 2008. Nebraska, like every other state in America, had just passed a safe haven law, sometimes also called a "Baby Moses law."[33] Safe haven laws allow a parent (or in some cases anyone authorized by a parent) to relinquish an infant legally (i.e., with immunity from prosecution) and anonymously at designated safe havens like hospitals or fire stations. Such laws have been passed in all fifty states since 1999 as a popular legislative response to horror stories of newborns being abandoned in places like garbage dumpsters or public restrooms. The hope is that safe, anonymous, and legal opportunities to relinquish babies will prevent women from abandoning or killing their children.

Particular features of safe haven laws vary from state to state, such as who counts as authorized personnel for receiving an infant and the age limit for determining which children can be relinquished. Most states limit safe haven laws to newborns. North Dakota currently has the highest age limit; it allows babies up to one year old to be relinquished in safe havens. In Nebraska in 2008, lawmakers did not want to set what they deemed arbitrary age limits, so their safe haven law did not say "infant" or "newborn," but simply "child." What happened next stunned and dismayed lawmakers, Nebraskans, and people across America. People began using Nebraska's safe haven law to relinquish their children, but the children were much older than anticipated. Indeed, none of them were infants. The thirty-six children relinquished under Nebraska's original safe haven law ranged in age from twenty months to seventeen years. Eight of them were between the ages of ten and twelve, and twenty-two of them were between the ages of thirteen and seventeen.[34] Some of the parents even traveled to Nebraska from states as far away as California, Washington, Michigan, and Georgia to deposit their children in Nebraska hospitals. Lawmakers wrestled with the legality of such relinquishments and wondered whether to wait until their next legislative session to amend the law. Eventually they called a special legislative session and changed the law so that only children up to thirty days old may legally be relinquished.[35]

Perhaps the only people who were not surprised by the events unfolding in Nebraska were beleaguered social workers, who saw the relinquishments as evidence of families in need and a system too small, understaffed, and underfunded to help them. Safe haven laws clearly involve a host of moral, legal, and social issues. My aim is not to investigate these here but to point to the act of safe haven relinquishment in order to raise some issues regarding moral language. The stories coming out of Nebraska invited plenty of condemnation for the parents (and a fair share for lawmakers, too) and some, though noticeably less, compassion. The relinquishments typically were called "abandonments." One story that tells of a parent walking down the hospital hallway away from her child, who was left crying, "I'll be good—I'll be good, I promise!" does not exactly dispel that characterization.[36] But some of the parents reported that they were relinquishing their children in the hope that they would receive better medical and social service interventions than the parents themselves or their home states could provide.

Consider what we know about two relinquishments under Nebraska's law. One case involved Gary Staton, who relinquished nine children, ranging in age from one to seventeen, at a Nebraska hospital. Staton found himself a single father after his wife died. He reportedly did not seek assistance from family members (one of whom is now in the process of adopting seven of the children), even though he saw one of them the day he relinquished his children. It was reported a short time later that he and his girlfriend were expecting a baby.[37] Another parent, Melyssa Cowburn, shared her story.[38] She parented a baby whose birth mother literally handed him over to Cowburn outside a Walmart store when he was sixteen months old. The boy eventually was diagnosed with reactive attachment disorder. He was prone to violent outbursts, once attacking another child with a hammer, and another time setting the house on fire. Cowburn and her husband struggled to pay for his medications; her husband even rejoined the military to help cover the costs. They were unable to get their insurance company to pay for mental health treatments for the boy. Cowburn was so desperate that she attempted suicide. She tearfully relinquished the boy, five years old, at an Omaha hospital, telling him she was taking him there so he could get better. She reportedly told him that she wanted him. Utilizing the safe haven law seemed the only way she could secure for him the treatment he needed.

These cases both involve parents stretched to the breaking point. There are, however, moral differences. Staton willingly brought his children into being; Cowburn did not. Staton's children were reportedly healthy and doing well in school, whereas Cowburn's child had a significant diagnosed mental health condition. Staton does not appear to have worked to create a network of caregivers, professional or familial. Cowburn struggled unsuccessfully to obtain necessary services for her sons. Is it appropriate to say in either case that these parents abandoned their children?

"Abandonment" conjures notions of harmful, even malicious, disregard and irresponsibility. Does it apply to the relinquishment a desperate parent makes when her own attempts to navigate social service and medical systems are failing her child? Does all child relinquishment count as abandonment? When might it in fact be an act of parental responsibility on behalf of the child? The utilization of safe haven laws helpfully points to the inevitable indeterminacy of our concepts, including our moral concepts. As is true of any empirical concept, moral concepts like abandonment have an open texture; they cannot exhaustively capture all the observations, facts, details, and future circumstances that might be relevant.[39]

Yet we could not employ such concepts at all unless they had some meaning or intelligibility. We know there is a moral difference between the way the birthmother turned her son over to Cowburn, disappearing into a Walmart, and the way Cowburn turned her son over to medical practitioners and Nebraska state family services. That we can reliably make such a discrimination does not settle moral inquiry, of course, but suggests the way we name moral practices by making conceptually rule-governed analogies. We know what it means to entrust, for example. We know that it can apply to actions like authorizing a sibling to be the guardian of one's children or appointing an employee to implement a new organizational initiative. We know that it does not apply to a vast array of other actions, like skiing, or driving within the speed limit, or recycling. We know this because concepts entail rules for speech and action. There are criteria for correctly using them, criteria grounded in intersubjective structures of meaning and usage.

Put differently, the practices of particular communities "provide the *immediate* and *necessary* context for the individual's comprehension and use of a concept." This means both that using and applying them involves "an irreducible element of discretion and judgment" and that disagreement about their application presupposes considerable consensus about the kinds of cases to which moral concepts and rules, like respect for life, do or do not apply. The concept of murder, for instance, "as we now employ it, is a distillation of an extended, rich process of reflection by which we have progressively drawn a line between permissible and impermissible forms of killing."[40] Disagreements about the moral propriety of destroying embryos, for example, presuppose consensus about the wrongness of murder, a consensus that takes shape by understanding murder with reference to paradigmatic cases of homicide and of killing other forms of sentient life, like animals. Moreover, concepts like "murder" and rules prohibiting it are paradigmatic examples of the even more generic concept of morality.[41] All this is to say that the concept of morality, along with more specific moral concepts and most empirical concepts in general, is analogical. "They can only be understood in and through a grasp of some formal element, in virtue of which the various instantiations of the concept can be recognized for what they are, that is, instantiations of *this* concept."[42]

The formal element of sin is its distinctively theological referent, disruption of proper relation with God. Because of this, serious attention to sin can theologically enrich moral reflection by supplementing moral resources like rules and virtues; its theological character refers us to the point of rules and virtues—they crystallize more basic considerations of the kind of life that responds fittingly to God and to neighbors in God. Attention to sin helps us to recognize the possibilities and limits of moral reason for and moral acting by creatures who are sinners in a world marred by sin. If we are saved while we are yet sinners, how can we attend adequately to the virtues, for instance, without considering how they modify a person who, though saved, remains a sinner?[43] Contemporary Catholic ethics, then, has rightly replaced the tradition's preoccupation with sins with a theology of sin. Does this serious attention to sin nevertheless require sustained reflection on particular sins?

Attention to sins is both compatible with and necessary for a theology of sin because sin and sins are analogical concepts. Attention to sin and to sins opens, rather than constricts, moral reflection. There are three reasons why this is so. First, as stated, the formal element of the concept of sin is its theological referent. As Alistair McFadyen argues, this theological referent yields a distinctive contribution to our understanding of pathology; for this reason, strictly secular descriptions of pathology are incomplete and inadequate. A theology of sin, rightly undertaken, should not operate within and on the terms of secular moral reflection, but should show how theological reflection makes our moral reflection more complete and true. Lust and gluttony, for example, designate particular disorders or pathologies; these vices have meaning with reference to allied notions like chastity and temperance. In other words, we understand these concepts in relation to other moral concepts. Moreover, to designate lust and gluttony as sinful opens our comprehension of them beyond moral considerations precisely by referring their meaning to God and by situating the person before God, thereby enabling us to understand them better.

Second, sin, as an analogical concept, has meaning and shape with reference to paradigmatic cases and kinds of actions—that is, sins. A theology of sin requires attention to sins, lest it become thin and abstract. Reflection on the kinds of actions and dispositions that may exemplify sin indexes it to the moral life.[44] Third, concepts that we may consider as sins depend on a more generic concept of sin. As a generic concept, sin encompasses both observable deeds as well as interior dispositions and proclivities. So to designate sinful actions as such cannot and ought never be a matter of identifying merely external acts.[45] Such concepts are interconnected with others, like rules and virtues, and, like them, are open textured. Sins derive their hermeneutic cachet from sin, the theological referent of which opens up moral reflection about acts to include theological matters. Thus, to attend to particular sins need not prompt a disregard for sin as a power or orientation. Rather, this attention asks after the ways sin as a power or state expresses itself concretely and keeps us mindful that the person as subject and agent is always negotiating her relationship with God. In this way it serves rather than thwarts the effort to attend to the totality of the person and the organic or narrative unity of the moral life.

Recall that for Curran, "at best one could use 'sin' analogously to describe the external act alone, but because of past distortions in the Catholic tradition it is much better to describe the objective act in itself as 'right' or 'wrong'" (192). Curran is not in principle opposed to identifying categorical acts as sins, but he is reluctant to do so because of the "past distortions" that reduced and yoked sins to external acts, thereby obscuring the properly relational character of sin and fostering premature judgments about the person and her relations on the basis of her acts. Curran, like other contemporary Catholic ethicists, expressly distances external acts from determinations of moral culpability. The analogous use of sin he grants (though nevertheless cautions against) is to remind us that sin, for him, most properly is alienation, which may or may not express itself in objective moral wrongdoing. This, as I have indicated, does not strike me as a difficulty. The difficulty I perceive is that this distancing of sin and moral culpability, as it is served and sustained by a standing inattention to sins, lets determinations of moral culpability severely limit what we can say about the theological significance of particular sorts of acts.

Catholic tradition's past distortions should not prevent us from saying a good deal, morally and theologically, about particular sorts of actions. Designating certain kinds of actions as sinful is an open-ended process of moral reflection that asks after the types of actions that typically express disruption of proper relation with God and others and that typically have certain kinds of effects on the agent and her relations.[46] Reticence to include this reflection in a theology of sin makes sin abstract. It also undercuts the very attempt to acknowledge that sin is not co-terminous with moral culpability because it halts our theological reflection on particular kinds of actions at the boundaries of moral culpability.

WHERE IS SIN? WHAT IS SIN?

Keenan argues that often sin is described as arising out of our weakness, the dis-order in our wills and lives. "Where you and I are weak, messy, and broken, we believe we sin. In those same areas we expend great moral effort and yet we name that part of our lives as our sinfulness."[47] Our association of sin and weakness is, says Keenan, profoundly self-deceptive. Insofar as we identify sin with weakness we also identify it with wrongdoing, as much of Christian tradition has done. What is self-deceptive about this is that believing sin to consist in wrongdoing leads us to domesticate sin, to parcel it into discrete acts we can itemize for a confessor, as in "I got angry three times . . . "[48] Keenan suggests that we would better understand sin if we recognized that it arises out of our strength, our ability to do otherwise. "Our sin is usually not in what we did, not in what we could not avoid, not in what we tried not to do. Our sin is usually where you and I are comfortable, where we do not feel the need to bother, where . . . we have found complacency, a compla-cency not where we rest in being loved but where we rest in our delusional self-understanding of how much better we are than others."[49]

Sin, for Keenan, is the failure to bother to love. Sin is therefore prior to our wrongdoing, antecedent to choice. Criticizing Aquinas's concept of sin, Keenan first grants with Aquinas that sin proceeds from the will and entails some disorder. "A disordered will is inclined to disordered behavior. But why is the will disor-dered?" Keenan goes on: "A disordered will has within it a disordered object. Its specific inclinations are wrong. But why? Is it due to error or to a failure to strive? Why does the alcoholic drink? Why does the wife-beater beat his wife? Why does the passive aggressive choose guilt-making objects or the timid person remain shy? . . . Disordered wills choose disordered objects, generally. But is that sin? Is the choice of disordered objects always rooted in a failure to move oneself, that is, a failure to bother? That is our question." Keenan locates sin not in wrongdoing but in our motivation, in the first movement of the will or "the end out of which [versus for which] we act."[50]

Keenan's account of sin is in keeping with the distinction he and other re-visionists draw between goodness or badness on the one hand and rightness or wrongness on the other hand. "Goodness is the striving out of love, charity, or duty for the right. But rightness, whether it focuses on a particular act, a class of rules or values, or even habitual character traits or virtues, measures not whether we strive, but whether we attain those standards."[51] As we have seen, sin properly concerns our badness, a failure to bother to love. And, according to Curran, if we extend talk of sin to refer to wrong acts, we ought to recognize that it applies only by analogy. I wonder if this means that the wrong we do is only a manifestation of sin if we were capable of doing better and chose not to, if the disorder and weakness in our hearts and lives is somehow separable and comprehensible apart from our knowledge of sin.

To be clear, I share Keenan's position that "we might not be as bad as our actions are wrong" and his not-incompatible claim "that we are probably greater sinners than we admit."[52] If I understand him, Keenan's description of sin as a failure to bother to love, a failure to strive, implies that there is some aspect of human freedom untouched by sin. To my mind this points to a difficulty in relating personal sin to sin as a power and force and to social sin. Granted, Keenan says that defining sin as the failure to bother to love is compatible with and even extends the concept of social sin because it defines sin in irreducibly social terms.[53] But neither motivation nor the relative (dis)order of our wills is construed in a way that renders its social situation and determination in dynamics of sinfulness and grace. How can we truthfully and comprehensively understand the disorder in our wills and the disordered action that arises therefrom in relation to God? How can we make sense out of the reflexive or self-determining character of our disordered choices?

Alistair McFadyen, whose work on sin began this chapter, also argues that sin is antecedent to choice. What he means by this is not that there is some exercise of freedom or movement of will prior to our choices. Rather, "sin *pre*-conditions freedom. It is a structural co-determinant of human being and action. Sin lies behind action, in the basic intentionality of the agent (indeed, in the biological and social processes which lie behind that), and not only in the acts themselves."[54] It is important to note that Keenan is discussing what is traditionally called personal sin, whereas McFadyen is discussing original sin. McFadyen criticizes moral approaches to sin that corral and tame original sin within the confines of a modern understanding of moral accountability. That is, McFadyen argues that contemporary Christian theology often moralizes sin so that imputing sin to an agent requires an understanding of freedom as the ability to have done otherwise. Original sin, and particularly Augustine's account of it, offers what McFadyen judges to be a more truthful understanding of human willing.

Sin always involves freedom or some engagement of our wills, but how ought we to understand that freedom? Strictly as the ability to do otherwise? By making this threshold of freedom the criterion for determining the presence or absence of sin in a given action, we forfeit inquiry into how sin as power, force, social process, and structure impinges upon us and our acting. We imperil our ability to speak about the disruption of proper relation to God when it does not fit neatly into assignations of blame, and underestimate our mutual implication in one another's sin. We will consider McFadyen's argument further in chapter 4. For the moment I want to describe the multidimensional reality of sin and argue that a theology of sin is incomplete and abstract apart from attention to particular sorts of sins.

Sin and Sins

Sin is the disruption of proper relation with God issuing in and resulting from the disruption of proper relation to ourselves, others, and the world, a disruption that does not, and cannot, fit neatly into determinations of moral culpability. Sin touches the person's multiple relations with God, self, neighbor, and world. It always involves a vertical estrangement or alienation from God, a reflexive disruption of one's self-relation, and a horizontal estrangement from neighbors and the world. Christian theology offers a wide and rich range of metaphors to designate this estrangement, like "pride" or "sloth," "folly" or "impurity."[55] Attempts to identify one foundational or overarching figure for sin are unnecessary and ill advised; the sheer plurality of images and metaphors helps us to apprehend various aspects and experiences of sin. Here I identify sin in terms of its disorienting, debilitating, and disintegrating effects; the following chapters describe various kinds of sin, such as infidelity and falsehood.

Sin, as an irreducibly theological concept, is the disruption of proper relation to a living God who has shown himself to will and to offer a mutual love relation. Because we were created to know and to love God, this estrangement takes the form of a disorientation, a turning away from our proper end or fulfillment. Scripture describes this turn from God as acquiescence to the desire to eat the forbidden fruit; doing so is a breach of trust in God and prompts Adam and Eve to hide from God (Gn 3). In the *Confessions* Saint Augustine compellingly renders his own disorientation and the confusion it effects as the conflictual and disordered love of the wrong things in the wrong way, even as this disordered love attests to the God for whom our hearts are restless. Because God is our true end, this disorientation bears the marks of falsehood and faithlessness, an idea we will explore further in chapter 5.

H. Richard Niebuhr notes that "the religious concept of sin always involves the idea of *disloyalty*, not of disloyalty in general, but of disloyalty to the true God, to the only trustworthy and wholly lovable reality. Sin is the failure to worship God as God. . . . [Sin] is not merely a deprivation, not merely the absence of loyalty; it is wrong direction."[56] This disorientation is a condition we inherit, in which the person's freedom, reason, and desire emerge. Hence, the force of sin preconditions our agency, affecting our free involvement with the goods of creaturely existence and with the God who gives them. The condition is also one with which we cooperate in our sins.

Thus, sin always also involves a reflexive dimension. Because persons are subjects and agents, our particular sins are more than manifestations of the condition of sin. Sins recoil in a way that involves us more deeply with sin. We cooperate with the reality of sin, in which we are already mired. "Sin lies *behind* action, in the basic intentionality of the agent (indeed, in the biological and social processes which lie behind that), and not only in the acts themselves."[57] We make choices by which we reflexively incorporate ourselves within the distorted economy of relations that sin effects. Because sin disrupts our relation with God, who is our good, because sin preconditions agency, and because by our agency we involve ourselves with it more deeply, we can speak of sins as debilitating. In and by them we reinforce our disorientation and resist the conversion to which we are continuously called. We further confuse the springs of our agency, our freedom, reason, and desire. We erode our capacities for knowing and loving what is truly good, and we constrict our imagination and harden our hearts against God and neighbor.

We cannot eradicate the force of sin through our own efforts. Saint Paul and Saint Augustine described this impotence in terms of the doubleness of the will. Moreover, our attempts to respond to our estrangement from God involve postures like pride and self-justification and dispositions and deeds through which we seek the fulfillment that we find, finally and fully, only in God. As the disruption and ongoing weakening of relations with God and others, sin is not rare. Because sins reflexively debilitate us, sin as an orientation should not be understood in ways that trivialize particular actions but as the unity and history of the person's freedom, which is always more than a moral tally of actions even as it is only wrought in them.[58]

Recognizing this brings us to the horizontal dimension of sin, the moral evil that mars our social existence and the world and that we bring about in our sins. Genesis 3, for example, describes the consequences of sin in terms of its problematizing our relations to one another (Eve must bring forth offspring in pain) and to the world (Adam must toil). Augustine describes the effects of sin at all levels of creation: in the family there is hatred, in the city, murder; among the states there is warfare, and among the angels, rebellion.[59] Sin creates enmity, discord, and vio-lence by breaking down trust, mutuality, and respect. The horizontal dimension of sin accounts for sin's transgenerational character, its pervasive and radical quali-ties, and for our ironic solidarity in sin.[60] Again, our particular sins are more than manifestations of the disintegrating effects of the power of sin. They are ways we involve ourselves more deeply with the economy of sin. They are also more than our own contributions to the presence of sin in the world. It is not as though we are, at the end of the day, only responsible for the deposits we have made. The per-sonal and socially disintegrating effects of sin mean we are deeply involved in one another's sins. Moreover, we cannot locate sin as a basic orientation in a reservoir of freedom that is untouched by these effects or this involvement. The effects of sin as a force operate not only around and on but in our free involvement with the goods and values of our social and creaturely existence, and affect our orientation toward the God who gives them.

Following chapters explore, without pretending fully to resolve, questions about the volitional character of sin. Certainly many additional questions arise re-garding, say, the relations between sin and finitude and the workings of social sin, questions I cannot pursue fully here.[61] My present aim is to show what attention to sins yields for a theology of sin and how such reflection theologically enriches our analysis of moral acts and ethics more generally. Toward that end, let me turn briefly to a particular sin.

The sin of lust provides a case in point, in part because its sexual character can help us to keep in mind that contemporary reticence to pay attention to particu-lar sins arises to some extent out of dissatisfaction with the traditional Christian preoccupation with sexual sins. As chapter 1 noted, contemporary Christian sexual ethics prefers to focus more on qualities or virtues of morally good sexual rela-tions rather than specific acts of sexual wrongdoing or indiscretion. Moreover, the example of lust helps us take note of the fact that moral acts are not limited to observable external events but also occur within the interior lives and dispositions of individuals.[62] Finally, this example also shows clearly that sin manifests itself in social relations, systems and practices, and institutions (e.g., reflection on lust can include attention to pornography and prostitution, sexual mores and gender roles, sexism, and so forth). Indeed, the following consideration of sinful, lustful acts figures in just this expansive, personally and socially integral context.

Lust names a disposition one might have and also an activity in which one might engage, both of which involve particular qualities or expressions of sexual desire. Lust objectifies the one who is desired in a way that is exploitative and distorting. To identify lust as a sin is not to deny the goodness and joy of bodily existence or sexuality; the concept of lust in fact implies some inordinate, polluted, or twisted expression of human sexual embodiment. The meaning of lust is allied to some consensus about sexuality, gender, and proper roles and bonds associated with human sexuality.[63] Its meaning is also allied to a range of virtues, like temperance, modesty, and chastity. Lust captures the sometimes seductive and deceptive character of sin because of the way lust can subordinate more considered judgments about the prudence and propriety of sexual relations and because the fulfillment or satisfaction it promises often in experience turns out to be empty or fleeting.

Typically, lust designates a disposition, a vice that expresses itself in, or at least inclines one toward, sexual sins.[64] Certainly it can express itself in acts like adultery or the use of pornography or in habits like sexual promiscuity. Lust can also designate an interior activity that does not transpire in easily observable external acts or issue in overt harms to oneself or one's neighbors. One may lust after a neighbor but interact with him with decorum. In this activity one beholds the other as an object; one's regard is acquisitive or instrumentalizing such that one seeks not union with but possession of the other. The sinfulness of lust resides in this manner of relating to another and in the manner of self-relation thereby entailed. Lust as a disposition may precede a particular act that instantiates it, but I think we would be mistaken to conclude that the sin lies in a choice prior to the act itself as, say, a failure to bother to love my neighbor appropriately. Rather, there is sin prior to the act itself insofar as the social processes whereby I receive and understand and live out my sexuality are themselves distorted by sin. It is not as though I stand outside them and choose whether or not to join myself to them, either at the level of my moral motivation or by intending to do some particular deed. My freedom is already co-opted and distorted so that I fashion myself in relation to God and others in a way that muddles moral culpability.

This is admittedly an incomplete description of lust, but, I think, a recognizable one. It is also a moral and not a theological description. What happens when we identify lust as a sin? Dante's *Inferno*, from his *Divine Comedy*, provides a classic and rich depiction of lust as a sin that helpfully illustrates sin's effects.[65] The disorientation of sin is signaled at the start of the poem, when Dante the poet reports having lost his way in a dark wood.[66] The dark atmosphere, chaotic activity, and treacherous landscape of hell also suggest this disorientation. In canto 5, Dante the pilgrim and Virgil his guide enter hell proper, having just passed through limbo. At this point stands Minos, a demon who hears the confessions of the damned, wraps his tail around them, and hurls them to their appropriate station in hell. The debilitating effects of sin are already suggested by the way the damned participate in their judgment through confessing, and they become more apparent in the correlation Dante the poet establishes between particular sins and their punishment.

55

In the circle of hell reserved for the lustful, for example, a terrible hurricane tosses about the damned, just as in their earthly lives they were swept away by desire. Among these poor souls, Dante the pilgrim sees Francesca and Paolo. He calls to them, hears their story, and swoons with pity over it. Their story and Dante's response to it signal the disintegrating effects of sin, our involvement in one another's sin.

Dante's exchange with Francesca and Francesca's love for Paolo are instances of desire begetting desire.[67] Paolo and Francesca's lustful interlude was, we learn, occasioned by their reading of Lancelot and Guinevere. "Several times that reading urged our eyes to meet and took the color from our faces, but one moment alone it was that overcame us. When we read how the longed-for smile was kissed by so great a lover, this one, who never shall be parted from me, kissed my mouth all trembling. A Gallehault was the book and he who wrote it; that day we read no farther in it."[68] As Sir Gallehault aided and abetted the adulterous affair between Lancelot and Guinevere, so did their story for Paolo and Francesca. Similarly, Dante the pilgrim is so enthralled by the tale Francesca tells that he, too, swoons. This hearkens back to a warning that Minos gave to Dante, "Beware how you enter and in whom you trust."[69] Dante the poet introduces a hermeneutics of suspicion—beware the story you enter—that complicates and celebrates the intertextuality of his *Comedy* and implies its heuristic value as a text that can teach us to listen and read well.

With all this in mind, let us see how asking after the sinfulness of an act like Paolo and Francesca's indicates the historicity, particularity, and provisionality of acts. Because sins paradigmatically exemplify sin, and because sin is an irreducibly theological concept, identifying sins places these acts in a personal relationship with a living God who offers forgiveness of and redemption from our sins. The *Divine Comedy* as a whole masterfully weaves human and divine history, notorious figures and ordinary folks. Its very structure and narrative sweep indicates that any particular part of the story must be read in light of the whole tale. Hell itself is bounded by the unbaptized and marked by Jesus Christ's passage through it. Moreover, the sin of lust is only intelligible in relation to other sins, as exemplified in the geography of hell, which itself is governed by the Christian story, such that we find Satan in the pit of hell, reserved for those who betray their benefactors.

Instead of fixing our attention on discrete acts, identifying sins indexes acts to human desire for God, to God's desire for us, and to the interplay of this mutual desire in salvation history. Placing acts in this history locates the person's relation to her neighbor there as well, thereby encouraging us to sustain genuinely theological attention to the divine ground of our social relations.[70] It also activates rich theological resources for apprehending, for example, the joy, beauty, power, and ambiguity of human sexuality (in contrast to, e.g., the courtly love with which Dante plays in canto 5 of the *Inferno* and in the *Comedy* as a whole through the figure of Beatrice). Attention to sins invites rather than neglects considerations like covenant fidelity and discipleship. Thus, it will refer us to our desire for God and to our neighbor as a fellow creature who shares our divine origin and end. In this way attention to sins prompts theological and moral reflection on how sin as a force preconditions desire, freedom, and reason, and the effects of grace on them, even as this attention keeps us mindful that sin is ultimately a matter of personal orientation in relation to God.

The historicity of, say, lustful acts points to their particularity. My acts arise from and contribute to my particular relationship with God. They belong to me as a unique individual and as the bearer of a particular (though in no way isolated) history of freedom. Paolo and Francesca's story becomes intelligible in light of its commonalities with and differences from their neighbors in hell, like Dido.[71] The particularity of Paolo and Francesca's deed also, of course, depends on its details. Francesca was married to Paolo's brother Gianciotto, who discovered the lovers together and killed them both. As the story goes, Francesca and Gianciotto were to be married for political reasons, but since Gianciotto was not altogether pleasing to behold, in order to insure that the marriage would be made his family sent Paolo to Francesca as a proxy. She was deceived into marrying Gianciotto under the pretense that Paolo was her betrothed. As Charles Singleton notes in his commentary on the *Inferno*, Bocaccio's own commentary makes much of this deception to exculpate Francesca.[72]

Attention to sins makes us mindful of their particularity. In my agency I negotiate a personal relation with a living God in a particular set of social, historical, and cultural circumstances. I experience the reality of sin as a persistent struggle or wound, one I come to recognize and accept as I apprehend its reflection in my concrete acts and relations and as I experience the transforming and healing effects of grace.[73] In individual moral and spiritual reflection, attention to particular sins belongs to a reflective, self-critical, open, and trusting responsiveness to God. Reflection on my acts of lust may disclose how I deny or evade the intimacy to which God calls me. I may come to realize, too, that certain moral failings that seem fairly disparate are in fact varieties or instantiations of a central struggle. In this discernment I may become friendly with the debilitating effects of sin, as deeper insight into my brokenness shows the futility of works righteousness and as attentiveness to the God who wills my transformation gives way to trust in the divine promises.[74] Moreover, the particularity of these acts as they bespeak and transact a life with God, lived among and with other creatures, invites rather than neglects considerations of vocation, integrity, responsibility, and so forth. Thus, attention to sins like lustful acts prompts theological, moral, and spiritual reflection on the meaning of acts within the tensive relation of sin as a force and sin as a basic orientation. And it does this by (rather than in spite of) enabling a self-critical and yet trusting responsiveness to God, in whom we live and move and have our being.

All this captures the provisionality of our acts. To identify a particular act as a sin is to place it in a relational context and to refer it to an ongoing struggle within an eschatological tension of the "already" and the "not yet." Granted, Dante the poet places Francesca and Paolo in hell for their deed. But he also has Virgil repeatedly rebuke Dante the pilgrim for the pity he feels for the damned.[75] Dante the pilgrim and we readers need to see the full sweep of God's merciful justice to understand the logic of hell. The moral evaluation of a particular act, however reliable it may be, is finally provisional because the full moral meaning of the act is hidden in the counsel of God. This appropriately relativizes our moral evaluation of the act in light of this context, struggle, and tension, even as we also attend to the real harms, fractures, and muddles the acts not only express but effect. Attention to sins also prompts ethics to be open to the insights of other disciplines without treating theological claims as additions to nontheological descriptions. And it makes specific moral issues more porous; for instance, asking after acts of lust highlights matters of intimacy and power that can illuminate the relations among, say, adultery and other forms of betrayal and exploitation. Thus, attention to sins will relativize and open our evaluation of acts even as we seek to specify such an evaluation via the historicity and particularity of our acts. It recognizes sin as a force that limits and perhaps infects moral evaluation and sustains the insight that the person's orientation cannot be reduced to any particular act or to the sum total of her acts.

It is important to note that lust involves dispositions and attitudes that express themselves in exterior and interior acts of lust, both of which have intersubjective effects. So attention to particular sins and the insight it yields into the individual's relation with God cannot occur apart from attention to the effects of sin in our lives with others and in the world. In other words, I am not suggesting that the discourse of sin and attention to particular sins is merely useful or important for individual moral reflection, but that it yokes this reflection to sustained considerations of the social and cosmic ruptures and harms in which we are embedded, by which we are co-opted, with which we cooperate, and to which we contribute. If I lust after my neighbor, this may eventually express itself in some fashion in my dealings with him (or with his spouse, or with mine). If I lust after a stranger, my regard for him still affects me internally, and this internal disintegration still affects the economy of social relations and the conditions of our social world.

In all these ways, attention to sins makes a theology of sin more concrete with-out losing sight of the power of sin or of sin's roots in the person's orientation. It recognizes that the person negotiates her relationship with God in the acts she performs. At the outset of this chapter I noted that talk of sin declined in recent decades in part because of worries about its rhetorical use to scapegoat and shame, to induce guilt in some and bolster self-righteousness in others. It now should be clear that practices of naming sins, reflecting on sins, and examining one's own actions and omissions with a readiness to discover, confront, and confess one's sins in fact permit considerable openness to pastoral and spiritual concerns and sensitivity. Recall that Curran argues that we should not identify acts as sins on the basis of an external act alone because we cannot know the effects of that act on one's relations to God, others, and the world. I say that we are bound in faith to seek to learn something about these very matters. And, in fact, we can do so along the lines I have suggested. Granted, it is important to avoid a minimalistic or physicalist sort of attention to sins, as though we could identify a sin merely by referring to a snapshot of the act or its departure from a particular rule.[76] My own position shares this and much else with Curran's approach.

My point is that asking after the presence of sin permits us to engage in a *lectio* of our moral acts and omissions precisely as a way to plumb the depths and dynamics of our relation to God. This attention does not reduce sin(s) to discrete, merely external events or constrict sin talk to matters of moral culpability. It per-mits us to pay attention to the moral and religious activity of our interior lives and to the real havoc and harm we bring to others. Attention to sins and their expres-sion in moral acts is essential if we are to understand and respond to the full reality of sin in a way that befits the person as subject and agent.

CONCLUSION

The language of sin is not a religious accessory to secular moral accounts of wrong-doing or evil, as though it merely embellished adequate moral descriptions without impinging upon their content; nor is sin a doctrine that Christian ethics can snub or simply avoid without costs. Given its irreducibly theological referent, sin talk is essential to a truthful account of the moral evil we encounter, perpetrate, and un-dergo. A theology of sin is essential to the work of Christian ethics, and attention to sins is an essential part of a theology of sin. Moral discourse should occur alongside and in conversation with the discourse of sin since the latter lends the former its so-teriological and ecclesial framework and context. Moreover, when we fail to name what is sinful about our actions and omissions, our dispositions, relationships, and social structures, we intensify the loss of God that any and all sin involves. In chapter 5 I will argue that when we truthfully name sin and sins as such, we speak healing words that reflect and partake in God's reconciliation of the world to himself. For the moment we need better to understand why and how a person's moral actions bear on her loss or gain of God. We will do so by examining the person's very self-relation as always deepening or eroding her intimacy with God.

NOTES

1. Mahoney, *Making of Moral Theology*, 27.
2. McFadyen, *Bound to Sin*, 24–42.
3. Mahoney, *Making of Moral Theology*, 31.
4. See, e.g., O'Keefe, "Social Sin."
5. The strands and thinkers I engage here are those influenced by fundamental option theory and/or arguments often grouped under the heading of proportionalism, both of which exemplify and have contributed to general trends in contemporary Catholic ethics that are discernible even in thinkers who expressly criticize and distance themselves from fundamental option theory and proportionalism.
6. McFadyen, *Bound to Sin*, 5.
7. Ibid., 4, 19.
8. Ibid., 38–39. McFadyen considers a range of positions and thinkers when making this point, from narrative and existentialist theologies to liberation theology.
9. In *Veritatis splendor*, nos. 65–70, Pope John Paul II criticizes proponents of fundamental option theory for separating the fundamental option from the choice of concrete behaviors. I think this charge is mistaken, though here I argue that the general Catholic emphasis on the person's orientation before God has often been used to distance the person's orientation or fundamental option from her specific moral actions.
10. Curran has made this point repeatedly. Here I focus on his recent synthesis of Catholic ethics, *Catholic Moral Tradition Today*. In the following discussion, references to pages in this work are given parenthetically in the text.
11. See Böckle, *Law and Conscience*.
12. Mahoney, *Making of Moral Theology*, 29, 32.
13. See ibid., 219 and 28–30; Keenan, "Spirituality and Morality."
14. Niebuhr, *Responsible Self*.
15. Rahner, *Foundations of Christian Faith*, 97.
16. An anonymous reviewer noted that Curran differs importantly from fundamental option theorists like Karl Rahner, Franz Böckle, and James Keenan, all of whom I engage in concert with Curran. To the extent that I risk conflating Curran's approach with a fundamental option approach, I may overlook differences among them concerning whether a categorical

act can be said to be a mortally sinful act. Rahner and others who are sympathetic to fundamental option theory argue that freedom is a unity of transcendental and categorical dimensions. Transcendental freedom, its total actualization in a fundamental option for or against God, cannot be separated from the exercise of categorical freedom. But it also cannot be reduced to categorical freedom, either as a choice alongside other choices or as the sum total of all categorical choices.

This leads many Catholic thinkers, including Rahner, Böckle, Keenan, and Curran, to insist that the fundamental option cannot be identified with any particular categorical act; e.g., we cannot say that such and such an act—say, abortion—is always a mortal sin and as such necessarily constitutes a negative fundamental option. Pope John Paul II criticizes moral theories like proportionalism, which he thinks separate the fundamental option from its determination in concrete choices and behaviors; see *Veritatis splendor*. Curran claims that the pope's criticism is mistaken, saying, "The theory distinguishes the transcendental and the categorical aspects, but it does not separate them" (98).

My concern is to probe matters that vex recent Catholic attempts to construe sin as an orientation, especially in relation to recognizing sin as a power, and as a counter to earlier Catholic tradition's focus on sins. Whether these attempts make appreciative use of the fundamental option or not, I attempt to show that the emphasis on orientation, as a counter to the earlier tradition, downplays sin as a force and winds up constricting and impoverishing our reflection on the theological significance of particular acts. These matters may be all the more vexing for approaches indebted to the fundamental option (though I think the theory has resources for addressing them), but they nevertheless trouble the "sin as orientation" approach even when it is not grounded in the theory.

17. See also the discussion of adverse virtue in my chapter 1.
18. Curran refers to the discussion of an invincibly erroneous conscience in Häring, "Theological Evaluation." See also Curran, *Invincible Ignorance*; Keenan, "Can a Wrong Action Be Good?"
19. James Keenan argues that neither mortal nor venial sin characterizes such an act; see *Goodness and Rightness*, 161.
20. Keenan, *Goodness and Rightness*, 16.
21. Of course, sin talk may be ill advised in a particular pastoral situation. I would think, however, that guided discussion about the meaning and experience of sin in one's life would be valuable for pastoral guidance and spiritual direction. At the very least, it would offer an opportunity to engage distorted and spiritually crippling understandings of sin.
22. See also Klubertanz, *St. Thomas Aquinas*.
23. Keenan, *Goodness and Rightness*, 155.
24. Böckle, *Fundamental Moral Theology*, 88.
25. Even this radical no is qualified, however, in fundamental option theory inasmuch as the no is predicated on a yes. See, e.g., Rahner's *Foundations of Christian Faith*, 99–102.
26. Böckle, *Fundamental Moral Theology*, 110.
27. This line of thinking is even more prominent when buttressed by fundamental option theory, but the passage I have cited from Curran makes it clear that such an approach need not depend on the theory.

28. Böckle, *Fundamental Moral Theology*, 111; see also Böckle, *Law and Conscience*, 124.

29. Though, of course, inquiry into impediments to acting might excuse the penitent.

30. See Pope John Paul II, "Reconciliation and Penance" (*Reconciliatio et paenitentia*; 1984), no. 18, accessed June 30, 2011, Vatican website, www.vatican.va/holy_father/john_paul_ii/apost_ex hortations/documents/hf_jp-ii_exh_02121984_reconciliatio-et-paenitentia_en.html. John Paul is discussing atheism and secularism, but we share a concern to root action theory in theology. I am grateful to an anonymous reviewer for alerting me to this particular passage.

31. See John Paul II, *Veritatis splendor*.

32. Keenan, *Goodness and Rightness*, 182.

33. National Safe Haven Alliance home page, accessed July 9, 2009, http://nationalsafehavenal liance.org/.

34. Joshua Rhett Miller, "Father Who Ditched Nine Kids via Safe Haven Law Has Twins on the Way," June 30, 2009, FoxNews.com, www.foxnews.com/story/0,2933,529597,00.html.

35. See the information on Legislative Bill 1 at "Safe Haven Bill," Nebraska Department of Health and Human Services, accessed July 9, 2009, www.hhs.state.ne.us/SafeHaven/.

36. Karen Ball recounts this story in "Defending Nebraska's Child Abandonment Law," *Time*, November 18, 2008, www.time.com/time/nation/article/0,8599,1859951,00.html.

37. Lynn Safranek, "Leaving 9 Kids under Safe Haven Law Was the Best He Could Do, Staton Says," *Omaha World Herald*, June 28, 2009, http://www.omaha.com/article/20090628/NEWS 01/706289910.

38. Nicholas Riccardi, "Nebraska Legislature Amends Safe Haven Law," November 22, 2008, *Los Angeles Times*, accessed July 9, 2009, http://articles.latimes.com/2008/nov/22/nation/na -nebraska22 (headline revised to "State Revamps Haven Law").

39. Chapter 5 will develop this discussion of moral concepts.

40. Porter, *Moral Action*, 27, 31, 21.

41. Ibid., 36. Porter argues that the focal meaning of morality is a commitment to nonmalefi cence. I am grateful to an anonymous reviewer for the suggestion that I consider whether this understanding of morality also provides an adequate understanding of sin. I suspect that it does not, or at least that the irreducibly theological referent of sin transforms a com mitment to nonmaleficence in transmoral ways, though I am unable to take this up here.

42. Ibid., 49.

43. Porter, "Virtue and Sin."

44. For a similar argument about Karl Rahner's account of salvific love, see Porter, "Salvific Love and Charity." I offer a reading of Rahner that endeavors to respond to Porter's criticism, and the criticisms of others, in *Self Love and Christian Ethics*.

45. References to merely external acts can be misleading. Subsequent chapters explore the way the idea of merely external acts or acts in themselves operates in debates between revisionist and traditionalist moral theologians.

46. Porter argues that there is no sharp line between virtues and rules, which implies that there is no sharp difference between describing proper relation to God and disruptions of it; see *Moral Action*, 125–38.

47. Keenan, *Moral Wisdom*, 52.

48. Ibid., 54.

49. Ibid., 57.

50. Keenan, "Thomas Aquinas," 408, 415.

51. Ibid., 412.

52. Ibid., 411; Keenan, *Moral Wisdom*, 53.

53. Keenan, *Moral Wisdom*, 62.

54. McFadyen, *Bound to Sin*, 28.

55. Consider feminist criticisms of Christian tendencies to identify sin as pride or self-love. Many feminists argue that women are more prone to the sin of sloth. See, e.g., Andolsen, "Agape in Feminist Ethics"; Plaskow, *Sex, Sin and Grace*; Grey, "Falling into Freedom."

56. Niebuhr, "Man the Sinner," 277.

57. McFadyen, *Bound to Sin*, 28.

58. This point reflects what has been called a shift from classicism to historical consciousness in Catholic moral theology; see Curran, *Catholic Moral Theology*, 103–4.

59. Augustine, *City of God*.

60. Andrew Sung Park uses the Asian concept of *han* to distinguish sinners from their victims. His argument speaks to the transgenerational character of sin; see *Wounded Heart of God*.

61. See McFadyen, *Bound to Sin*; Alison, *Joy of Being Wrong*.

62. Charles R. Pinches offers an exploration of omissions that is also pertinent; see *Theology and Action*, chap. 7.

63. This point can keep us mindful that reflection on sinful, lustful acts can and should include attention to sin as a power that, e.g., affects our thinking about sexuality, gender, and proper interpersonal roles and bonds.

64. As such it may characterize disorder in a basically good orientation, or it may express an orientation away from God.

65. References to the Italian text and translation are according to line number. References to the commentary are according to page number.

66. Dante, *Inferno*, pt. 1, canto 1, lines 1–3.

67. Ibid., canto 5, lines 76–87, 103–5.

68. Ibid., lines 130–38.

69. Ibid., lines 19–20.

70. See McFadyen, *Bound to Sin*, chaps. 7–9.

71. Dante the pilgrim's pity for Francesca echoes Augustine's tears for Dido; see Augustine, *Confessions*, bk. 1.

72. Dante, *Inferno*, pt. 2 commentary, 84.

73. See Alison, *Joy of Being Wrong*; Kelsey, "Whatever Happened to the Doctrine of Sin?"

74. Hauerwas, *Peaceable Kingdom*, 30–34, 46–49.

75. See, e.g., Dante, *Inferno*, pt. 1, canto 20, lines 19–27.

76. See Porter, "Moral Act."

analysis of
moral action

tradition of
moral acts +
development of
persons

CHAPTER THREE

INTIMACY WITH GOD AND SELF-RELATION

Attending to particular sorts of actions (sinful or not) may and should alert us to their historicity, particularity, and provisionality. Properly mindful that any human action is historical, particular, and provisional, we are rightly modest, compassionate, and open to correction in what we venture regarding their import for one's relationship with God. Too often, however, theologians invoke these features of moral actions to forestall or limit what we say about their theological significance; modesty gives way to an unfitting agnosticism, compassion gives way to pastorally and practically enervating subjectivism, and openness to correction gives way to anxious defensiveness about the ethical theories that corral and constrict moral theology today. The previous chapter attributed these moves to an understandable dissatisfaction with earlier Christian preoccupation with sins. This preoccupation entailed mistaken views of sins and fostered premature judgments about persons on the basis of their actions. As we saw, however, the concern to avoid focusing on and arriving at hasty judgments of moral culpability has led to theologies of sin that nonetheless permit determinations of moral culpability to dictate what we may say, if anything, about the theological or religious significance of particular moral actions. Moreover, those determinations of moral culpability depend upon problematic modern accounts of autonomy and responsibility.

This chapter explores the connections among particular moral actions, the agent's moral identity, and the significance of those actions for the agent's relationship with God. What is the relation between the objective rightness or wrongness of particular actions and the person's subjective moral goodness or badness—that is, her orientation toward or against God? How do particular actions affect growth in or erosion of personal relation with God? Answers to these questions require an account of human freedom that surpasses modern moral autonomy, one that affirms the intimate nearness of God within the very structure of the person's agency without obscuring the necessarily embodied exercise of that freedom. The notion of intimacy helpfully renders the truth that we live, move, and have our being in God (Acts 17:28). God wills intimate relation with us; indeed, we are made for it. In our acting we embody and negotiate our free response to God's self-offer. The person's moral willing and acting involve her in the world of goods that God authors and negotiate her response to God, the origin and end of her freedom.

INTIMACY WITH GOD

The point of reflection on persons and moral actions is to understand better and orient ourselves in faithful responsiveness to God's self-offer, so let us begin by considering the intimacy God wills to share with us. God's presence, as Saint Augustine described it, is "more inward than my most inward part and higher than the highest element within me."[1] It is written within my self-relation. More intimate than the person's self-presence is the presence of God. It is not as though the person stands before God unrelated and makes a decision about whether to take up a relation *to* God. This would deny God's immanence and suggest a sovereign self-possession that the person, as a creature, does not have. Rather, the person's self-relation, situated as it is within and vis-à-vis God's self-offer, depends upon and always already involves relation with God. God's self-offer, as an invitation, precedes and bears our response to it.

Self-relation and relation to God are intertwined such that the person comes to herself as she responds to others, the world, and, in doing so, to God. The person becomes aware of herself, understands herself, and fundamentally determines herself in and through her encounters with and responses to others, the world, and God. The person's self-relation encompasses her interpretive, evaluative, and embodied self-determination as a creature who reflexively fashions herself in and as a response. That is, the person takes up and negotiates who she is in and through these encounters and responses in the full and embodied range of her understanding, valuing, and acting in the world with others. As she plans for her future, discerns her vocation, takes on or abandons social roles, chooses her pursuits, makes, forsakes, keeps, and forgives her friends, samples cultural wares, undergoes what she suffers, and prepares for death, she is all the while responding to the living God. The fundamental and inextricable connection between self-relation and relation with God means that our exercise of freedom, in its particulars and as a whole, is always responding to God's desire for intimacy with us and, thus, that the person experiences the gain or loss of God in her self-relation.

Intimacy consists in the self-gift of persons who are different. Genuine intimacy does not obliterate this difference, but makes it a gift to be received, welcomed, and revered. It requires dependence in freedom—we are free when we embrace our dependence on others to be who we are, at least to make an offering of ourselves to them. It also requires freedom in dependence—we are intimate when we learn to be dependent in a way that preserves freedom. Intimacy with God is an utterly gratuitous possibility, as is all intimacy. In creating us for intimacy, God depends upon us in order to be for and with us in the way God freely wills to be. This does not mean that there is anything about us that requires God's self-offering, but rather that God's sovereignty and transcendence express themselves in the divine willing of immanent self-communication. Since God establishes our freedom, it is realized and fulfilled in dependence on God. Intimacy with God is possible for humans precisely as creatures made to know and love God.

Intimacy has a constitutively historical or narrative character. It is possible only between and among persons who are bearers of freedom and, as such, negotiate relations in history as they forge histories with others. The mutual self-presence of intimacy is possible by virtue of and takes its shape and tenor from the history or story of approach and withdrawal, communion and alienation, availability and evasion that persons weave together. The "always already" of God's self-offer comes to us in creation and covenant, in the person, death, and resurrection of Jesus, and in the gift of the Spirit. It is encountered and mediated in our experience of and personal histories with God, others, and the world. So intimacy with God involves coming to know more directly the history of God's saving love as one's own history.

As a mutual self-gifting intimacy can only be particular. Because relation with God is written into the person's self-relation and because intimacy is constitutively historical, the self-gift the person makes is not the offering of a self that is finished or independent. The self that is given emerges in the relationships she negotiates for better or worse. The person is made by them in her making of them. In intimate relations our very selves are at stake. Intimacy cannot be exacted or demanded— when it is, we surely experience only a counterfeit of it—though it exacts and demands everything. The particularity of any intimate relation encompasses who we are; it is not a sharing of part of ourselves but of the whole of ourselves. Yet it begets something new, transforming us into ones we could not be without giving ourselves to a particular other and without receiving this particular other as a gift. Intimacy with God, then, requires a person to love God with her whole heart, mind, and strength (Mt 22:37) and accordingly requires her to make herself as one receiving and ever more made by God's self-offer.

Because intimacy is this free self-gift of particular persons in history, who make a history, it is never finished or episodic, however many moments might be decisive for the relationship. There is a certain provisionality to intimacy. It is polarized toward ever greater degrees, toward a fullness that is not finally possible in this world. Intimacy with God must be incomplete short of the beatific vision. And because this intimacy is with a living God, it beckons us continually toward an ongoing conversion. At every moment God invites us into deeper intimacy. The provisionality of intimacy with God arises from, rather than qualifies, the fidelity or steadfastness of God's self-offer. And, of course, this provisionality is due to our freedom to accept or reject God. Our particular free choices can honor, deepen, and substantiate intimacy with God or betray, evade, and diminish it. Sin and weakness and fear, human finitude and incompletion, and the person's plurality and complexity all make intimacy provisional. But this provisionality does not mean that our choices can be undone; although we remain free (albeit in varying degrees), since intimacy is constitutively historical, these choices matter and persist.

Because we are made by God and for God, we can speak properly of God as the source of freedom and value. God's intimate presence in the depths of our self-relation founds our freedom, and founds it for the sake of deeper intimacy. The God who is the source of our freedom is also our highest good, the true end of our freedom. We can only encounter God's desire for intimacy in the gift of our creatureliness, and we see it manifest supremely in the Incarnation. We know that God affirms the goodness of creation and wills its flourishing. As our creator and as our highest good, God is the source of value. We make intimacy with God and others in a world laden with divine gifts given for the sake of the divine self-promise. Indeed, our experience of and response to God's self-offer are mediated by the objective goods and values that constitute our lives. So our intimate involvement in and with this world is always also an involvement with the God who gives it and loves it and us.

The person responds to God in and through the full range of her creaturely existence in the world. Because intimacy with God is necessarily historical, particular, and provisional, the person's moral willing and acting fashion a response to God that is always in the making and is always meant to be a movement into deeper intimacy. And because God is the source of both freedom and value, we cannot separate the person's self-relation, her response to God, and her involvement in a world thick with goods and values.

FREEDOM AS A FUNDAMENTAL OPTION

This section introduces fundamental option theory and discusses debates about it between Pope John Paul II and revisionists.[2] We consider fundamental option theory because it is an instrument of the recent theological distancing of persons from their actions. Although the fundamental option is no longer fashionable in contemporary Roman Catholic ethics, it significantly influenced post–Vatican II moral theology, and a diluted version of it persists in theological talk of the human person's basic orientation to God. Here we want to consider recent debates between John Paul and revisionists concerning the relation of the fundamental option (the person's basic orientation toward or against God) and particular decisions and actions. Revisionists distinguish between the objective rightness or wrongness of particular acts and the subjective goodness or badness of the person's motive (whether or not she strives to love God as best she can). John Paul takes this distinction as evidence that revisionists separate particular actions from the fundamental option, such that what the person chooses, a concrete behavior, has no bearing on the fundamental option. Revisionists argue that the pope misunderstands the fundamental option as an act; he fails to appreciate the athematic character and irreducibility of transcendental freedom.[3]

These respective charges concern, on the one hand, the way particular actions not only express but constitute the fundamental option, and on the other hand, the fact that the fundamental option, as the total self-determination of the person in response to God, is irreducible to any particular act. As we will see, John Paul argues that the free choice of particular sorts of actions determines the will of the agent who performs them, and thus, *what* the agent chooses to do may crucially determine her fundamental option. Revisionists stress that we cannot determine what an agent chooses in performing some action without attending to the totality of her intentions and the morally relevant circumstances, and that the objective rightness or wrongness of that action does not tell us whether the person acted with a subjectively good or bad motive. Hence, for revisionists, the import of particular actions for the fundamental option depends importantly on what is going on *in the choosing* of those actions. Even so, they argue, transcendental freedom—and so the person's fundamental option—cannot be reduced to her particular choices and actions. Both sides offer insights worth retaining, yet neither side adequately renders the dialectical relation of the person's response to God, her fundamental option, and her free involvement with the creaturely goods God gives. Attending to the reflexive character of human self-relation helps us to understand better how human acts, in the choosing of what is chosen, are (1) more engaged with our fundamental option than revisionists allow or can explain, but (2) less regimented to it by what is chosen than the pope imagines. The fundamental option both expresses itself in particular choices and actions and is always being decided in them.

The Fundamental Option and Moral Actions

Fundamental option theory emerged in dogmatic theology but has considerably influenced moral theology. Karl Rahner, drawing on Jacques Maritain and Joseph *not just about the action & consequence — Obeying law or not, but our actions say something about us, our relationship to God*

CHAPTER THREE

Maréchal, developed the idea of the fundamental option by investigating the conditions for the possibility of revealed truths, like the Incarnation. In doing so he set the stage for moral anthropology on the terms of God's self-communication. Knowing what we know of God, what can we say about ourselves as creatures who have received this gracious revelation? Rahner argues that the human person has a receptive potential for it—we are created as ones who can receive God's self-communication.[4] God is our true end, our highest good, the fulfillment of our aspirations and longings.

The fundamental option articulates this recognition of God in an account of human freedom. Because God is the source of our freedom and its ultimate orientation, freedom is basically and always a freedom vis-à-vis God.[5] It has a transcendental depth or dimension. It consists in more than freedom of choice; it is a capacity to decide about ourselves in response to God's self-offer. This means that transcendental freedom is not reducible to particular categorical choices or to their sum total—the transcendence of freedom eludes such a complete objectification.[6] Yet, as bodily, social, historical, and finite creatures, we only experience the transcendental ground and orientation of freedom categorically—that is, as spirits in the world. Transcendental freedom "as the freedom of the subject about himself and towards himself and from himself as a single whole . . . is not a freedom which lives behind a merely physical, biological, exterior and historical temporality of the subject. Rather, it actualizes itself as this subjective freedom in a passage through the temporality which freedom itself establishes in order to be itself."[7]

The fundamental option refers to the unity and interpenetration of transcendental and categorical freedom. Transcendental freedom expresses itself in but is not reducible to categorical freedom. Categorical freedom is the constitutive medium of transcendental freedom. If we limit freedom to the categorical choices of objects, we cut short its reach and may overlook its unity, which abides through the individual and disparate choices we make. If we disassociate transcendental freedom from these categorical choices, freedom becomes an abstraction and we risk denying the unity of the person as an embodied spirit in a world endowed with value, who reflexively fashions herself in and through these choices.

The theory has prompted analyses of moral acts that, despite differences, basically insist that if we are to understand the moral meaning of particular actions, we must consider them in light of the fundamental option—that is, the present direction of a freedom that is yet unfinished.[8] This is quite evident in revisionist uses of the theory. Klaus Demmer, for example, argues that individual decisions are "interpretations" and "ratifications" of the person's fundamental option.[9] Similarly, Franz Böckle calls them "constitutive signs." According to Böckle, while the fundamental option can only be expressed and actualized in categorical choices, the person "can neither understand himself as a whole nor fail as a whole by means of an individual decision."[10] Thus, we cannot say that the choice of some categorical object necessarily posits a negative fundamental option.

Josef Fuchs insists that acts manifest only a part of the person and "never touch more than a rather small area of the full horizontal reality of the individual, or of humanity, or of the subhuman world." Fuchs argues that we can and should distinguish the moral status of the person, as one fundamentally open or closed to God and so good or evil, from the rightness or wrongness of her acts—that is, their "fittingness" to "the good of the person and of his world."[11] This means that we may and must distinguish between goodness and rightness, the person's fundamental moral identity and her concrete actions. Because freedom is a unity, there is no separation between goodness and rightness.[12] But morality is really about persons, not "actions as such." Goodness disposes us to seek and to realize what is right. Wrong behavior does not "directly involve" goodness or salvation, for "one who does what is unfitting, but does this in error or in good faith can be morally good and can be saved in his relationship with God."[13] We will return to the distinction between goodness and rightness.

There are several important, interrelated moral theological insights in fundamental option theory. First, it emphasizes the relational character of grace and salvation, and it befits a developmental understanding of the moral life as growth in (or the erosion of) relation with God and others. It thereby helps to account for erratic and mistaken actions and behaviors, the existential possibilities and limits of the person as an acting subject, and so forth. Second, the theory stresses the unity and history of the person's freedom. The person is an acting subject; she has a totality and a complexity that underlie, abide in, and absorb her particular acts. Thus, we ought to avoid construing the moral life atomistically—that is, as a series of discrete acts. Third, the person's fundamental option, as a transcendental and so athematic self-determination in relation to God, eludes complete and fully conscious objectification. The ineffability of her fundamental option prompts agnosticism about the relation of any of her particular acts to it. This agnosticism, when appropriate, can express a faithful recognition of God's sovereignty, our finitude, and the open texture of human freedom. Finally, fundamental option theory is particularly amenable to the relations between the moral and spiritual life. The person has the task of integrating her individual choices with her basic decision, of engaging in an ongoing conversion.[14]

This tensive relation between transcendental and categorical freedom is the great merit of fundamental option theory. Nevertheless, recent debates about persons and acts suggest that it could be deployed to better effect. In his 1993 encyclical *Veritatis splendor*, Pope John Paul II affirms the fundamental option as

a self-determining response of faith to God's self-offer but worries over certain
formulations or deployments of the theory wherein the distinction between the
fundamental option and deliberate choices of concrete kinds of behavior can tend
to appear as a separation.

> *Particular acts* which flow from this option would constitute only partial and
> never definitive attempts to give it expression; they would only be its "signs"
> or symptoms. . . . There thus appears to be established within human acting
> a clear disjunction between two levels of morality: on the one hand the order
> of good and evil, which is dependent on the will, and on the other hand spe-
> cific kinds of behavior, which are judged to be morally right or wrong only
> on the basis of a technical calculation of the proportion between the "pre-
> moral" or "physical" goods and evils which actually result from the action. . . .
> The properly moral assessment of the person is reserved to his fundamental
> option, prescinding in whole or in part from his choice of particular actions,
> of concrete kinds of behavior.[15]

Proponents of fundamental option theory, particularly revisionists, offer rejoinders. Thomas Kopfensteiner, for instance, says the theory posits "no such separation between goodness and rightness or person and act." By suggesting that it
does, the pope fails "to appreciate the interpenetration of the transcendental and
categorical levels of action."[16] This failure leaves him, and others who worry about
such a separation, open to the charge that they remain in the grips of a reductive
neo-scholastic analysis of acts. And, says Kopfensteiner, these thinkers are the ones
who are prey to culpable demarcation between the subjective and objective dimensions of the moral life, inasmuch as their focus on the phenomenal structure of the
act fails to attend to the human subject.

Fuchs says that because the fundamental option and specific choices "happen
on different levels of the same person," it is "just not possible for us to examine
the core of our person from the outside so as to establish whether we are fundamentally good or evil . . . [though] we can to some extent conclude by a conjecture
based on our actions." Moreover, "it is not as easy for a good person to change his
or her fundamental option as it would be to swap morally good particular actions
for morally bad ones," though individual decisions and actions "can nevertheless
gradually bring a person to a point at which he is now committed to the contrary
of his previous direction and disposition. When this happens, his fundamental option is reversed."[17] The pope's failure to appreciate the necessarily athematic character of the fundamental option leads him to suggest that it is "a precise, definite,
determinable *act*" and to assume that we can morally judge a person on the basis

of her free and conscious acts. So he sees a split or dissociation in the positions of his interlocutors that simply is not there. Fuchs argues that "precisely because the fundamental option and moral choices are on different levels, the theory stresses rather their mutual relationship and interpenetration." The problem is how to relate acts "to the ethical status of the person as a whole, which is on another level."[18]

Of course, the pope also thinks the problem is how to relate the acts of the person to her fundamental self-determination before God. But, for him, this means the fundamental option *"is always brought into play through conscious and free decisions. Precisely for this reason, it is revoked when man engages his freedom in conscious decisions to the contrary, with regard to morally grave matter."*[19] This passage gives the lie to rejoinders that say the pope fails to appreciate the interpenetration of the fundamental option and particular choices, though he may render it in too tight and punctual a fashion.

Revisionists, for their part, are right to say they do not separate the fundamental option from individual choices or acts, though as a reply to *Veritatis splendor* this insistence is unhelpful. The worry that the fundamental option drags attention away from the person's social and historical situation and from her particular acts is common and persistent among both detractors and proponents of the theory.[20] It places the onus on those sympathetic with the theory to better articulate the interpenetration of transcendental and categorical freedom. How can we avoid, on the one hand, a reductive analysis of acts that locks the fundamental option into them, and, on the other, a more nuanced analysis of acts that implies a separation of the fundamental option from them? We need to consider more directly some of what the pope and revisionists say about moral acts.

Moral Action Is Reflexive

Recall that the following insights emerged in our initial consideration of intimacy with God. Self-relation and relation with God are inextricably connected, such that we experience and respond to God's self-offer in and through the full range of our creaturely existence. Because intimacy is historical, particular, and provisional, our actions disclose and negotiate, express and constitute who we are in relation with God. The meaning of any particular act for our self-determining response to God depends on the history and future of that relationship, even as it contributes to the loss or gain of intimacy with God. This is because God is the source and end of human freedom and the source of those goods and values that he himself gives for the sake of our creaturely good in intimate relation with him. Since our free actions are self-determining or reflexive, our involvements with creaturely goods are always also involvements with God. With these points in mind we can consider further the debates between John Paul and revisionists regarding the import of particular actions for the fundamental option.

We will see that John Paul understands this import in terms of what the person chooses when she acts—the object of her act—and its order or disorder in relation to the human good and to God. On the basis of this account, the pope judges that revisionists separate particular actions from the fundamental option. Revisionists think the pope prematurely judges persons' wills on the basis of their acts (thus, they charge him with physicalism). Revisionists construe the import of particular actions for the fundamental option in terms of distinctions between rightness and goodness, intention and motive. These distinctions permit an understanding of persons, acts, and relation with God that is more attentive to the historical, particular, and provisional character of intimacy with God than the pope's argument allows. Yet they also show how revisionists undercut the reflexivity of human acting and so distance particular acts from the person's response to God, because they do not allow for or explain how the objective rightness or wrongness, order or disorder, of particular acts redounds upon the person as a creature growing in or eroding intimacy with God in and through her involvements with the goods God gives.

In *Veritatis splendor* John Paul's worry about the fundamental option becomes clearer in his subsequent discussion of the moral act. He argues that human acts, insofar as they are deliberate choices, morally define the person, and that the morality of acts depends on the relation of these free choices to the person's good and to God. "Activity is morally good when it attests to and expresses the voluntary ordering of the person to his ultimate end and the conformity of a concrete action with the human good as it is acknowledged in its truth by reason. If the object of the concrete action is not in harmony with the true good of the person, the choice of that action makes our will and ourselves morally evil, thus putting us in conflict with our ultimate end, the supreme good, God himself."[21] The pope repairs to the traditional fonts of a moral act (intention, circumstances, and object) in order to argue that, while intention and circumstances matter, they are insufficient for morally judging a concrete choice. "*The morality of the human act depends primarily and fundamentally on the 'object' rationally chosen by the deliberate will. . . .* In order to be able to grasp the object of an act which specifies the act morally, it is therefore necessary to place oneself *in the perspective of the acting person.*" The object is "the proximate end of a deliberate decision," a "freely chosen kind of behavior" which "determines the act of willing on the part of the acting person."[22] It must be capable of being ordered to the person's good; such an act is therefore capable of being ordered to God and is ordered thus by the will through charity.

Some acts are "intrinsically evil"—that is, incapable of being so ordered. They cannot be justified by a good intention or anticipated good consequences. The pope therefore rejects a thesis he finds in some moral theories, that we cannot identify deliberate choices of specific acts as evil "*apart from a consideration of the intention for which the choice is made or the totality of the foreseeable consequences of that act for all persons concerned.*" John Paul thinks this thesis is characteristic of proportionalism; it is discernible in revisionism more generally. According to him, revisionism suggests that "concrete kinds of behavior could be discerned as 'right' or 'wrong,' without it being thereby possible to judge as morally 'good' or 'bad' the will of the person choosing them." Revisionists tend to separate the fundamental option from the person's particular choices "when they expressly limit moral 'good' and 'evil' to the transcendental dimension proper to the fundamental option, and describe as 'right' or 'wrong' the choices of particular 'innerworldy' kinds of behavior: those, in other words, concerning man's relationship with himself, with others and with the material world."[23]

Revisionists contest the pope's presentation of their arguments—for instance, rightly rejecting the claim that they separate the fundamental option from particular actions.[24] Several note that no one wishes to deny what the pope affirms.[25] Nevertheless, *Veritatis splendor* poses a challenge to anyone seeking to construe the relation of persons and acts. John Paul repeatedly returns to the capacity of acts to be ordered to the human good, and thus to God as the final end of the person, and says, "Clearly such an ordering must be rational and free, conscious and deliberate."[26] His sustained focus on the deliberate choice of particular acts and on the voluntary ordering of the person to God indicates his principal concern: whether particular sorts of intentional involvements with goods respond fittingly to God, who made us and wills our good in him as the creatures we are.[27]

In their responses to *Veritatis splendor*, some revisionists run past the pope's challenge in large part because, to them, the way the pope casts it embodies an unacceptable physicalism that regards acts apart from our moral willing. The physicalism that these revisionists discern in the encyclical (and in the magisterium's moral teaching on sexual ethics) suggests that one can morally evaluate an act on the basis of the act in itself—that is, as a physical occurrence—without knowing the person's intention or considering all the morally relevant circumstances and consequences. Moreover, as the pope seems to suggest, we can morally evaluate not only the act, but the will of the person who performs it insofar as the act is freely chosen. Physicalism seems either to imply a picture of acts out there in the world, shorn of persons who are acting subjects within them, or to collapse persons into particular acts as though the acts were totally determinative of the person and of her relation to God.

Charles Pinches has argued recently that the charge of physicalism does not stick to the pope's argument in *Veritatis splendor*. Since the pope speaks of the perspective of the acting person and of the will's involvement in the person's choice of particular actions, he clearly does not mean to be physicalist.[28] John Paul does acknowledge the charge of physicalism and suggests that it arises from a modern tendency to oppose freedom and nature.[29] In fact, following Martin Rhonheimer, Pinches argues that it is the revisionists who are physicalist.[30]

Whatever the verdict on physicalism, revisionists are manifestly concerned with the relation of persons and acts and with the person's relation to God. But their arguments fall short of the challenge *Veritatis splendor* makes. This is not because they separate the fundamental option from particular choices, but because in their formulations of the theory and, subsequently, in their analysis of moral acts, they do not attend sufficiently to the reflexive character of acting. Their arguments tend to emphasize the irreducibility of transcendental freedom to its categorical objectifications. This undercuts the reflexive or constitutive character of those objectifications for the fundamental option and thereby distances them from the person's response to God, who at every moment calls her into deeper intimacy in and through her categorical, creaturely existence. We can see this distancing by moving from claims revisionists make about particular acts back to claims they make about the fundamental option.

Revisionists insist that if we are to morally evaluate an act we must consider it in its totality. They are not saying, as the encyclical accuses, "that *morally wrong actions (ex objecto)* can be justified by the end." Indeed, revisionists reject the very idea that an action can be identified as wrong by virtue of its object prior to consideration of the agent's intention or the circumstances that surround the action. "An action cannot be judged morally wrong simply by looking at the material happening, or at its object in a very narrow and restricted sense."[31] We cannot know the object of a given act, what the agent chooses in her choice to perform it, unless we consider not only the material happening but the agent's intention and the morally relevant circumstances.[32]

Sometimes the agent's intention crucially determines the object. By way of example, Richard McCormick draws a distinction between masturbation for sperm testing versus for self-pleasuring. Says McCormick, "They are different because of different reasons for the act, i.e., different goods sought and aimed at different intentions. Intention tells us what is going on."[33] (Note that, though McCormick is surely correct, his point does not settle whether the agent's intention in, say, masturbation for sperm testing is a willing involvement with the desired good, presumably procreation, that responds fittingly to God.) Sometimes circumstances crucially determine the object. For example, in an act in which one person kills another, it is not "a mere circumstance that the killer is an authorized executioner and the victim is a duly convicted criminal."[34] Revisionists do not quarrel with the claim that there are intrinsically evil acts, acts that are always wrong by virtue of their object, "*if the object is broadly understood as including all the morally relevant circumstances*."[35] Like the pope, revisionists are concerned with what the person chooses in her acting. For them, this requires consideration of the act in its totality.

But even once we have considered an act in its totality we are only yet in a position to speak of the act's rightness or wrongness, its order or disorder with reference to the human and common good. According to Fuchs, "Rightness of conduct is not directly related to the personal morality of the human person, i.e., to his moral goodness, but refers as such to the good of the human being (of mankind) in his horizontal dimension." Goodness disposes the person to seek to identify and realize right behavior, to incarnate her goodness, but inevitable failures in this discernment and realization do not circumscribe the perennial possibility of being good.[36] The distinction between goodness and rightness helpfully forestalls premature moral judgments about persons on the basis of their acts. The person sometimes acts mistakenly but in good faith. Note, however, the movement from goodness to rightness, but not back from rightness to goodness. If the question that concerns us is the import of some act for the person's God relation, any answer must wait because "rightness of conduct is not directly related to" personal morality, which concerns the person's response to God.

We are not without help, however, because we can consider a distinction some revisionists draw between motive and intention. "Goodness pertains to the former, rightness to the latter." Rightness, says James Keenan, "has two realms: the executed act (choice) and the agent's reason for acting (intention)."[37] From here we can go some way in discerning how it is or is not ordered to the human and common good. But this will not tell us the agent's motive. Motive "explains [one's] fundamental disposition"— that is, "whether one moves oneself out of charity or benevolence to realize oneself or one's acting rightly." What's more, "moral goodness depends solely on the motivation of the person."[38] This is more helpful. Goodness tells us something about the person's response to God in this decision and action, and rightness tells us something about its fittingness to the human good. Again, note the movement from the person's goodness to rightness, but not from rightness back to goodness. Rightness in conduct may express, manifest, and incarnate goodness. Wrongness in conduct, if accompanied by a good motive, signals, perhaps, error on the person's part, or limitations of existential or innerworldly varieties, or disorder in the person because of a vice like greed. It does not alter, or evidently even touch, her motive.[39]

This is all the more evident when we link the person's response to God in a given act to the fundamental option. The fundamental option (and so the person's relation to God considered most properly) is not separate from her choice in acting. Indeed, the choice may express it. Then again, it may not. Whatever the case, a particular act is a partial expression and actualization of transcendental freedom. This means that it is probably insufficient to revoke or reverse the fundamental option unless the act "attain[s] to the same non-conceptual level."[40] And, in any event, the person's fundamental option is inaccessible to her since it is necessarily athematic.

Revisionists rightly insist that the person is required to integrate her choices, actions, and relations with her fundamental option for God.[41] Categorical choices are partial exercises of the one, total freedom the person has and is. Franz Böckle calls actions constitutive signs of the fundamental option. The picture revisionists give is one wherein actions ferry the fundamental option into the categorical realm. But the emphasis falls on the fundamental option as expressing itself in particular actions. The ferry ride, as it were, does not appear to make a return trip. Emphasizing the irreducibility of transcendental freedom to its categorical objectifications undercuts the reflexivity of the person's acting, which effectively distances her response to God from the particular choices she makes in acting. Moreover, inasmuch as the rightness or wrongness of particular acts does not directly affect goodness, it is unclear how it affects the person's growth in or the erosion of her God relation or her future capacities to respond fittingly (i.e., to act rightly and with good motives) to God. Given the reflexive character of acting, categorical freedom is not simply a realm of partial appearances of transcendental freedom but its constitutive medium.

John Paul's argument in *Veritatis splendor* faces difficulties of its own. The pope argues that the correct identification of the object of a moral act is sufficient for morally evaluating it and the person's will, insofar as the act is freely chosen. He notes that factors may limit the person's subjective guilt. But he nonetheless gives the impression that in deliberate choices of specific acts, persons act with relatively unified wills; in this way he may eclipse the complexity of the person as an acting subject. In other words, he does not offer a sufficiently rich account of self-relation. Certainly John Paul recognizes that as persons work out their self-relation, they make choices that reverberate in—indeed, that can decisively affect—their relation with God. Yet the pope's approach to moral acts is overly punctual or episodic. He rightly attends to the will's involvement in the person's choices, but may overplay its determination by these choices given the historicity, particularity, and provisionality of any act as it transacts our relations with our selves, God, and others in the world.[42] He risks subsuming the person, and hence her response to God, into her acts, rather than locating her acts in her complex and historical self-relation as this fashions a response to God.

Neither side separates the person's response to God from her involvement in a world thick with goods and values. Revisionists, nevertheless, stress this response in a way that burrows it into the person. By undercutting the reflexivity of the person's acting, they do not address sufficiently the way those actions bear on her response to God. John Paul, for his part, stresses our involvement in the world in a way that absorbs, even locks in, the person's response to God. He thereby constricts self-relation, and so the fundamental option, to particular acts. Neither the revisionists nor the pope render adequately the dialectical relation of the person's response to God and her involvement in the world.

INTIMACY IN THE WORLD OF GOODS GOD GIVES

My aim is not to resurrect fundamental option theory. We have considered it because of its important role in post–Vatican II theologies of sin and in Catholic theological moral anthropology. At its best, fundamental option theory reminds us that God is closer to us than we are to ourselves. Good poetry succeeds inasmuch as it breaks language out to spark an appreciation of our affective and spiritual depths, while at the same time rooting language in the possibilities and perils of our everyday activity in the world. The appeal of fundamental option theory consists primarily in its invitation to reverent wonder, to join the psalmist in crying, "O Lord, you have searched me and known me. . . . You hem me in, behind and before, and lay your hand upon me" (Ps 139:1, 5).[43] Such knowledge is "too wonderful," surpassing our full understanding, but is knowable in part as wonderful indeed (Ps 139:6).

The God who hems us in does so in a merciful cradle. The God who knows us completely also *likes* us.[44] The God whose hand lays upon us faithfully wills our good in and with him. This invitation to reverent wonder is not the only asset of fundamental option theory; as we noted earlier, the theory offers a view of human freedom that accounts for freedom's unity in and through the person's erratic behavior. Nonetheless, various deployments of fundamental option theory constrict such appreciation and undercut the significance of our embodied life and living. Many thinkers, Protestant and Catholic alike, understandably take the theory to imply, incorrigibly, a reservoir of human freedom, untouched by culture and untainted by sin, a freedom oriented to God as its highest good but curiously untouched by our involvements with the creaturely goods of human life. Many Christian ethicists today look to alternative approaches to affirm the moral agent's reflexive self-determination while simultaneously locating the agent in a shared history or story that shapes her identity even in the springs of her agency.

Contemporary narrative and virtue ethics offer such alternatives. They helpfully oppose modern moral notions of autonomy that would lead to an atomistic conception of moral action in relation to the agent's identity. Stanley Hauerwas, for example, has called for an ethics of character that recognizes how we form ourselves by our actions to meet future situations in a particular way.[45] Rather than construe the moral life as a series of dilemmas and decisions, virtue ethicists render the moral life as the task of becoming a particular sort of person, cultivating certain sorts of dispositions and habits. The emphasis, in short, is on being, not doing. Character, then, is not a mere persona that covers, even mediates, an authentic self hidden below the surface. Nor are our actions mere performances that exemplify this subterranean self. Rather, character "is the very reality of who we are as self-determining agents."[46] Granted, the contingent historical, social, and psychological factors that situate and shape us are part of the character we acquire, but they constitute our identity as we interpret them, endorse them, and embody them in our acting.

Narrative and virtue ethics also rightly grasp the teleological character of human freedom, affirming that persons act in pursuit of some apparent good. Virtues perfect our being by properly actualizing our potentiality, disposing us to act in certain ways so that we do the right thing for the right reason and in the right manner. In this respect virtue ethics promises to affirm the goodness of creaturely life and does so more directly and robustly than many deployments of fundamental option theory. Grace perfects nature, which is to say that the intimate union with God for which we are intended is possible for and as the creatures of God that we are.

Our moral acting is reflexive or self-determining and is so in a religiously or theologically significant way. Narrative ethics captures this well by describing selfhood as storied. Hauerwas, for example, argues that "story is a more determinative category than self. . . . We can only make sense of our lives, to the extent we can make sense of our lives at all, by telling stories about our lives." Moreover, "to be able to 'make sense of our lives' is primarily an exercise . . . of retrospective judgment. Such judgments are by necessity under constant negotiation just to the extent we must live prospectively, with a view to the future. We are able to go forward just to the extent we can look back."[47] Hauerwas rejects the inflated sense of autonomy central to modern accounts of agency. Character is something we fashion as we choose and act, but often the choices we make are ones whose meaning continues to unfold for us. But we do not make these choices as unfettered, independent, and intact selves. We coauthor our own stories, responding to God, who has already acted on our behalf, and interacting with others whose stories intersect with and sometimes overlap ours. "The Christian life so understood is not made up of one isolated 'loving' act added to another. Rather it ought to be the progressive growth of the self into the fuller reality of God's action in Christ."[48]

Narrative and virtue ethics sharply counter the modern subject, that paradigmatic self-creator, whose acts of will make and remake value, whose powers of reason prescind from the messy contingencies of bodies and history. A crucial element in this counter is the centrality of moral vision to these ethics and its corrective promise for Christian ethics. In his important essay "The Significance of Vision," Hauerwas charges that Christian theological readiness to exalt human freedom and make human will the source of value drives God to the universe of the "wholly other" and makes Christian ethics "inevitably Pelagian" since "the aim of the Christian life becomes right action rather than the vision of God."[49] For Christians, moral action must "adhere to and locate the self in respect to basic affirmations about God and man. A Christian does not simply 'believe' certain propositions about God; he learns to attend to reality through them." Hauerwas goes on to say, "It is not a matter of transforming the language to fit the world in the name of relevancy; but it is a matter of transforming the self to fit the language. The problem is to become as we see."[50] Moral and theological virtues enable us to see truthfully, which is to say they enable us to see charitably. Subsequent chapters will develop the importance of truthfulness before God. The point here is to recognize God's nearness to us in the depths of our self-relation and to locate the springs of our agency in relation with God (and in salvation history), such that our involvements with the goods that God authors and gives redound upon our involvement with God, ourselves, others, and the world. A literary example may illustrate and extend this point.

The narrator of Marilynne Robinson's *Gilead* (set in Iowa in the mid-1950s) is John Ames, an elderly, dying pastor writing a journal to his young son. The journal is meant to give his son an account of their forebears and to prompt Ames to tell the boy things he will not have the opportunity to say and might not otherwise have said. In point of fact it is a meditation on the "two occasions when the sacred beauty of Creation becomes dazzlingly apparent, and they occur together. One is when we feel our mortal insufficiency to the world, and the other is when we feel the world's mortal insufficiency to us."[51] By the novel's end the reader comes to see that negotiating one's identity is linked tightly to recognizing and responding fittingly to the gratuitous beauty of the world God gives and in which he meets us.

Ames begins the journal with accounts of his own pacifist minister father and abolitionist minister grandfather and the gulf of misunderstanding that separated them. He recounts the loss, when he was a young man, of his first wife and child and the decades of loneliness and longing that followed until late in life he met, married, and welcomed a son with his current (much younger) wife. The journal takes a turn as Ames reports the arrival of his namesake, John "Jack" Ames Boughton, the veritable prodigal son of Ames's dear friend Boughton, who named the boy on the assumption that the aging, widowed Ames would never come to have a son. Ames wonders whether or not to warn his wife and son to stay away from Jack and how much of Jack's bad behavior to reveal. He struggles as well with their warm reception of Jack. As Ames prepares for his death and laments the poverty in which he will leave his family, he worries whether they will come to some harm by Jack. "People," he writes, "are fairly and appropriately associated with their histories, for human purposes. To say a thief is a brother man and beloved of God is true. To say therefore a thief is not a thief is an error" (156). When Jack was in college, Ames reveals, he impregnated a poor girl and abandoned her and the child to live in squalor with her family. The Boughton family made overtures to welcome and raise the child in his stead, but were refused, and after a few years the child died from an infection that could easily have been prevented by a cleaner environment and better care.

Ames writes that it is not for him to forgive Jack, since "that one man should lose his child and the next man should just squander his fatherhood as if it were nothing—well, that does not mean that the second man has transgressed against the first," and in any case Ames does not forgive him (164). Ames does not know what Jack has done during the twenty years he has been away, but thinks "he doesn't have the look of a man who has made good use of himself" (160). Useful is what Ames prays his own son will be as a man. To be useful is to be generous, and being generous requires the bravery "to acknowledge that there is more beauty than our eyes can bear, that precious things have been put into our hands and to do nothing to honor them is to do great harm" (246). Bravery is required because of our mortal insufficiency to the world and its mortal insufficiency to us. Beholding the beauty of God's creatures, and thereby glimpsing our own, we know this beauty to be gratuitously given but nonetheless to oblige us. We know that we will fail fully to do justice to others, and that they will fail us in turn, but these failings—of sheer finitude, of inadvertent and deliberate fault—may, God willing, sharpen our apprehension of and gratitude for the precious things God puts into our hands.

For most of the book Ames simply finds Jack provocative and mean. Jack's history provides the hermeneutic through which Ames interprets every smile, every word, every deed of Jack's. Ames endeavors to be more cordial, and when he feels that this only amuses Jack as a mere performance, he endeavors prayerfully to think more graciously of Jack. He appeals to Calvin's belief "that each of us is an actor on a stage and God is the audience," which he likes because it "makes us artists of our behavior, and the reaction of God to us might be thought of as aesthetic rather than morally judgmental in the ordinary sense" (124). More specifically, Ames likes it because it suggests how God enjoys us, something Ames likens to enjoying the *being* of a child even when that child is a thorn in your heart. By moving beyond acting better toward Jack to thinking better of him, which not only will enable but already amounts to a new degree of acting better toward him, Ames finds "the chance to show that I do in some small degree participate in the grace that saved me" (ibid.).

Following a series of failed attempts by the two men to engage each other, Jack tells Ames what brought him to Gilead. He has met a black woman and married her "in the eyes of God," and together they have a son. "I also have a wife and child," he tells Ames (219). Jack's past misbehavior—his drinking, his debts—has made it difficult for him to provide for them, but these difficulties are exacerbated by the prejudice they encounter as an interracial family. Jack managed to secure a job and a modest home, and for eight months they lived as a family, until one afternoon while they were enjoying the park Jack's boss saw them together and fired Jack. Jack hit his boss, and though he tried to make amends he had to send his wife and son to Tennessee to live with her family. It becomes clear that Jack has not come to Iowa to help his sister care for their father, Boughton, whose health is failing, or to cause trouble, or even to hide. Jack, knowing that Iowa does not have antimiscegenation laws, knowing that Gilead was a site of abolitionist activity, and knowing that Ames's grandfather was a leader in this cause, hopes that Gilead might be the sort of place where he can make a home with his wife and son. In a turn that would be surprising if by then the reader had not already become acquainted with Ames's steadfastly appreciative outlook on others and the world, Ames concludes that Jack is "a better man than [Ames] ever thought he could be." So Ames tells him that he is a good man, "And he gave me a look, purely appraising, and laughed and said, 'You can take my word for it, Reverend, there are worse'" (231). Ames records all this for his son, risking pastoral indiscretion, because Jack "is a man about whom you may never hear one good word, and I just don't know another way to let you see the beauty there is in him" (232).

After learning that his wife and son have moved on to a new life without him, Jack decides to leave town, leaving his father to die and his sister to live without him. Ames understands both how unforgivable Jack's departure is—unforgivable perhaps for anyone but Jack's father—and why Jack has to leave. Ames even reports feeling grateful for all his "old bitterness of heart" toward Jack for squandering his fatherhood the first time around and toward others for their happy, noisy families and homes (240). Ames's own years of living with the loss of and longing for a wife and child enable him to appreciate what it would be like for Jack to remain at his father's house while all his siblings arrive to say their goodbyes and mourn: "The house will fill up with those estimable people and their husbands and wives and their pretty children. How could he be there in the midst of it all with that sad and splendid treasure in his heart?—I also have a wife and child."

Ames understands because, as he writes to his son, "I could never thank God sufficiently for the splendor He has hidden from the world—your mother excepted, of course—and revealed to me in your sweetly ordinary face. Those kind Boughton brothers and sisters would be ashamed of the wealth of their lives beside the seeming poverty of Jack's life, and he would utterly and bitterly prefer what he has lost to everything they had" (237–38). That Ames can see the beauty in Jack's seemingly impoverished life, or the splendor in his boy's ordinary face, is in keeping with his view of creation in the light of his faith:

> It has seemed to me sometimes as though the Lord breathes on this poor gray ember of Creation and it turns to radiance—for a moment or a year or the span of a life. And then it sinks back into itself again, and to look at it no one would know it had anything to do with fire, or light. . . . But the Lord is more constant and far more extravagant. . . . Wherever you turn your eyes the world can shine like transfiguration. You don't have to bring a thing to it except a little willingness to see. Only, who could have the courage to see it? (244)

The transfiguration of Jack in Ames's estimation culminates in an act of blessing Jack as he departs town. Ames, awkwardly sitting with Jack waiting for the bus, offers him a book and a few dollars.

> Then I said, "The thing I would like, actually, is to bless you."
> He shrugged. "What would that involve?"
> "Well, as I envisage it, it would involve my placing my hand on your brow and asking the protection of God for you. But if it would be embarrassing—"
> There were a few people in the street.
> "No, no," he said. "That doesn't matter." And he took his hat off and set it on his knee and closed his eyes and lowered his head, almost rested it against my hand, and I did bless him to the limit of my powers, whatever they are, repeating the benediction from Numbers, of course—"The Lord make His face to shine upon thee and be gracious unto thee: The Lord lift up his countenance upon thee, and give thee peace." Nothing could be more beautiful than that, or more expressive of my feelings, certainly, or more sufficient, for that matter. Then, when he didn't open his eyes or lift up his head, I said, "Lord, bless John Ames Boughton, this beloved son and brother and husband

and father." Then he sat back and looked at me as if he were waking out of a
dream.

"Thank you, Reverend," he said, and his tone made me think that to him
it might have seemed I had named everything I thought he no longer was,
when that was absolutely the furthest thing from my meaning, the exact opposite of my meaning. Well, anyway, I told him it was an honor to bless him.
And that was also absolutely true. In fact I'd have gone through seminary and
ordination and all the years intervening for that one moment. (241–42)

We can mine this passage for some insight into how we respond to God's intimate nearness to us through our active involvement with the world of goods
God gives. It helps first to refer this blessing to an earlier one Ames gave when, as
a child, he and his friends baptized some cats. "Everyone has petted a cat, but to
touch one like that, with the pure intention of blessing it, is a very different thing.
. . . There is a reality in blessing, which I take baptism to be, primarily. It doesn't
enhance sacredness, but it acknowledges it, and there is a power in that. I have felt it
pass through me, so to speak. The sensation is of really knowing a creature, I mean
really feeling its mysterious life and your own mysterious life at the same time"
(23). So when Ames blesses Jack he does not enhance Jack's sacredness or beauty
but acknowledges it, which is to say that he really knows Jack. And although Ames
thinks the blessing from Numbers is sufficient he winds up extending and specifying
it by naming Jack precisely in terms of those earthly bonds that Jack appears to have
failed, which have grieved him and others, but in which he is loved. This specification
is enabled by Jack's persistence as one receiving blessing; by keeping his eyes closed
and head bowed he invites a deepened intimacy between himself and Ames in which
God is called upon by concrete reference to Jack's mysterious life and loves.

Moreover, this shared moment permits Ames to know his own mysterious life
in a new way, such that his history as a minister somehow climaxes in this blessing.
An old sermon Ames gave on the prodigal son is illuminating here. "Jesus puts His
hearer in the role of the father, of the one who forgives. Because if we are, so to
speak, the debtor (and of course we are that, too), that suggests no graciousness in
us. And grace is the great gift. The other half is that we also can forgive, restore, and
liberate, and therefore we can feel the will of God enacted through us, which is the
great restoration of ourselves to ourselves" (161). Ames is restored to himself when
and because God enacts the divine, reconciling will through him. Of course, there
remains some possibility of misunderstanding—Jack's tone of voice might suggest
a misinterpretation of Ames's naming—but this is part of our mortal insufficiency
to the world and the world's mortal insufficiency to us. We are at once staggered by
the surfeit of beauty in the world (our insufficiency to it) and by what it portends,

what it can do to and for us beyond itself (the world's insufficiency to us). We and the world are blessed and broken; recognizing one of these facts makes our experience of the other more acute.

Gilead provides a helpful moment to revisit the distinction between goodness and rightness, both to affirm what it rightly captures and to reach for insights it should not cause us to overlook. Goodness, some revisionists argue, pertains to one's motivation or striving to love. Rightness or wrongness concerns how ordered or disordered one's actions are. Goodness and rightness do not always keep company with each other. Failing to appreciate this often leads to mistaken judgments about one's character as a sinner. A moral theology that is blind to the distinction typically "labels as sinners those who lack well-ordered lives, self-possession and healthy self-esteem. Moral theology specifically identifies the spiritually and emotionally poor and downtrodden as sinners. . . . Contrariwise, the more successful people are, the more therapy they can afford, the more integration they enjoy, the more this moral theology hesitates to refer, even think, of these people as sinners. Only those whose lives are victimized by repeated failures are called 'sinners.'"[52] Jack would seem to fall prey to this sort of moral theology. His history of misdeeds and the present disorder in his life invite the judgment of Ames and other townsfolk that Jack is a sinner. Ames's eventual recognition that Jack is a good man therefore seems to affirm the difference between goodness and rightness. Jack may have done wrong—drinking, fighting, leaving his dying father—but one cannot charge him with the failure to bother to love. He strives to love, but for many reasons (some of which consist in the sinful racism of others) Jack has been unable to order his life. He has done wrong, and some of that wrongdoing (neglecting his first child and her mother) is undoubtedly also sinful, if by that we mean he failed to bother to love. But now at least he loves and tries to love better. So he is good.

The distinction between goodness and rightness does not cancel the truth of Ames's earlier observation that people are rightly associated with their histories, though it reminds us that we are not privy to the whole of those histories and that we can misunderstand even the part we do know by viewing it through the lens of our own longings and grievances. Indeed, Ames's estimation of Jack—initially and in the end—says more about Ames than it possibly could about Jack. This brings us to two insights we might otherwise overlook were we to stop with the legitimate moral distinction between Jack's goodness and the wrongdoing that in some measure continues to characterize his life. First, Ames strives to love Jack better and he is able, occasionally, to act rightly toward Jack in large measure because of the vision his faith provides and the manner of self-relation God's grace and his free response have wrought. Ames's journal for his son is simultaneously a self-interpreting dialogue with God. By it Ames takes up his own life in preparation for his death and in eager anticipation of eternal life; he celebrates with sincere gratitude the gifts of his family, his ministry, his congregation and friends as he entrusts their future to God's providence; he reflects critically on his motives and choices, referring them and himself to God; and in his own endeavors to be "useful" he experiences the gain of living intimacy with the living God. Moral vision precedes our acting—our striving or not, our right or wrong execution—and mediates our being in the world. We negotiate our relationship with God in the full breadth of our self-relation, not simply in momentary actions; we thematize, without fully encompassing, our fundamental exercise of freedom in and through our moral vision. Hence our moral vision is also ratified or modified by our acting.

The second point we may draw from *Gilead*, that the distinction between goodness and rightness does not itself occasion, is that because the person responds to God in and through the full range of his creaturely activity, he experiences the loss or gain of God in the depth and breadth of his self-relation. Ames participates in the grace that has saved him by endeavoring to think graciously of Jack, by forgiving him, by blessing him. He participates in the grace that has saved him by preaching, by parenting, by being a friend, by studying scripture, and by contemplating nature. In and through his involvement in a world he believes to be and experiences as sacred, he responds to God, the source of his freedom and of the goods and values he encounters. The God he encounters and to whom he responds in the world is the God in whom he lives and moves and has his being.

Because God is closer to us than we are to ourselves, the person's experience of and response to God's self-offer are inextricably bound up with her self-relation, encompassing her free self-understanding and responsiveness to others and the world prior to, in, and beyond any particular actions she performs. The very springs of agency—freedom, reason, and desire—are always already set within her relation to the God who made her, who meets her in particular circumstances and in a world marked by the distorted relations of sin. Thus, human freedom is always, so to speak, "in gear"; there is no neutral resting place for freedom's appetite, just as reason cannot take its view from nowhere.[53] Accordingly, the person's growth in or resistance to intimacy with God is not confined to explicit acts and endeavors to respond to God, such as prayer. It occurs in all of her (self-)interpretation, in what she considers, neglects, and takes for granted, in all she chooses and apprehends, seeks and avoids, accomplishes and omits, and in all her responses to what she undergoes. The person responds to and negotiates her relationship with God in the way she interprets and undergoes suffering, in her estimation of her talents, in the comforting daydreams she indulges, in the phone call to a lonely relative she repeatedly defers. Growth in or resistance to intimacy with God occurs in all her processes of moral deliberation, in the way she presents a situation to herself, as she determines whether and how to consult relevant norms, authoritative sources, or moral exemplars, in the goods and values she intends to realize and those with which she unwittingly involves herself.

Intimacy with God is possible for and as a creature of God. Given the inextricable connection between self-relation and relation to God, in her exercise of freedom the person must order herself to God, her highest good, and her acts ought to be ordered to her human good as a person in a community of persons, a point both the pope and revisionists make. Revisionists tend to emphasize the person's ordering of values associated with the human good in the rightness of intention and execution of acts. The pope tends to emphasize the conformity of free and rational acts with the human good as an order of goods. As we have seen, they differ on the import of particular actions contrary to the person's good for her fundamental option. Virtue ethics stemming from Thomistic and narrative theology affirm that the theological virtues of faith, hope, and love and moral virtues such as temperance, fortitude, justice, and prudence order the person's intellect and will, rightly relating the person to herself, to others, and to her supernatural end. The historicity, particularity, and provisionality of intimacy with God capture these various insights.

Intimacy with God occurs in history. The person encounters and responds to God's call to intimacy in her relations with others and the world. The respective histories she makes there are part of the one history that is hers and hers with God. The meaning of any act becomes clear only within this narrative context. It remains open to reinterpretation in light of future information and insight, especially the more truthful perspective conversion brings. And in some sense its meaning awaits the completion of the story. This does not mean, however, that we are unable to reach reliable descriptions or understandings of acts until then. Indeed, our endeavors in this regard are part of the history we make with others and God and are accountable to them. Intimacy with God requires such conjecture in the form of prayerful and open inquiry into the state of the union. It also enables such conjecture and purifies it of self-deception and scrupulosity.

The particularity of intimacy with God emphasizes that the person's acts are *her* acts. Whatever the reach of any instance of categorical choice, the person responds to God both as the one she is and has been up to now, and as one called to become herself more authentically. Her free activity expresses her fundamental option or discloses something of the relationship she and God have made thus far. In this activity she continues to make this relationship and so contributes something to the fundamental response she fashions. Intimacy with God heightens our sense of the particularity and meaning of any act and its relation to a person's fundamental option. This particularity emphasizes rather than qualifies the person's obligation to consider how her acting bears on the God relation by considering the wisdom, experience, norms, and exemplars of her community.

The provisionality of intimacy relativizes the meaning of particular acts inasmuch as the person remains free to accept or reject God. It heightens their meaning because they bring about something new for her God relation, which matters and persists precisely because the person fashions her response to God with her life. Growth in intimacy includes moments of marvel and delight as we welcome the gift the other makes of herself and as we come to discover who we are, as the other's delight shows us to ourselves. Because intimacy is polarized toward ever greater degrees, growth in it also includes acute pangs as we apprehend its incompletion and wrenching challenges as we confront (and are confronted by) obstacles to it. These obstacles include more than explicit and fairly discrete choices against intimacy's demand to deepen; they include a variety of implicit terms or conditions we bring to the relationship, the inertia of patterns of relating, and the distorted images we project onto the other. Growth in intimacy with the living God confronts us with such obstacles, inviting and challenging us in each moment to accept the grace that enables our ongoing conversion. Each moment in an intimate relation is both expressive of the relation and an opportunity to fashion it further.

Intimacy, in short, is a living bond forged by mutual self-giving that withers or flourishes depending upon whether the parties involved do and may offer themselves freely and fittingly and receive the other in the same manner. The actions by which we deepen or evade intimacy are precisely those by which we share or withhold ourselves and welcome or refuse the other. This means that our actions contribute to the gain or loss of the other, that we experience that gain or loss not as an extrinsic verdict on our actions but as their inner reality.

Because God is the source of freedom and value, our creatureliness is an encounter with the goodness of God's work and with the harm and muddle that violations of it beget. It sets parameters within which intimacy with God is possible. This is why both the pope and revisionists are concerned with what the person chooses in her acts and its order to the human good. Because God wills deeper intimacy with us in and through our choosing, a theologically adequate understanding of persons and acts concerns itself not only with what is chosen and its order to the good, but what is going on in the choosing. Revisionists help us to appreciate that more is going on in the choosing than the pope's argument in *Veritatis splendor* shows. The pope, for his part, helps us to appreciate that whatever is going on in this willing and choosing is yoked to what is chosen, given the person's unity as body and spirit. I have suggested that revisionists risk undercutting our moral willing in choosing a specific action as it fashions a response to God, while the pope risks constricting it.

More generally, reflecting on intimacy with God—aided by our consultations with fundamental option theory—has led us to appreciate the embodied range of human freedom vis-à-vis God. Human freedom not only expresses itself in particular choices in acting but plays out in the springs and full range of the person's activity. It informs her self-understanding, reason, and desire, all of which influence the way she presents any decision to herself, considers the expectations and norms of her community, and seeks, avoids, or violates particular goods. Intimacy with God indicates why and how what goes on in her choosing of what is chosen expresses and fashions the person's response to God's self-offer. In and through her free involvement in a world thick with goods and values, the person responds to God, the source of her freedom and of the goods and values her moral willing orders and is ordered by. Once we dialectically relate the person's response to God and her involvement in the world, we see that because the person responds to God in and through the full range of her creaturely activity, she experiences the loss or gain of God in the depth and breadth of her self-relation. The God she encounters and to whom she responds in the world is the God in whom she lives and moves and has her being. The experience of our loss or gain of God in our self-relation is always also an experience of God inviting us into deeper intimacy.

CONCLUSION

God created us to know and love him and wills our acceptance of the divine self-offer at every moment and for eternity. This chapter's narrowly defined task was to locate fundamental option theory within this basic claim about the divine-human relation and thereby to recalibrate it. More broadly this chapter initiated an account of the moral agent's embodied freedom that the next chapter will develop. Reflecting on the intimacy God wills with us enriches our understanding of the person's innermost, fundamental response to God precisely by binding it more closely to her moral actions. Because God is the source of value, and of our freedom, our disordered and disordering involvements with creaturely goods are fittingly considered in terms of fidelity to God.

NOTES

1. Augustine, *Confessions*, 43.
2. *Veritatis splendor* uses the term "proportionalism," not "revisionism." I typically use the latter because some revisionists reject the label of proportionalism when it is applied to them

and because revisionism designates a wider body of Catholic moral theology that evinces a debt to the foundational principle of proportionalism.

3. Theologians sympathetic to fundamental option theory differ on how athematic one's fundamental option is.

4. In other words, grace presupposes and perfects nature. See Rahner, *Foundations of Christian Faith*, 132 and 218; Rahner, *Hearer of the Word*. See also Dych, *Karl Rahner*; Kelly, *Karl Rahner*; Kilby, *Karl Rahner*; Losinger, *Anthropological Turn*.

5. Rahner, "Theology of Freedom," 180.

6. See, e.g., ibid., 186. See also Rahner, *Foundations of Christian Faith*, 95–97.

7. Rahner, *Foundations of Christian Faith*, 94.

8. See Demmer, *Living the Truth*, 126. Fundamental option theory has played an important role in Catholic theologies of sin, developed against neo-scholastic tendencies to emphasize sins—i.e., to construe sin and the moral life chiefly in terms of particular acts. See, e.g., Fuchs, *Christian Morality*; Böckle, *Fundamental Moral Theology*; O'Keefe, "Social Sin."

9. Demmer, *Shaping the Moral Life*, 51.

10. Böckle, *Fundamental Moral Theology*, 108, 110.

11. Fuchs, *Christian Morality*, 116–17, 107.

12. Ibid., 26. See also Keenan, *Goodness and Rightness*.

13. Fuchs, *Christian Morality*, 21, 111. See also Graham, "Rethinking Morality's Relationship to Salvation."

14. O'Keefe, *Becoming Good*, 47–48.

15. John Paul II, *Veritatis splendor*, no. 65. This problem relates to other criticisms of proportionalism and revisionism that the pope makes in *Veritatis splendor*: that they deny there are intrinsically evil acts and that they offer excessively "creative" accounts of conscience. See also reservations about the fundamental option in Congregation for the Doctrine of the Faith, *Persona humana*, Vatican website, accessed November 10, 2010, www.vatican.va/roman_curia/congregations/cfaith/documents/rc_con_cfaith_doc_19751229_persona-humana-en.html, and "Reconciliation and Penance."

16. Kopfensteiner, "Theory of the Fundamental Option," 130.

17. Fuchs, "Good Acts," 23–24.

18. Ibid., 24.

19. John Paul II, *Veritatis splendor*, no. 67.

20. See Metz, *Faith in History*. See also Curran, *Directions in Fundamental Moral Theology*, 87–89.

21. John Paul II, *Veritatis splendor*, no. 72.

22. Ibid., no. 78.

23. Ibid., nos. 80, 79, 75, 65.

24. See, e.g., McCormick, "Some Early Reactions to *Veritatis splendor*," 20.

25. See, e.g., McCormick, "Killing the Patient." See also Curran, "*Veritatis splendor*."

26. John Paul II, *Veritatis splendor*, no. 73.

27. See also Wojtyla, *Acting Person*.

28. Pinches, *Theology and Action*, 63–69. See also John Paul II, *Veritatis splendor*, nos. 75 and 78.

29. See John Paul II, *Veritatis splendor*, nos. 46–48 and 78.

30. See Rhonheimer, "Intrinsically Evil Acts"; Rhonheimer, "Intentional Actions."

31. McCormick, "Killing the Patient," 18. See John Paul II, *Veritatis splendor*, nos. 79–82, where the pope suggests that revisionists think morally wrong actions can be justified by good intentions. See also Gaffney, "Pope on Proportionalism"; Curran, "*Veritatis splendor*"; Hoose, "Circumstances, Intentions and Intrinsically Evil Acts."

32. Janssens, "Theology and Proportionality"; Selling, "Context and the Arguments of *Veritatis splendor*"; Demmer, *Living the Truth*, 10.

33. McCormick, "Some Early Reactions to *Veritatis splendor*," 18.

34. Porter, "Moral Act," 283. Revisionists have made appreciative use of this essay.

35. McCormick, "Killing the Patient," 19. See Fuchs, "Absoluteness of Behavioral Moral Norms."

36. Fuchs, *Christian Morality*, 108–9.

37. Keenan, *Goodness and Rightness*, 13, 14.

38. Ibid., 14.

39. See Porter, "Virtue of Justice."

40. Fuchs, "Good Acts," 25.

41. Fuchs, *Christian Morality*; e.g., 150–53.

42. Thinkers like Charles Curran sometimes contrast traditionalist and revisionist approaches in terms of classicist and historically conscious methodologies, respectively. See Curran, *Directions in Catholic Social Ethics*, 6–22. See also Johnstone, "Revisionist Project."

43. See Demmer, *Living the Truth*, 122, where he relates the fundamental option to self-interpretation.

44. Alison, *On Being Liked*.

45. Hauerwas, "Toward an Ethics of Character," 49.

46. Ibid., 59.

47. Hauerwas, "Going Forward by Looking Back," 101.

48. Hauerwas, "Toward an Ethics of Character," 67. See also Loughlin, *Telling God's Story*.

49. Hauerwas, "Significance of Vision," 31. See also Ottati, *Jesus Christ*.

50. Hauerwas, "Significance of Vision," 46.

51. Robinson, *Gilead*, 245. In the following discussion, references to pages in this work are given parenthetically in the text.

52. Keenan, "Thomas Aquinas," 416.

53. McFadyen, *Bound to Sin*, 179.

CHAPTER FOUR

FIDELITY TO GOD AND MORAL ACTING

God has acted graciously on our behalf—in creation, in covenant, and in Christ—by offering us a share in the divine life. We respond to God's initiative with our lives. Our response to God is more than any isolated deed we perform, more than the sum total of all our deeds. It is finally the self we freely fashion in the world and with others. And yet that self is wrought through our active self-relation as we seek to understand and respond to everything that we undergo.

Chapter 1 considered Christian moral tradition's early and enormously influential association with the sacrament of confession, which contributed to a significant and in some respects unfortunate focus on moral actions. Protestant ethics and post–Vatican II Catholic moral theology generally pay less attention to moral actions as such and more to persons. There are real benefits and real costs that accompany this shift. The costs centrally include tendencies to neglect the importance of concrete actions for affecting our orientation toward or against God or to treat human actions in a way that distances the agent-before-God from her own actions.

Chapter 2 argued for this diagnosis by considering recent theologies of sin. They endeavor to take sin more seriously by refusing to reduce it to sins. Yet their dissociation of personal sin from wrongdoing limits what we can say about the theological significance of our actions. Moreover, they fail to relate personal sin to sin as a power or force and social or structural sin. This dissociation arises from and contributes to problematic approaches to human freedom. Recovering some attention to sins (the sorts of actions that typically express and contribute to the disruption of proper relation to God) could actually enrich Christian ethics substantively and pastorally, given the theological referent and analogical character of "sin" as a concept.

Chapter 3 explored a debate about how concrete actions relate to the person's basic orientation toward or against God. Put differently, the debate concerns how our intentional involvements with goods respond fittingly to God. Because God is intimately near to us, and because our acting is reflexive, we respond to God's self-offer through what we choose to do and through what transpires in our choosing. Indeed, we respond to God through the whole breadth and depth of our self-relation. The selves we fashion come to be in a material world that they encounter, experience, and impact through a mediating moral vision. That vision is shaped and sustained by the communities we inhabit, the practices that structure the lives of those communities, the languages we learn to speak, and the stories we tell.

This chapter endeavors to tie together various threads of the argument to explain better our moral acting in relation to God. By our moral actions we involve ourselves with material and relational goods in ways that form our wills and contribute to the gain or loss of God in the depths of our self-relation. The moral significance of our actions centrally concerns our fidelity to God.

FIDELITY TO GOD

Our fidelity to God finds its possibility in God's faithful love for us. God initiates a relationship with us, first by creating us and then by acting in history to forge a history with us. God makes us and acts in history on our behalf because God wills for us a share in the divine life. God is our origin and end, our ground and our good. Our fidelity to God finds its parameters in our creaturely nature and in the particular history God makes with us.

With regard to our creaturely identity, those parameters consist of stable features of human existence, like needs, capacities, and the goods that correspond with them. Human beings, for instance, have basic bodily needs, like food and shelter. Across history and culture, different communities will meet these needs in diverse (not necessarily equally morally worthy) ways and will assign them diverse cultural meanings.[1] Yet, as the Aristotelian-Thomistic tradition affirms, "moral debate and even consensus are reasonable intercultural goals, because all peoples and all cultural differentiations have at their core a shared human way of being in the world, one closely linked to our bodily nature; to our abilities to reflect, to choose, and to love; and to our intrinsic dependence on a community of other human beings, not only for survival, but also for meaning."[2] Because humans are social creatures, the human good is necessarily tied to the common good such that the flourishing of one person is bound up with that of others. The human and common good sets parameters that help to specify what fidelity to God requires because God loves us for our own sake and wills our good.

While human needs, capacities, and goods cut across cultural and religious traditions, Christians interpret and are empowered to promote the human and common good in light of God's saving action in Jesus Christ. God's self-disclosure in salvation history reveals us to ourselves. We know ourselves as creatures made in God's image, as partners in the covenant God established with Abraham, as sinners forgiven in Jesus Christ, and as recipients of God's Spirit. Accordingly, we know that we are called to a manner of life that reflects and responds to God's gratuitous decision to be God for us and with us.

By covenanting with human beings God "makes an unconditional promise of unconditional love to human persons."[3] God promises a relationship and accordingly a future. Christians place their faith and hope in God's fidelity, displayed through God's steadfast love for Israel and in Jesus's willingness to die for us while we were yet sinners (Rom 5:8). God's unconditional promise of unconditional love does not mean that God is indifferent to our response. Our response does nothing to secure God's commitment to us, but "there is something about the *goal* of the Covenant that cannot be realized without it. That is, human response can make a serious difference only if the goal of the Covenant (and of God's love) includes a relationship that is mutual and if mutuality between God and human persons depends on the free response of human persons."[4]

Indeed, God's faithfulness toward us makes our fidelity to God possible. This is because the former consists in God's choice to be unconditionally God *for* us. The Incarnation reveals that God is God *with* us, taking on flesh and dwelling among us (Jn 1:14). In the death and resurrection of Jesus, God is for and with us even in the darkness and desolation of sin, in the forsakenness of death.[5] This good news is efficacious. It changes our possibilities, liberating us from the alienating dynamics of sin and incorporating us into an alternative, reconciling economy of relations. We thus undergo a process of being born again (Jn 3:7) that is not an extrinsic imputation of righteousness but an intrinsic transformation that reorients, liberates, and integrates the springs of our agency.

Our incorporation into a new economy of relations is nothing less than our incorporation into a people. "I will take you as my people, and I will be your God" (Ex 6:6; 2 Cor 6:16). Our transformation occurs through new patterns of relationship made possible by God's grace. We are introduced and invited into and empowered to replicate ways of mutual presence that faithfully imitate God's presence for and with us. In Leviticus 19:33, for example, we find God commanding Israel not to oppress aliens; the commandment comes with a reminder that Israel had been aliens in Egypt and were delivered from bondage by God, who elected Israel as God's own people. Christian scripture tells us that Jesus, the night before he died, washed the feet of his disciples, telling them, "You ought also to wash one another's feet" (Jn 13:14) and giving them a new commandment to love one another as he loves them (Jn 13:34). Fidelity to God, while necessarily personal, cannot be separated from one's membership in the people of God, a people characterized by a manner of life compatible with and perfective of their creaturely status yet disclosed in its particularity in the history of God's self-giving as one for and with us.

The sine qua non for this manner of life is a prohibition of idolatry. "I am the Lord your God, who brought you out of the land of Egypt, out of the house of slavery; you shall have no others gods before me. You shall not make for yourself an idol, whether in the form of anything that is in heaven above, or that is on the earth beneath, or that is in the water under the earth" (Ex 20:2–4). The prohibition of idolatry indicates several things about the substance of fidelity to God. Idolatry is principally relational, consisting in our self-disposal in a manner of being that actively or performatively denies God *as* God.[6] That said, as a performative self-disposal idolatry necessarily involves beliefs about reality and axiological convictions. Put differently, it is inextricably tied to the person's hermeneutic stance. The prohibition of idolatry is a comprehensive moral norm, which is to say that no part of human life falls outside it. Idolatry therefore involves devotion of our personal energies to something other than God or to an idolatrous version of God such that we understand and relate to it apart from the reality of God. This devotion confers an identity upon us insofar as we performatively make ourselves ones who live apart from God. Fidelity to God consists in singleness or purity of heart, our self-disposal in loving devotion to God as our God. We can sum up fidelity to God in the commandment, "Hear, O Israel: The Lord is our God, the Lord alone. Your shall love the Lord your God with all your heart, and with all your soul, and with all your might" (Dt 6:4–5; see also Mk 12:30; Lk 10:27). And since loving God means loving what God loves, fidelity to God includes and is instantiated in loving our neighbors as ourselves (Lv 19:18; Lk 10:27; Mk 12:31).[7]

Fidelity involves both the direction of our personal energies and the enactment of loyalty in behaviors that are consistently appropriate to the relationship we occupy and the commitment we have made.[8] These two demands—direction of personal energies and consistently appropriate behaviors—point to the possibility of internal and external human actions.[9] Human beings act in ways that cannot be observed externally and sometimes are not easily demarcated into temporally discrete acts. One can daydream or ponder, nurse a grudge, offer thanks to God, or turn away from an uncharitable thought, all without performing external actions clearly and definitely associated with these activities. One can envy another, hope for a state of affairs to come to pass, and trust in God. "Envy," "hope," and "trust" often refer to dispositions or character traits that influence or qualify action. But they also designate interior activities that one can perform. Each entails an exercise of the will in relation to particular objects. While we may possess envy or hope as a vice or virtue, and while character is rightly a fundamental moral concern, the fact remains that we can consent to or refuse to engage in activities like envy or hope. Moreover, we shape our character and our relationships with others thereby. So internal actions involve the direction of our personal energies, the exercise of our will, in ways that may transpire without inviting (immediate) notice from others but that endure insofar as they shape our character and relationships.

Our external actions need to be consistently appropriate to the relationship we occupy and the commitment we have made. External actions are observable human actions or behaviors. To matter morally our wills need to be operative, as Thomas Aquinas argued in distinguishing human acts from acts of man, those involuntary human actions like blinking or digestion.[10] External actions instantiate that relationship or commitment in the present in a way that establishes the future. When they are faithful, external actions are signs or signals of the relationship, expressions of the commitment. These deeds incarnate our fidelity, which has no lasting reality apart from its faithful expression in a manner of life. Indeed, our covenantal commitment to love God and others entails a commitment to some framework, to a way of living out that love.[11] God gives Israel the law as a gift that specifies for them how to live in a way that is faithful to the covenant.

As we noted in chapter 1, Christian scriptures speak in diverse ways about the import of law for discipleship of Christ Jesus. The mutual love relationship at the center of God's covenant is unconditionally valid and comprehensively normative for his covenant partners. Some laws, like a prohibition of idolatry, strike to the substance of that relationship. Others point to the conditions that generally are conducive to fidelity in our personal energies and in our imitation of God's way of loving. Accordingly, some laws are essential and others are relative to the gifts and demands of the covenant as a living, ongoing, unfolding relationship between God and human partners. They matter and oblige us because and inasmuch as they "are not rules extrinsic to its life [but] are formative of the relationship that is its goal."[12] Our free choices ratify the commitment, build up or strengthen the relationship, and bear it into the future. As we ratify our commitments we acknowledge that our freedom, though unfinished, is obliged.

In sum, our actions matter for our fidelity to God because they are ways we invest and commit ourselves in relation to God's creation. We are, of course, covenant partners who live in between the efficacious promise God makes and the fulfillment of that promise. We are sometimes unfaithful to God in our thoughts, words, and deeds. Our hearts are conflicted in misdirected and inordinate loves. In the tension between what God already has done and what has not yet been fulfilled, our fidelity to God involves having faith in God's promise and relying hopefully on the belief that God's charity will accomplish our full union with God.[13] Put differently, as the pilgrim creatures we are, among the ways we enact faithfulness to God are repenting for our sins, entrusting our brokenness to God, and endeavoring to grow in intimacy with God. Saint Paul captures this pilgrim fidelity in his letter to the Philippians: "Not that I have already obtained this or have already reached the goal; but I press on to make it my own, because Christ Jesus has made me his own. Beloved, I do not consider that I have made it my own; but this one thing I do: forgetting what lies behind and straining forward to what lies ahead, I press on towards the goal for the prize of the heavenly call of God in Christ Jesus" (Phil 3:12–15).

With this account of fidelity to God in mind, let us explore moral action as our intentional involvement with material and relational goods in ways that form our wills and contribute to the gain or loss of God in the depths of our self-relation.

OBJECT, INTENTION, AND THE PERSON'S PARTICIPATION IN HER ACTIONS

Significant segments of contemporary Christian ethics neglect moral actions. Some recent work by revisionist moral theologians deals extensively with moral action, but as I have argued, it does so in a way that effectively distances the person and her God relation from the concrete actions she performs. Other moral theologians—traditionalists—tend to overlook the disparate character of human willing and tie persons and their God relation too tightly to particular actions. We will revisit this debate one final time to draw appreciatively from these theologians' respective insights and to move beyond their difficulties toward an understanding of human acting, the will's conformation by good and evil, and the significance of the person's moral actions for her relationship with God. Then we will turn to some alternative treatments of moral action, human freedom, and responsibility.

Chapters 2 and 3 explored revisionists' distinctions between the person's subjective moral goodness or badness and the objective rightness or wrongness of her actions, as well as their deployments of fundamental option theory. Recall that for revisionists, one can be good yet do something that violates a moral principle; one can act in conformity with moral principles but with a bad or malicious motive; and wrong and/or bad acts, where they do exist, may be uncharacteristic or misrepresentative of the person's basic orientation toward God. The objective rightness or wrongness of an action does not necessarily signify the person's subjective goodness or badness. Moreover, any particular act in which the person is good or bad (because she strives to act rightly or does not bother to do so) is only a limited expression of the person and probably is insufficient to determine accurately her basic orientation, fundamental option, or character.

Revisionists rightly worry that identifying the object of an action in terms of the material happening invites premature moral judgments about the person as she stands before God. Traditionalists, for their part, rightly worry about obscuring and undercutting the import of concrete actions for the person's God relation.

If one side risks presumptuousness, perhaps the other risks an undue agnosticism about human actions. My aim in this section is not to resolve this debate so much as to mine the resources each side offers in order to sketch an account of our agency before God, in relation to others, in the world God gives. Revisionists offer us a battery of resources for grappling with the disparate character and degrees of human willing. Traditionalists alert us to the importance of the will's conformation by the goods and values with which the person consorts in her actions. An adequate understanding of our willing needs to include their respective contributions if we are to do justice to the range, complexity, and significance of our willing as our intentional involvement with creaturely goods.

What Do We Choose When We Act? Relations among Premoral Values and Disvalues?

Revisionist arguments initially unfolded around the importance and meaning of the principle of double effect. As Christopher Kaczor notes, "The purpose of double-effect reasoning is to determine whether or not an act is ethically permitted."[14] There are various forms of double-effect reasoning, but it basically consists in a method for determining the objective rightness or wrongness of an action in a conflict situation in which the action in question produces both good and bad effects. Revisionists name these effects premoral values and disvalues, and they are sometimes also called nonmoral, ontic, or physical goods and evils or values and disvalues. The terminology easily confuses, and not only because of its plurality. I will simply use the language of premoral values and disvalues. Louis Janssens offers a definition (his preferred term is "ontic evil"): "We call ontic [premoral] evil any lack of a perfection at which we aim, any lack of fulfillment which frustrates our natural urges and makes us suffer."[15] These imperfections result from human finitude and from the presence of sin in the world. Premoral disvalues include things like pain, death, and disfigurement. Calling them premoral does not mean they are neutral or unimportant. As James Walter puts it, "When they emphasize the prefix 'pre' in premoral values and disvalues, proportionalists refer to the fact that these values/disvalues really do exist independently of our free will. When they emphasize the 'moral' aspect in premoral values and disvalues, revisionists point to the fact that these values/disvalues are always relevant to our moral activity and therefore must always be taken into account."[16] Causing another's pain simply to satisfy a sadistic or vengeful impulse is wrong; causing another's pain in order to disinfect her wound is right. Killing a person in order to obtain your victim's new sneakers is wrong. Killing a person in self-defense can be right, provided the death does not result from excessive force. The disfigurement caused by torture results from a wrong act. The disfigurement caused by a life-saving mastectomy results from a right act.

The point is that bringing about premoral disvalues does not in itself mean we have acted wrongly. As Richard McCormick argues,

> causing certain disvalues (nonmoral, pre-moral evils such as sterilization, deception in speech, wounding and violence) in our conduct does not by that very fact make the action morally wrong, as certain traditional formulations supposed. These evils are said to be premoral when considered abstractly, that is, in isolation from their morally relevant circumstances. But they are evils. Thus theologians sometimes say that they are morally relevant, but not morally decisive. They are morally relevant because they ought to be avoided as far as possible. The action in which they occur becomes morally wrong when, all things considered, there is not a proportionate reason in the act of justifying the disvalue.[17]

Premoral evil should be avoided and minimized when possible. Moreover, says Janssens, "we never have the right to will the ontic [premoral] evil as the *ultimate end of our intention*"—that is, as the final or remote end of our inner act of will; yet it can be right to will premoral evil as the proximate end of our inner act of will provided we have a proportionate reason to do so.[18] The surgeon who performs a mastectomy on a woman stricken with breast cancer does so for the sake of removing cancerous tissue from her body, not for the sake of disfiguring her.

Revisionists argue that all human actions produce good and bad effects, which means that the principle of double effect is not reserved for rare moral quandaries but is instead an appropriate means for reasoning about everyday moral decisions.[19] According to this principle, actions are morally permitted when "(1) the act *directly* performed is in itself good or at least indifferent; (2) the good accomplished is at least as immediate as the evil; (3) the intention of the agent is good; (4) there is proportionate reason for causing the evil."[20] Accounts of proportionate reason vary among revisionists, but in general revisionists hold that the means used to achieve an end cannot contradict that end, or that the end cannot be achieved through alternative means that would cause fewer premoral disvalues. Paulinus Odozor claims that revisionists understand proportionate reason to be governed by the *ordo bonorum*, or hierarchy of values. Premoral values are not absolute values, and so their relative precedence can vary from one situation to another. A restaurant patron in the middle of negotiating a business deal rightly abandons his work to perform the Heimlich maneuver on another patron who is choking. Life takes precedence over work. In other cases life might rightly be subordinated to other values, as when a patient refuses burdensome medical care that promises no overriding benefit to her in order to prepare more lucidly and peacefully for her death.

According to Kaczor, "the presence or absence of commensurate reason will determine what one morally chooses, what one intends morally."[21] Intention, understood as proportionate reason, differentiates human actions in part by demarcating them in a world of conflicting premoral values and disvalues. McCormick offers some examples to illustrate this: "Most people would not view the removal of a kidney from a living donor as an act separate from its transfer to the ill recipient. They would view the whole process as an act of organ transplantation. Contrarily . . . they would judge aborting fetuses for population control, killing for world peace, etc., as fully constituted acts (therefore, with their own intentional objects) aimed at by ulterior intent to a further end."[22]

McCormick argues that "intention makes the act what it is."[23] A human action may include a range of intentions, some of which are the proximate or immediate ends for which the person acts, and others of which are the "remote ends" (what McCormick here calls motives) for which the act is done. McCormick quotes Josef Fuchs to clarify his point: "The object of the ethical decision for an action is, therefore, not the basic (e.g., physical) act as such (in its ethical relevance, such as killing, speaking falsehood, taking property, sexual stimulation), but the entirety of the basic act, special circumstances, and the chosen or (more or less) foreseeable consequences."[24] To understand the person's participation in her actions requires an "expanded notion of the object" that includes "foreseen and intended consequences."[25]

McCormick is making a point common among revisionists, that the object of a moral action (that which makes, say, this act of killing a murder versus self-defense) cannot be determined apart from some knowledge of the agent's intention and the relevant circumstances. Recall from the previous chapter that Pope John Paul II insisted that "*the morality of the human act depends primarily and fundamentally on the 'object' rationally chosen by the deliberate will. . . .* In order to be able to grasp the object of an act which specifies the act morally, it is therefore necessary to place oneself *in the perspective of the acting person.*" The object is "the proximate end of a deliberate decision," a "freely chosen kind of behavior" that "determines the act of willing on the part of the acting person."[26] Like the pope, revisionists are concerned with what the person chooses in her acting. For them, this requires consideration of the act in its totality.

The principle of totality prompts revisionists to be wary of talk about intrinsically evil actions and absolute moral norms. Manualist moral theology held a number of moral actions to be intrinsically evil, actions that cannot be redeemed morally by a good intention or desirable consequences. Intrinsically evil acts would correspond with absolute moral norms or exceptionless prohibitions. It would be difficult to identify particular actions as intrinsically evil or particular norms as absolute insofar as doing so seems to require extracting actions from their circumstances and the agent's intention. According to McCormick, we cannot say that "A killed B" is wrong because "killing" does not convey the agent's intention or any of the circumstances surrounding the act.[27] Such a physical description might even refer to an involuntary act—A killed B when A fell off an observation deck and landed on B.

John Paul lists intrinsically evil acts, including murder, along with items that are not actions as such but conditions created through actions and omissions, such as "subhuman living conditions" and "degrading conditions of work."[28] Lisa Cahill then points out that John Paul's list does not name "acts in the abstract" because a term like "murder" already has circumstances built into it (versus "killing" or "homicide").[29] It is what ethicists sometimes call a synthetic moral term, yoking a physical act (killing) to a moral evaluation of that act (unjustified killing). One could say that murder is intrinsically evil, but that amounts to a tautology: unjustified killing is unjust. The relevant moral question is whether a particular killing counts as murder, and that is something we can only know by consulting the agent's intention and the circumstances surrounding the act.[30] As we will see in the next chapter, synthetic terms like "murder" actually do more work than a tautology.

Charles Pinches thinks that Cahill's reference to acts in the abstract typifies revisionist views of human actions as basically neutral events to which intentions and circumstances must be added. "This is once again the idea that there is a 'premoral' world—in effect, a neutral physical world in which are to be discovered a variety of act/movements that have, in themselves, no moral significance. To this world human beings come, as minds, as having intentions and a capacity for moral judgment, and, with the moral or immoral acts, make this world a morally better or worse place."[31] Should Pinches's reading seem entirely unfair, note that Bernard Hoose, a revisionist, points out that reticence regarding intrinsically evil acts could make the first criterion of double-effect reasoning (that the act directly performed be good or at least indifferent—i.e., not intrinsically evil) unnecessary; if there are no intrinsically evil acts, all actions are either indifferent or good.[32]

Note as well that revisionists do not understand the world to be a neutral field of human action. Premoral values and disvalues really are good and evil, but the moral assessment of the actions that cause them cannot be determined apart from the agent's intention and relevant circumstances. Yet revisionists do say things that invite readings of them as consequentialists and subjectivists, for a number of reasons. These reasons include their indebtedness to Aquinas and his account of the human act, which we will consider below. Focusing (with traditionalists) on whether there are intrinsically evil acts and absolute moral norms also means asking questions that create these confusions rather than resolve them. They set us up to demand lists of evil acts or norms only to quarrel with whatever is furnished. We would do better, as Jean Porter notes, were we to recognize that we have a concept like murder precisely because we already judge some kinds of killing to be intrinsically wrong; what is needed is more careful and sustained reflection on moral concepts like murder and the collaborative processes by which they emerge and are applied to particular actions.[33]

Revisionists also invite charges of consequentialism or subjectivism because of the way they speak about human actions in terms of the effects they produce and values to be balanced. I am not objecting, as Germain Grisez, John Finnis, and others do, to comparing, balancing, or sacrificing a good or value for the sake of another. I am objecting to the rather depersonalized and detheologized way these unavoidable tasks are envisioned. It seems that the moral quality of a person's action inheres in the relationship between its good and bad consequences, so that it concerns more the transient effects of her actions than who she is making herself to be through them, or the relationships she takes up with regard to human goods and to others. And all this seems far removed from her relationship with God and with the world as the arena in which she necessarily encounters and responds to God, a world created good, distorted in sin, and being reconciled by grace.

What Do We Choose When We Act? A Relationship to Good or Evil?

Despite all the resources revisionists offer for attending to the person's participation in her actions, Martin Rhonheimer, a traditionalist, argues that revisionist analyses of human actions "put aside . . . the acting person as a subject which *intends* something *in* doing x."[34] Rhonheimer thinks that for revisionists, "what one chooses are mainly the consequences of one's actions (actions therefore conceived as simple behavioral performances), but not the actions themselves." And this means that "the acting subject disappears as a subject that *chooses* and thus willingly performs concrete acts, acts that are not simply events causing consequences, but proximate ends of a choosing will."[35] Thus, "following [revisionist] methodology . . . one omits focusing on what is going on in the acting and choosing person, precisely where moral evil comes about." Now, in the previous chapter I argued that revisionists actually do attend to what is going on in the choosing of what is chosen, and I have suggested that their conceptual distinctions helpfully point to the degrees of human freedom and the disparate character of our wills. What Rhonheimer means is that the acting subject is "willingly 'taking a position' with regard to 'good' and 'evil' *in* choosing this or that particular action."[36]

Why is this so?

As soon as the agent relates *practically* to goods/bads as life, health, physical integrity, truth, property, it is no longer possible to call those goods or bads *adiaphora*, indifferent things or "extra-moral" goods; for the practical relation itself involves, with regard to them, one willingly taking a position on the basis of a judgment of practical reason; and it is precisely this which determines the quality of the *will* as a good or an evil will. So precisely insofar as a good is a *practical* good (or object of a free will orientated to action) it *cannot* be a non-moral good *because it is impossible that the will relates to "good" in a non-moral way.*

Thus, "the acting subject, that is, its *will*, takes a position with regard to good and evil already by *choosing* concrete actions that bring about such consequences. This taking a position relates to the agent's own person and to other persons (including God). . . . *In the will* of the agent the properly moral qualities of 'good' and 'evil' may also appear *independently* from the whole of foreseeable consequences."[37] Rhonheimer grants that persons may do the right thing but with an evil will and can mistakenly do the wrong thing but with a good will. Such a distinction, however, does not inform us of the structure of moral action, but rather arises in the context of concerns about moral norms and cases of conflict. Rhonheimer describes his own approach as focusing instead on the conditions necessary for goodness or wickedness of appetite and will.[38]

Differences between revisionists and traditionalists are often characterized as a disagreement regarding the commensurability of human goods. Revisionists think we may sometimes sacrifice some human goods in order to attain or protect others. Traditionalists like Grisez contend that it is always wrong to act against human goods. Recall that Grisez's approach posits self-evident basic goods (even goods like marriage, which clearly cannot be experienced apart from the social construction of it[39]) grasped by practical reason, along with modes of responsibility that specify morally appropriate and inappropriate ways of setting our wills in relation to these goods. Porter argues that practical reason simply does not operate as Grisez's theory would necessitate.

We desire and seek objects or states of affairs, and these are desirable to us because they fit into ongoing needs, desires, projects, and long-standing commitments, whether our own or those of people, communities, or ideals toward which we are committed. Even if these desiderata could be analyzed without remainder into a set of basic goods (and this is not apparent), we do

not desire them simply *as* instantiations of basic goods; we desire them because they promote the overall well-being of people and other entities about
which we have some concern, or avert harm from them. By the same token,
we inevitably find ourselves weighing different desiderata against one another
in the light of our overall concerns and commitments, and this process will
on occasion lead us to "act against" some goods, precisely in order to preserve
other weightier or more urgent desiderata.[40]

Porter's criticism shows that Grisez and company overstate practical reason's apprehension of human goods—reducing this complexity into a list of basic goods—
and in doing so misrepresent the way we desire human goods. Our desire for
human goods is intimately woven into our care for ourselves, our projects, other
persons, and things.

Rhonheimer better describes practical reason's apprehension of human goods
and the import of this for understanding and evaluating moral action. For Rhonheimer, "we do not live in a world of nonmoral goods that are then made moral
through our own agency," as he thinks revisionists hold, nor do we simply discover
"an objective order over and against us."[41] Take the good of life and our inclination
for self-preservation as an example:

> For whom is "self-preservation" ever simply something given, a good only to
> be "taken into account" or a mere state of affairs, no matter how desirable?
> For whom is it ever a "non-moral" good, that is, a good which does not con-
> cern him *as* a person striving for the fulfillment of his being? . . . The goods
> of natural inclinations are never simply a set of given facts, and man is not
> simply the sum of various inclinations. They rather constitute the proper
> practical self-experience of persons as *a certain kind* of being. They form a
> whole, grasped by intelligence as "my" being. So, the practical self-experience
> of man as naturally striving for goods is precisely what constitutes the *iden-*
> *tity* of a person as a *human* person: every inclination and its proper good are
> experienced as correlated to *my own* striving and not as something alien to
> me, as, e.g., nature which surrounds me, the world in which I am placed, my
> environment.[42]

We apprehend human goods in our practical relation to them, and this relation
constitutes our experience of ourselves. Rhonheimer's approach therefore links
practical reason closely to virtue. For example, Rhonheimer's moral evaluation
of contraception includes assessing how contraception would form us as agents.
Rather than evaluate contraception according to an account of the conjugal act's

ends, Rhonheimer looks to the virtue of temperance. With regard to human sexuality, he says, temperance includes the virtue of procreative responsibility. Accordingly, one reason he thinks contraception is wrong is because it circumvents the need for virtuous moderation of our sexual desire.[43]

Rhonheimer's approach not only links practical reason to virtue, it points to the social relationships and practices that constitute our human moral world. The will's taking of a position in the choice of a concrete action demarcates human actions, whatever further intentions the acting person might have, and locates them not in a world of premoral values and disvalues, but "in the context of definite 'moral relationships,' the relationships between concrete persons (fellow-men, friends, married persons, parents and children, superiors and subordinates, employer and employee, creditor and debtor, physician and patient, partners in a contract, persons who live in a particular community, etc.)."[44] In this regard Rhonheimer's approach can find points of contact with narrative ethics, as Rhonheimer himself notes.[45]

In order to be intelligible actions need to have a home, which means they need to belong to a narrative context or to a shared way of life. According to Pinches, "no human action (or omission) can be understood apart from the place it has in the moral/human world."[46] For example, "when we speak of a particular action, like kissing, we know it as such precisely because we know about how kissing fits into human life. (Note that there is not just one place it fits, but many.)"[47] The fact that actions have homes in a shared moral world relates directly to Rhonheimer's insistence that moral action is intentional action, the person's will taking a relation to good or evil. Says Rhonheimer, "'What' we do is always a 'why' we do something *on purpose*. It is a 'material doing' ('*materia circa quam*') chosen *under a description*, while it is the 'description' which actually contains the intentional content of the action."[48] While I think Rhonheimer is right to say that we always act under a description, we can act willingly yet with conflicted wills, with diminished freedom, in self-deception, and so forth.

Aquinas and Human Action

Revisionists and traditionalists both work out of the Thomistic natural law tradition, and a treatment of moral action would be incomplete without some attention to Aquinas's account. I reserve that attention for this juncture in the argument because a consideration of Aquinas at this moment can highlight the import of my contention that our moral actions involve us with goods in ways that form our wills and contribute to the gain or loss of God in the depths of our self-relation.

Aquinas insists that all human actions are moral actions, precisely because they proceed from free will.[49] Human actions differ from acts of man, involuntary things we do like digesting our food.[50] Human actions involve deliberation and choice. They proceed from us as their cause. Thus, all human actions are by definition intentional. We act for particular ends, which is why "what" we do always involves a "why" or "what for." To say that human actions are moral actions is to deny that morality can be treated as a separable component of human life. Contemporary Western culture often treats it as such. Deciding whether to terminate a pregnancy or carry it to term is a moral decision, but things like choosing a college to attend, getting a tattoo, or going to see a movie do not necessarily seem like moral decisions. It should be clear by now that I understand the moral life far more expansively. Nevertheless, while all human actions are moral actions, they are not all equally morally significant.[51] The boundary line between morally significant and insignificant actions cannot be determined in isolation (we can disagree about whether something was a trifling matter) or fixed permanently.[52]

Aquinas discusses human (which is to say moral) actions as consisting of three parts: object, end (often termed "intention"), and circumstances. We have seen how disagreements regarding the interplay of these parts figure in revisionist-traditionalist debates. These three aspects of a moral action bear on each other. The object and end are particularly closely related, as we will see. For Aquinas the object of an action is what makes it this deed versus that one, an act of kicking versus washing, or daydreaming versus gardening. The object explains why a set of actions, taken together, may constitute a single intelligible action: breaking eggs, measuring flour, whipping butter and sugar, and turning on an oven can all add up to baking a cake. The object of an action locates it in a species of actions. As Daniel Westberg notes, "because the object gives the basic specification of an action, it is possible to speak of certain types of action as good, bad, or indifferent."[53] Although, Pinches notes, Aquinas asserts that some actions are morally indifferent as regards their *species* (e.g., taking a walk versus murder), every *individual* human action (every walk I choose to take) will be morally right or wrong.[54]

The term "circumstances" refers to "whatever conditions are outside the substance of an act, and yet in some way touch the human act."[55] Circumstances include details such as who acted, where, and when. Sometimes particular circumstances have a significance and relevance that helps to determine an action's object. Westberg uses the example of driving someone else's car to work without their knowledge or consent.[56] The fact that the car is not yours and that the owner has not granted you permission to drive it makes the principal object of your action stealing even if you are also driving to work.

The end refers to the agent's purposes, that toward which her will is directed. The end of an action is closely related to its object. Aquinas says that moral actions consist of both an exterior objective and an inner act of the will.[57] The exterior objective (sometimes called the external act) is the object of the act (running, baking a cake, and so forth). Notice that the exterior objective implies an intention on the part of the agent. Running is an intentional action—I want to get from here to there, and quickly—whatever its end may be. Yet the inner act of the will individuates the act, such that it distinguishes one instance of running from another—A's running is exercising, while B's running is fleeing a crime. The will's act could also morally individuate a single action into a collection of moral acts: making a phone call is a single action during which the will may engage in a number of acts, like gossiping and expressing gratitude, each of which can be morally evaluated in its own right.[58] The inner act of the will consists in the end of the act, the purpose for which I act.[59] The object (exterior objective) and end (inner act of the will) usually are intrinsically related, such that the will's object and the act's object are identical. Aquinas gives the example that fighting well is ordained to victory.[60] But the two might not have any intrinsic relation; Aquinas gives the alternative example of stealing to commit adultery. Though the inner act of the will and the exterior objective differ, and the act has two objects, Aquinas insists the agent still performs one act.

In cases where the inner act of the will and the exterior objective differ, the will's end may determine the moral quality of the action, while in other cases the exterior objective does so.[61] The exterior objective is already an intentional human undertaking. When that exterior objective is indifferent in its species, like running is, the inner act of the will makes a particular instance of running morally right or wrong. But it is also possible that the inner act of the will is wrong while the act chosen as its means (the exterior objective) is (according to its species) right. Consider seeking praise through almsgiving.[62] Alternatively, the will's act can be good (teaching one's child to stay safely in sight in a public place) while the exterior objective is wrong (hiding from one's child so that she becomes scared of being lost or left behind).

The next chapter addresses naming moral actions. For the moment we can note three things. First, we note that moral actions may fall under multiple true descriptions—running may also be fleeing, teaching a child can also be an instance of manipulating him, and so forth. Any truthful description sticks, but moral evaluation of a given act may well involve determining which description is primary. For Aquinas the primary description is the one that refers to the action in relation to good and evil ("exercising" or "fleeing" implies this relation more than "running" does).[63] Second, Aquinas argues that "for a thing to be evil, one single defect suffices, whereas, for it to be good simply, it is not enough for it to be good in one point only, it must be good in every respect."[64] Therefore, an act in which the inner act of the will is right but the exterior objective is wrong is, taken as a whole, wrong. So too is an action that consists of a wrong act of the will and a right exterior objective. Third, as Westberg notes, revisionists and traditionalists accent different elements of Aquinas's account. Revisionists emphasize the inner act of the will in a way that sometimes neglects the intentionality of the exterior objective. Traditionalists sometimes emphasize the intentionality of the exterior objective so that it subsumes or dictates the will's end. Both sides sometimes speak as though determining the object of a moral action is a starting point for moral evaluation rather than an outcome of it.[65]

I do not think their disagreement can or needs to be adjudicated finally over the question who reads Aquinas more faithfully. Westberg is correct that revisionists and traditionalists amplify some aspects of Aquinas's account at the expense of others, as any reader of Aquinas is probably likely to do. Both revisionists and traditionalists presuppose that the person acts in a morally imbued world. Revisionists tend to speak about human goods and values as things we cause, construct, and relate as we act to protect or enhance human well-being in the world. Traditionalists tend to speak about human goods and values as an established order to which we must conform ourselves through our actions. Revisionists better render the way persons act with degrees of freedom and multiple intentions and motives. As a traditionalist, Rhonheimer better captures the way we experience human goods and evils not as things apart from us, but within the experience of our cares—indeed, as written into our self-relation. An adequate account of our acting would clarify our apprehension of, (dis)inclination for, and experiences of these goods and evils within a broader account of human self-relation as our self-constitution in response to God. That means closing the distance revisionists create between the person-before-God and her moral action without yoking them as punctually as traditionalists do. That, in turn, means asking some critical questions of the revisionist distinction between goodness and rightness.

How Do We Choose When We Act? Are We Striving or Failing to Bother?

Recall that "goodness means that out of love we strive to live and act rightly. Rightness means that our ways of living and acting actually conform to rational expectations set by the ethical community." Goodness "does not ask whether a person *attains* a greater degree of freedom or order, but whether one *strives* to attain it." Rightness concerns the relation between intention and the chosen act an agent performs. "One can actually have the right intention but, lacking prudence, make the wrong choice; or one can make the right choice even if one's intention is not completely ordered. Rightness has two realms: the executed act (choice) and the agent's reason for acting (intention)."[66]

Even if both our executed act (i.e., the object or exterior objective) and our intention (the inner act of the will) are disordered, that does not settle the question of our goodness or badness, which is solely a matter of whether or not we strive to realize ourselves and our actions rightly. For this reason, James Keenan uses the language of motivation to refer to our striving or failure to bother. Motivation, morally speaking, "concerns whether one moves oneself out of charity or benevolence to realize oneself or one's action rightly." As such, moral motivation, says Keenan, differs from psychological motivation. An example he provides illustrates the difference and what is at stake in it:

> A greedy person, for instance, is psychologically motivated to act greedily. In this way, neither the person nor the person's actions are rightly ordered. But being greedy is not necessarily an indication of badness. Whether the person is bad depends on whether the person has failed to strive to be free from greed in order to serve God and neighbor. The person's striving to be free makes the moral (or formal) motivation good, though the psychological (or material) motivation is wrong to the extent that it remains greedy. The person's goodness is solely dependent on whether that person has been trying to overcome the greed; the person's rightness is dependent on whether that person has overcome the greed.[67]

The goodness/rightness distinction thus permits an understanding of degrees of personal freedom. On the one hand, "due to nature, nurture, economics, luck, and other causes, some people are more capable of realizing right activity than others."[68] Thus, different degrees of personal freedom account for varied capacities among persons for living and acting in a rightly ordered fashion. On the other hand, since goodness or badness is solely a matter of striving to be and to act in a rightly ordered manner, and not a matter of attaining rightness, persons remain perennially free to be good or bad, to strive or not.

The goodness/rightness distinction indicates, again, that causing disvalue does not necessarily mean that a person acts wrongly, and that even if she can be said to act wrongly, she is not *by virtue of that wrongdoing* bad. (She might be bad, but the badness would precede the wrongdoing.) While this distinction has the great merit of attending to the acting person's endeavor to respond lovingly to God, and rightly recognizes that she may do so sincerely while still experiencing disorder in her inclinations and executing actions wrongly, in my judgment the distinction needs to be drawn less sharply in light of several factors that the rest of this chapter will explore: the way the springs of human agency (and, thus, the person as an acting subject) emerge within social processes of sin and grace, the reflexive or self-constituting character of human action, and the way our inclinations to human goods and our intimate experience of God are woven into our experience of ourselves—that is, our self-relation as embodied, social, self-interpreting creatures.

Revisionist-Traditionalist Debates about Moral Action: An Assessment

I consider the revisionist-traditionalist debate as a shared—though too often acrimonious—endeavor to demarcate human actions so as to locate them in the world and with respect to the agent's free transactions with goods and values she encounters and constructs there. Each side of the debate thinks the other conscripts human willing into an insufficient account of intention. By attending to what is happening in the person when she chooses concrete actions in an intentional human world laden with human goods and ends, traditionalists alert us to the importance of what happens to the person by virtue of these choices—her will is morally determined by the goods and evils to which it relates. Revisionists, of course, do not deny that the person's choices are self-determining. The conceptual frameworks they sometimes use (particularly the goodness/rightness distinction and fundamental option theory) indicate that we should not understand this self-determination punctually or reductively. Whatever the rightness or wrongness of a person's choices or her intentions or motives in choosing, she may strive to love God and neighbor as best she can, and, in any case, her particular choices are only partial expressions of the total freedom the person has and, to recall an insight from fundamental option theory, the freedom she finally *is*.

Yet Rhonheimer is on to something in his charge that revisionists put aside the person as an acting subject. For revisionists, the presence or absence of proportionate reason establishes the moral rightness or wrongness of my acts, and the values and disvalues that my actions cause certainly can include effects on me. But none of this determines or even directly involves my goodness or badness. Whether or not I strive to love rightly, whether or not my freedom is fundamentally oriented toward God—these matters establish most properly and fully who I am morally. In effect, my participation in my actions is thus marked out by distancing me from the actions themselves. What's more, the values and disvalues my actions produce appear as effects on me and my relationships, rather than consisting in my identity and relationships as I have negotiated and reconstituted them.

Keenan is right that I may struggle against a particular vice or compulsion, and this struggle indicates a striving that makes me good. But what he does not really address is the possibility, even the likelihood, that my weakness can be a real aspect of how I withhold part of myself from God, how I cling to an old, false, sinful self (the "flesh," as Saint Paul might say), a deeply rooted hostility to God or idolatrous center that has yet to be won over by grace. Indeed, whether we act rightly or wrongly in a given situation, because our wills are in the process of being unplugged from sinful dynamics and reoriented and integrated by grace, our striving can be sincere but sluggish. Prayerfully asking after the connection between my free wrongdoing and my striving refers that wrongdoing to my self-understanding in relation to God. My brokenness, my weakness, my mess then become an invitation into deeper intimacy with God, an occasion for accepting the grace God offers, for putting to death the old self and being born as a new creature in Christ Jesus.

SOCIAL SIN AND MORAL AGENCY

If we are adequately to understand the theological significance of particular ac-tions for the person in her relationship with God, then we need to situate the springs of her moral agency within the realities of sin and grace. Chapter 2 argued that recent Christian ethical discussions of sin tend to construe personal sin in terms of the person's orientation toward or against God rather than in terms of sins. Moreover, the description of personal sin often displays a modern tendency to posit some reservoir of human freedom untouched by sin as a power or by social or structural sin. Without reverting to earlier Christian tradition's equation of sin and wrongdoing, we want to understand better how sin and grace precondition our willing and what this means for our moral responsibility. I use the language of responsibility because, as we will see, it can be understood as encompassing more of our agency than determinations of culpability. For all their concern to move away from earlier Christian tradition's "gloomy gestalt,"[69] in their debates revisionists and traditionalists remain preoccupied with securing or forestalling determinations of culpability, thereby missing our mutual implication in one an-other's goodness and badness, rightness and wrongness, and, indeed, the way sin and grace operate in social processes that make and unmake us as selves.

Sin preconditions freedom because we become selves through social processes that are themselves sinful. Structural violence provides a helpful starting place. The term "structural violence" refers to the systemic, institutional, and cultural shape human violence acquires in organized society.[70] Through institutional and cul-tural mechanisms human beings are able to harm and oppress one another. They establish and sustain hierarchical relations that unduly limit some persons' access to basic resources, render certain groups vulnerable to direct forms of violence or assault, and obstruct their participation in social, economic, political, and cultural life. Examples of structural violence include racism, sexism, heterosexism, ageism, and economic oppression.

Structural violence is socially constructed. Individual and collective choices create and sustain systems that organize access and participation, distribute social status, and engender vulnerability. Structural violence is therefore a product of human freedom. This means that the mechanisms that instantiate and transmit structural violence are subject to change, that social life could be organized differently, more justly.

And yet structural violence challenges our thinking about responsibility for such changes in several respects. Because structural violence occurs in given or standing features of society and culture, the mechanisms and value judgments that make up structural violence can appear benign, unavoidable, even necessary. As Julia Fleming notes in an essay on the right to a good reputation, "denunciations of [marginalized persons'] character, work ethic, values, customs, and even hygiene explain why such people are 'not wanted here.' Claims of self-defense thus obscure both the damage to the victim and the impoverishment of the community that is denied his/her contribution."[71] Violence in the form of unjust injuries to the reputations of marginalized persons is thus deceptive. It entails lies about the character and basic dignity of marginalized persons, as well as the lie that the common good is served rather than undermined by their exclusion or oppression. Moreover, the unjust injuries to reputation that marginalized persons confront render "marginalization the exclusive problem and responsibility of the marginalized. . . . If the poor can be blamed for their own suffering, then the affluent have little responsibility to alleviate that suffering. In particular, the poor's bad repute allows the rest of us to avoid asking whether we benefit (or, more accurately, seem to benefit) from social policies that promote marginalization."[72] It can therefore be difficult to recognize these structures and conventions as violent. Structural violence lulls us into believing that change is not possible, that current ways of organizing society and distributing social and material goods are more or less the way things must be.

Structural violence extends the reach of our agency so that our choices affect more people, many of whom are otherwise quite removed from us. Structural violence also attenuates our agency, masking the effects of our choices. For example, Vincent Miller discusses the way commodification affects consumers. He defines commodification "as the evaluation and use of things without considering their fuller stories: where they come from, who made them, what impact they have on the environment. Commodities are disconnected things, lacking any context."[73] Our economy hides from view information about where and how things are produced and distributed, the labor practices and workplace conditions affecting the people who grow, process, manufacture, package, and ship our purchases. What is the moral impact of commodification? Miller doubts "whether our decisions about commodities can be considered to be moral acts at all. Insofar as commodity distancing insulates us from knowledge of the full effects of our acts, we are not making a full moral decision in any given act of consumption."[74]

Above I said that structural violence results from free human choice. Yet these structures are already in place, and human freedom takes shape and is exercised amidst them as givens. So structural violence, though built through human freedom and extending the impact of human freedom, also situates and constrains human freedom. Structural violence limits our agency and hence our responsibility. Moreover, it does this not only by making it more difficult to act knowingly—with basic information and reasonable awareness about the circumstances surrounding our choices—but by dispersing our responsibility through the social structures that mediate our interactions with and impact upon other persons. Because structural violence affects our perceptions and value judgments, in order to recognize, limit, and deconstruct these social mechanisms we must undergo a moral conversion that illumines reason and reorients will. I will say more about that below.

Another way to name structural violence is "social sin." The language of social sin is relatively recent, though the insight that institutions and features of social life can be sinful is not. As a theological concept social sin refers human social mechanisms and systems to God, thereby opening us to a more complete and truthful understanding of structural violence. As a manifestation of sin, structural violence involves more than systemic mediation of human conflict and oppression. It expresses our radical, fundamental alienation from God. Understood properly, social sin names more than institutional structures built atop human freedom. Social sin names the alienating processes by which we become selves in relation to others.

> We receive the means for acting in a manner capable of moral evaluation (i.e., freely) through the processes of social reproduction. But these processes are themselves distorted by sin, and so we receive the distortions of our situation alongside—or, rather, at the very heart of—our personal being. We do not therefore enter the stage of personal action with a clean slate, morally in neutral as it were, but already infected with the pathologies of our situation, alienating us from God and the good. We stand already, prior to any action on our part, in a pathological relationship to God—in sin. Furthermore, through our subsequent, active participation in corporate sin, we ourselves contribute to the building up of a distorted and distorting common life, which passes these distortions on to others.[75]

What the language of sin helps us to see is that the very conditions of our moral agency—reason, freedom, desire—are distorted by sin.[76] This distortion affects us in relation to the very ground of our being, God, who is our good. Any fitting sense of responsibility must acknowledge that we depend utterly on a solution beyond our own making. Moreover, since social sin simultaneously discloses our mutual implication in one another's sinful alienation and points to our utter impotence to redeem this social economy through our own efforts, any fitting sense of responsibility needs to encompass our indebtedness to all of creation and our dependence on a gracious and redeeming intervention in this economy.

FREEDOM AND RESPONSIBILITY

Gerald McKenny argues that the concept of responsibility is actually a modern one, expressing something that traditional concepts can't capture. That something is a more intense and expansive sense "in which a matter of morality or the whole thereof is 'up to us.'" The emergence of responsibility is "correlative to the modern withdrawal of God from the world."[77] As God exits the scene, our perceived field of action expands; more and more of the world falls under our power. This is true in at least two senses, both of which imply a morally neutral world as the arena or field of human action. The first, often attributed to Dostoyevsky's Ivan Karamazov, is that as divinely ordained moral norms ostensibly evaporate, more is permissible to us. The second way we perceive more of morality as up to us is through an uncritical faith in progress. For instance, developments in scientific knowledge and technological know-how increase our confidence that we can master many of the world's problems.[78] Without some sense that God or the world or features of human nature set moral constraints on our acting, the fact that something is technologically possible also settles the question whether it is permissible. While versions of responsibility may employ or borrow from traditional moral concepts, then, "responsibility" designates a more acute sense of our agential prospects than McKenny thinks traditional concepts allow. With McKenny I want to show that a modern view of freedom as autonomy leads to an acute sense of human agential prospects that then has implications for understanding moral responsibility.

First we need to consider what responsibility generically encompasses. According to McKenny, responsibility in general involves three "modes, which can be designated *imputability* (that actions can be ascribed to one), *accountability* (that one is answerable to someone), and *liability* (that one is answerable for something or someone). . . . The three aspects and the single reality [of responsibility] can be expressed schematically in a single sentence: *x is responsible to y for z*."[79] It follows that the overarching question of how much is up to us will depend upon the conditions for imputing actions to us (i.e., whether we act freely or from some necessity or determination), whether or not we are accountable to anyone beyond ourselves, and the claims and consequences for which we must answer. As we will see, since what is up to us depends upon convictions about what is the case, our agential prospects for responsibility appear quite different when examined in light of Christian faith.

Modernity depicts and prizes human freedom in a particular manner, as autonomy. Freedom as autonomy has several characteristics. It is perhaps first and foremost freedom in the sense of freedom from external determination. On this view freedom requires immunity from influence, a neutrality only had in the absence of dependence, constraints, or interference. This freedom is freedom of choice. It is self-determining choice in the sense that nothing outside the self is understood to determine the will's capacity to choose from among available objects or options; the self alone determines the exercise of freedom. But autonomy is not self-determining in the sense of developing an agential history that internally conditions or disposes one's freedom. Autonomy is thus atomic or episodically exercised, lacking a personal history of cumulative self-determination. Autonomous freedom is also an individualistic freedom. The free person is essentially unencumbered and unfettered, independent and self-sufficient. The self thus exists prior to relationships, community, or society and remains capable of transcending these sufficiently so that freedom remains intact.

Freedom as autonomy leads to what McKenny calls a "strong" view of moral responsibility, one I would also label as "narrow" or "inadequate." Strong theories of responsibility "give a more ambitious account of the necessary and sufficient conditions for imputing actions, requiring that these actions be not only voluntary (uncoerced) but also free (spontaneous)." As I said above, freedom as autonomy means that our choices are not only free from interference, they also lack a history of self-determination or self-disposal. McKenny notes that other strong versions of responsibility construe it as "the act of a subject who makes himself responsible or asserts responsibility. . . . Responsibility is an act of self-assertion by which one posits or constitutes oneself as a subject over against what is other."[80] Note that such a view of responsibility is compatible with a recognition of structural violence, though not with social sin. One can acknowledge the pervasive presence and complexity of structural violence yet espouse a strong theory of responsibility by asserting the possibility of opposing or resisting its influence. People sometimes express such a view when public discussion of gratuitous sex and violence occurs ("Just because I play video games/watch movies with sexual or violent content doesn't mean I go out and act on it"), all the while missing the fact that sexual objectification or violent dehumanization of others is not an object of choice presented to an otherwise neutral will but is built into the perceptions and value judgments that structure reason and will. Moreover, because responsibility here is moral self-constitution "over against what is other," a modern understanding of moral agency assumes that our separation from one another is more real than our interdependence. Opposition rather than relationality is basic to responsibility.

A strong sense of responsibility means we are responsible for our choices and actions only when we have the ability to do otherwise. Only on this condition are actions legitimately imputed to us. Alistair McFadyen tries to capture this by saying that on this view our acts are personal. "What makes for a *personal* relationship to action, what makes acts *our* acts, acts of our *person*, is that, in their commission, we are acting freely: *we* are their self-determining cause. Hence, moral evaluation concerns itself with action that is freely willed, and we escape moral responsibility where our acts may be shown to be compelled, determined or otherwise unavoidable."[81] A modern understanding of moral responsibility thus reduces determinations of imputability (X is responsible) to determinations of culpability (X is excused/to blame/deserving of praise). This is a narrow understanding of responsibility that excludes or hides from view important aspects of human willing, like the way it is socially, culturally, and historically situated and therefore conditioned, the way freedom emerges within an economy of sin and thus is always already disoriented. It sets the bar unrealistically high with regard to the necessary conditions for imputing responsibility.

Freedom as autonomy also distorts the two other modes of responsibility, accountability and liability. Insofar as autonomy implies an unencumbered, unfettered moral agent, accountability is not a standing feature of selfhood. If we are accountable to anyone other than ourselves it is because we elect to be so, and that accountability depends on our ongoing willingness to make ourselves so. Our relationships with others rest in our consent; even given relationships like kinship require our free endorsement of them as making some claim upon us.[82]

So it is, then, with responsibility as liability, or that for which we must answer. McKenny identifies three senses of liability. We are liable for those persons and things in our care—that is, those persons and things that make some claim upon us. But here, too, such claims are contingent upon our consent. Second, we are liable for the consequences of our actions. Because our free actions originate from us, our liability for their effects boils down to imputing those actions to us and meeting with praise or blame accordingly. Hence, even granting a sense of responsibility as the self's moral self-constitution (responsibility as imputability), morality is here narrowed to determinations of culpability. Finally, we can be liable for the actions of others. This sense of liability is difficult to square with a strong theory of responsibility. If the actions of others can be traced causally to us and the conditions for imputability are satisfied, perhaps we can be held accountable for the actions of others. For instance, we might hold a manager responsible for the actions of his employees when they follow his workplace policies.[83] But this sort of liability stops well short of the mutual implication and complicity that social sin involves.

McFadyen contrasts this modern view of freedom and responsibility with Saint Augustine's understanding of the will. For Augustine, in McFadyen's words, the "will enjoys a neutrality of independence neither from the desires of the agent nor from the attractive power of the good; hence neither is it arbitrarily self-motivating and self-moving. It is always 'in gear', as it were ... drawn towards that identified as the good." Since sin preconditions freedom, since it involves an internal disorientation prior to action, our will is properly understood as operative but not free, bound but not incapacitated.[84]

McKenny regards Augustine's approach along with others that talk of the bondage of sin as "weak" theories of responsibility. Weak theories allow actions to be imputed to an agent even given the influence of desire, inclination, habit, and so forth, so long as "the action originates in the agent's power to act or not act."[85] For McKenny, in weak theories of responsibility the "ability to act otherwise" simply means the absence of external coercion; apart from this the agent acts freely and thus is responsible for her action, even if internally she is bound to act sinfully. William Schweiker offers a more nuanced account. He identifies Augustine's understanding of freedom as "evaluative" and contrasts it with the voluntarism of autonomy. An evaluative account of freedom sees the will as divided in its attraction to conflicting apparent goods. Schweiker says that on this view the "ability to do otherwise" refers not to choice but to the evaluation and formation of our wants. "An evaluative theory argues that an agent is free if and only if she or he acts on what is most basically valued, what really matters to her or him, and not simply what is desired or wanted. ... The fact that what we value might be shaped by social roles, conventional beliefs, natural desires, and needs does not negate moral freedom if we come to endorse those values."[86] Here, too, the person constitutes herself as a moral agent. The difference is that she does so in relation to something identified as good or valuable. Instead of solitary choice in a neutral field of action, moral selfhood emerges responsively in a world independently imbued with value.

At this point we need to return to the effects of social sin. McFadyen's study of sin identifies an important feature of the will's bondage. Social sin does not only constrain and disorient our willing. Social sin blocks our moral self-transcendence. By engaging us in distorted patterns of relationship, by striking down into the conditions for moral agency, by alienating us from the very ground and good of our being, sin obstructs our access to normative reference points that would enable us to evaluate these patterns differently. Sin gives us a world. Or, perhaps better put, it involves us in sharing a world that is perversely related to the one God gives us. Because sin obstructs our access to normative reference points that would reveal the falsity and pathology of the world we share in sin, our capacity to evaluate our conflicting wants, to endorse the ones that matter most to us, certainly should not be understood as a reservoir of freedom untouched by sin. That capacity is created in us by the grace God offers in the forgiveness of our sins and the gift of his Spirit. Grace replaces the social processes by which we emerge as selves in relation to others. Because grace gives us a share in God's own life, it reconciles us to the ground and good of our being and incorporates us into a new economy of relations with others and the world.

MORAL SELF-TRANSCENDENCE, FAITH, AND FIDELITY TO GOD

Grace makes possible the moral self-transcendence that sinful dynamics block. The Holy Spirit liberates and reorients our wills by incorporating us into an alternative economy of relations, one that is reconciling us to our true good. Importantly,

> the Spirit does not illuminate the good so that we may then decide whether to pursue it from a position of neutrality; rather the Spirit instills love of God and therefore of the good. This makes the will good. That is to say, the will is reoriented *internally*. . . . Although the will's independent and unaided power is insufficient to do and will the good, the action of the Spirit empowers and reorients the will so that subsequent willing and acting do not happen without the will's own (aided) power and active engagement. The power of an individual will is a necessary but insufficient condition for good willing and action.[87]

Grace, then, engages our wills so that we find ourselves drawn toward God our good. It does not replace or determine our subsequent willing but redirects and integrates it. Grace makes it possible for us to consent to the gift of faith. Understanding ourselves through the light of faith "has the effect . . . of binding our power as self-understanding agents to specific norms that concern the recognition, respect, and well-being of finite life."[88]

Christian faith thus determines the three modes of responsibility. The first is determined by asking, How is it that I am responsible? This is the question of imputability, of being assigned and of assuming responsibility "to *y* for *z*." The gracious initiative God exercises in offering us a share in the divine life summons us to respond. We must answer this call, decide about this offer. For the Christian this means locating herself as an agent before God, in a world already laden with moral value, and in relation to fellow agents who are likewise God's image, fellow sinners, and extended the same loving forgiveness and sanctifying grace on which she depends. Our assumption of responsibility is responsive to and finds its order in our reliance upon God. Thus, as responsible agents we must engage in the ongoing task of discerning God's plan for us, the particular vocation to which we are called. We must look for God's presence and activity in others' lives and in our communities, for here we discover how we are called to responsible action. We must also therefore discern the concrete measure of that responsibility, so that we neither shirk nor presume what is up to us.

Imputability necessarily involves answering a second question: To whom am I responsible? Who legitimately holds me accountable or makes a claim on me? This question receives a clear answer: "I am the Lord your God, who brought you out of the land of Egypt, out of the house of slavery; you shall have no other gods before me" (Ex 20:2–3). Accordingly, "you shall love the Lord your God with all your heart, and with all your soul, and with all your mind" (Mt 22:37). In the Gospel of Matthew Jesus follows this command with a second: "You shall love your neighbor as yourself" (v. 39). Taken together, these two commands sum up the law (v. 40). They blur the distinction between our accountability to one another and our liability in the sense of those persons who claim our care. Moreover, our accountability to our neighbors is part of our accountability to God. The way we treat others, especially the least among us, bears directly on how we respond to God (Mt 25:40). The New Testament specifies these commands in a number of ways, teaching, for example, the radically inclusive scope of neighbor love (Lk 10:25–37) and the radically giving scope of neighbor love (Jn 15:13). Christian tradition offers many resources for translating these aspects of neighbor love into concrete courses of action and ways of life, such as looking to orders of creation for an apportioning of our responsibilities to specific neighbors. Our responsibility to others has limits, too; our accountability to them is authorized, but also ordered by our primary responsibility to God (Mt 5:30).

Accountability to others thus brings us to the third mode of responsibility, liability: For what am I responsible? What is entrusted to me? What is the character or content of my responsibility; that is, what shape does it take in my dealings with others? What is the aim of my responsibility—what am I to bring about? What task is entrusted to me? For the Christian these questions basically concern how her agency meets God's, how she is called to participate in salvation history. Put differently, responsibility in all its modes can only be understood by locating ourselves in the story of God's reconciling work. This means avoiding any idolatrous posture that would deny God as God. It means embracing the gospel as the primary hermeneutic for understanding one's own life. It means acting—relating—in ways that replicate God's self-giving presence with and for others.

Involvements with God and Goods

God is the source of freedom and value, the good in which all other goods partake. We are not free when we delude ourselves into thinking that we are unfettered, that good is an arbitrary object of choice, that creation in no way obliges us. Freedom consists in the orientation and integration of our wills in devotion to God as God.[89] Because God is the source of all goodness, including that which pertains to us as creatures made in God's image and adopted as God's children, our free involvements with the material and social goods God gives us are part of our response to God. God has chosen to be present in the world, actively to sustain it, to work in history to draw all things unto God. When we set our hearts against that which is good, when we relate to it in postures of inordinate attachment, instrumentalization, and irreverence, our hearts move in resistance to God's presence and active solicitude. When we fittingly desire, estimate, attain, and share these goods, we taste the goodness of the Lord. Because we are persons who constitute themselves through their actions, our involvements with these goods reverberate within our experience of ourselves as agents. We gain and lose God who is intimately near to us in the depths of our own self-relation.

Our actions determine the concrete limits and possibilities of our relationships with others. Granting that they are provisional moments set within larger histories that we share with others, they nevertheless calibrate those relationships. They impact the interpersonal conditions for social interaction, such as building up or eroding trust, understanding, and respect. When I lie to you, my communication with you becomes partially determined by a need to maintain the lie or to undergo the consequences of having my lie revealed, quite apart from the question whether the lie was morally justified. When I listen to you, I help to create conditions in which I can receive you as who you are rather than who I make you to be. When I allow myself to be used by you, I have to live with the smallness I have made of myself.

Sometimes our actions impact the material limits and possibilities for our relationships as well. A parent who neglects her child, failing to provide adequate nutrition, to read to him, or to take him to the dentist, is one who communicates to the child the message that he is unworthy of basic care and by her actions makes him less healthy and less prepared for education than he otherwise would have been. In these and other ways our actions affect the degree and quality of our relationships. They make and unmake us, they build up and break down others. Accordingly, we cooperate with and contribute to the reconciling dynamics of grace or the alienating dynamics of sin. The covenant relationship God establishes with us requires our response in order for its goal to be fulfilled; that goal consists in our being God's people. Hence, when we diminish and obstruct the mutual presence that faithfully replicates God's way of being with and for us, we resist God's self-offer and impede our common good.

Sin preconditions choice. It precedes our action. Wrongdoing does not necessarily indicate badness or make us bad. But, given the reflexive or self-determining power of our acting, persistent wrongdoing *can* make us bad. It can be part of a pattern of acting—and hence habituation—by which we act ourselves into coldheartedness, indifference to others, hostility toward God, or an idolatrous attachment to some person or cause or creaturely good. Short of habituation, in one who sincerely and manifestly is striving to love God and neighbor and faithfully to live out this love in right action, wrongdoing can signal her ongoing involvement in sin even as grace is working out her reorientation toward God, integrating her will, and delivering her from the debilitating effects of sin. Importantly, the way sin operates in our acting cannot be understood properly if we think of actions only as discrete deeds that are in principle observable by others. We act upon ourselves and in response to others in myriad ways that cannot be observed by others but crucially impact our character and future actions.

Grace preconditions choice as well. It too precedes our actions. Doing right does not necessarily indicate goodness or make us good. But it *can* make us good. Doing right can be part of a pattern of self-determination or habituation by which we cooperate with the grace God gives us and experience in our inclinations and relationships—in our self-relation—the effects of that grace. We do not earn that grace; we do not secure it by our good works. That is neither possible nor necessary. When we do right, it is cause for gratitude that God is working in and through us. Our right acts are ours yet empowered and energized by our participation in an alternative economy of relations, which we help to intensify by the addition of our personal energies and by acting (which is to say, relating) in ways that help to create conditions conducive to others' right relation.

Fidelitas interrupta

A return to Marilynne Robinson's novel *Gilead* can draw this portion of my argument to a close and position us to consider the work of naming moral actions. Recall from the previous chapter that *Gilead* tells the story of Rev. John Ames, a dying pastor writing to his son. Ames struggles with the arrival of his friend Boughton's son and Ames's namesake, Jack, a man with a checkered past. Ames wonders whether to warn his young wife about Jack and struggles with what he takes to be an understanding between his wife and Jack. After a number of misunderstandings and offenses, Jack finally confides in Ames that he is separated from his own wife and son and has returned to Gilead with the hope of being able to settle there with them. Those hopes are dashed and Jack leaves town, but not without some measure of reconciliation between him and Ames.

Throughout the novel Ames reflects on the many years following the loss of his first wife and child and the loneliness and longing that marked them. More than once he writes to his son about his struggle with the sin of "covetise," avarice in response to what another has. Ames says that the commandment against covetise is unenforceable and then says that it can be instructive precisely because it offers undeniable evidence of our fallenness. He describes covetise as "that pang of resentment you may feel when even the people you love best have what you want and don't have." Ames writes that over the years he didn't keep the commandment against covetise so much as spare himself the experience of disobeying it by keeping to himself so often. He would have been a more effective pastor had he accepted covetise as something in himself and been present to his flock in their moments of joy (134).

Ames later recounts the first time he had occasion to bless Jack, when he baptized him as an infant. Ames's friend Boughton surprised him in the midst of the ceremony by announcing that he would name the child after Ames. Ames describes his reaction: "If I had had even an hour to reflect, I believe my feelings would have been quite different. As it was, my heart froze in me and I thought, This is *not* my child—which I truly had never thought of any child before. I don't know exactly what covetise is, but in my experience it is not so much desiring someone else's virtue or happiness as rejecting it, taking offense at the beauty of it" (188). Ames reflects on the admittedly "foolish" thought that Jack could feel Ames's reserve during the baptism. Then he wishes he could bless Jack all over again. What is interesting here is that Ames does not wish the blessing simply for Jack's sake but also for his own. What he wants to correct is the experience of having set his heart against Jack, thereby foreclosing the possibility of experiencing—of knowing—Jack's "mortal and immortal being," the essential thing about him (197). What Ames wants is to correct the way his own reserve in blessing Jack meant that he missed out on "that sacredness under my hand that I always do feel [during baptisms], that sense that the infant is blessing me" (188).

This is rectified at the novel's end when Ames blesses Jack as he prepares to leave town. Ames, in a real spiritual sense the father to Jack, names Jack as God would name him: as one beloved. At one point in *Gilead*, while sitting in Ames's church, the same church where Ames's father had preached, Jack says, "It is an enviable thing, to be able to receive your identity from your father" (168). This, I think, is precisely what happens to Jack when Ames blesses him, though there remains some question about Jack's experience of the blessing. Ames's account certainly suggests that the reserve he felt when baptizing Jack has vanished. In its stead is an apprehension of Jack that simultaneously delivers Ames to himself, allowing him to taste for a moment a mutual presence in the Lord, even if Jack is unable fully to recognize himself as beloved.

Notice that covetise is a sin that does not transpire outwardly, though it may manifest itself in outward or observable actions. Some might object and say that covetise names a particular inflection of desire and thus is something we may have rather than do and, moreover, a desire that by nature or nurture some might be more prone to experience than others. That argument does not square with the description of self-relation offered here and in the previous chapter. Persons have active interior lives in which they make choices and engage in interior activities that are crucially self-determining and bear importantly on any outward actions and responses. We respond to God in and through the breadth of our self-relation. Ames responds to God in his covetise, in how he handles his covetise, in his subsequent reflection on it. Indeed, what originally alienated him from others and from himself, what occasioned forms of evasion or avoidance, becomes an occasion for grace; Ames is able finally to receive Jack, to let go of his suspicion and grievances against Jack, to love Jack as Boughton had always wished (244). The sin of covetise becomes a *felix culpa*, a happy fault, though not without Ames's actively and persistently referring it—and thereby himself—to God in prayers of supplication.

What does this mean for understanding our moral actions under the rubric of fidelity to God? We began by noting that God's fidelity to us makes our fidelity to God possible. Ours, though, is unavoidably imperfect, a *fidelitas interrupta*. But since fidelity to God is comprehensively normative, since there is no part of our lives or selves that does not fall under it, how we try to understand and deal with our own infidelities is no less an occasion for faithfulness than the one wherein we fell short. To consider this let us remember how Ames's sin of covetise was amplified by Jack's sin, the way he "dishonorably" took up with a poor young girl and then abandoned her and their child (166–67). Until Ames learns that Jack, as an adult, has a wife and son from whom he is painfully separated, until Ames's covetise is transformed into compassion, Ames feels personally aggrieved by Jack's treatment of the girl and child, his "squandered" fatherhood (164). But as Ames "puts before the Lord" his ruminations on Jack's baptism, he comes to an insight he wants to record for his son:

Existence is the essential thing and the holy thing. If the Lord chooses to
make nothing of our transgressions, then they *are* nothing. Or whatever reality they have is trivial and conditional beside the exquisite primary fact of
existence. Of course the Lord would wipe them away, just as I wipe dirt from
your face, or tears. After all, why should the Lord bother much over these
smirches that are no part of His Creation?

Well, there are a good many reasons why He should. We human beings do
real harm. History could make a stone weep. I am aware that significant confusion enters my thinking at this point. . . . Though I recall even in my prime
foundering whenever I set the true gravity of sin over against the free grace
of forgiveness. If young Boughton is my son, then by the same reasoning that
child of his was also my daughter, and it was just terrible what happened to
her, and that's a fact. As I am a Christian man, I could never say otherwise.
(190)

The true gravity of Jack's sin is tied to what he did. He used a girl, then dismissed
her. He fathered a child, then did nothing to provide for it. Sin would have preconditioned such choices, but the choices themselves instantiate sinfulness. They
literally are failures to bother to love, disruptions of proper relation to God and
others. What's more, they initiate a legacy of hurt and harm for a number of people
that crucially determines the interpersonal prospects for Jack's relationships with
them. That said, "if the Lord chooses to make nothing of our transgressions, then
they are nothing." What we are looking for is a way to speak about the true gravity of sin and the free grace of forgiveness together. To speak of them together
is to speak truthfully about our actions. Our endeavors to do so—even, perhaps
especially, when that involves naming our sin as such—are themselves instances
of fidelity to God.

CONCLUSION

In the range and complexity of human willing the person involves herself with
material and social goods that form her will. Her choices form and gradually constitute who she is in response to God and others. They help to establish the concrete limits and possibilities of these relations. They instantiate fidelity to God or
its opposite, but not because they keep or violate a norm (they may or may not do
that) or because they involve trade-offs among human goods. Our actions instantiate fidelity to God or its opposite because in them we set our hearts and direct
our freedom, and we take up relationships toward ourselves, others, and God, who

is offering us a deeper share in his life through our creaturely existence and the goods associated with it.

Morally interpreting or understanding our actions—right and wrong—is a task best undertaken in stable relationships of personal intimacy such as friendships, faith-based fellowship, pastoral counsel, and spiritual direction, particularly when these relationships are supported by regular practices of personal and communal prayer, reading of scripture and availing oneself of the sacraments, and in practices of seeking and offering forgiveness. As I will argue in the next chapter, the work of naming our moral actions is a collaborative endeavor, itself a moral enterprise, and one that can be an entrée into the deeper intimacy with God and others that truthfulness makes possible.

NOTES

1. Klemm and Schweiker, *Religion.*
2. Cahill, *Sex, Gender and Christian Ethics,* 51. See also Hollenbach, "Human Rights"; Schweiker, "One World, Many Moralities."
3. Farley, *Personal Commitments,* 113.
4. Ibid., 119.
5. Weaver, "Death."
6. McFadyen, *Bound to Sin,* 221–29.
7. Vacek, *Love, Human and Divine.*
8. Margaret Farley makes this point, describing the direction of personal energies in terms of one's "presence" to the other; *Personal Commitments,* 46.
9. Aquinas, as we will see, argued that human actions consist of the external performance of a deed and an interior act of the will; see *Summa theologiae,* pt. I-II, question (hereafter, q.) 18. I have no quarrel with this. My point here, however, is that human actions might not involve observable deeds but nonetheless reflexively shape us in relation to God, others, and the world.
10. Aquinas, *Summa theologiae,* pt. I-II, q. 1.
11. Farley, *Personal Commitments,* 124.
12. Ibid., 124–27, quotation on 120.
13. Aquinas speaks of hope in terms of our status as wayfarers; *Summa theologiae,* pt. II-II, q. 17.
14. Kaczor, *Proportionalism,* 31.
15. Janssens, "Ontic Evil and Moral Evil," 45.
16. Walter, "Foundation and Formulation of Norms," 129. I am grateful to an anonymous reviewer for directing me to Walter's passage.
17. McCormick, "Killing the Patient," 17.
18. Janssens, "Ontic Evil and Moral Evil," on 70; see also 69.
19. Ibid., 60–66.

20. Odozor, *Moral Theology*, 211. The emphasis is in the original text. Odozor uses it to indicate a distinction between direct and indirect action that some revisionists came to draw. See, e.g., Schüller, "Direct/Indirect Killing"; McCormick, "Commentary on the Commentaries."

21. Kaczor, *Proportionalism*, 32.

22. McCormick, "Some Early Reactions to *Veritatis splendor*," 27.

23. Ibid., 18.

24. Fuchs, "Das Problem Todsünde," as translated in McCormick, "Some Early Reactions to *Veritatis splendor*," 23. See also Demmer, *Living the Truth*, 10–11, 42–46, 136–38.

25. McCormick, "Some Early Reactions to *Veritatis splendor*," 24.

26. John Paul II, *Veritatis splendor*, no. 78.

27. McCormick uses "A killed B" as an example in support of the principle of totality. See also Odozor, *Moral Theology*, 226.

28. John Paul II, *Veritatis splendor*, no. 80. John Paul is quoting from *Gaudium et spes*, no. 27, in Flannery, *Vatican Council II*.

29. Cahill, "Accent on the Masculine," 58.

30. Ibid., 57–58. See also Porter, "Moral Act," 285; Porter, *Moral Action*.

31. Pinches, *Theology and Action*, 74–75, quotation on 79.

32. Hoose, *Proportionalism*, 34.

33. Porter, *Moral Action*.

34. Rhonheimer, "Intrinsically Evil Acts," 12. For a helpful introduction to Rhonheimer's approach to natural law, see William F. Murphy Jr., "Aquinas on the Object and Evaluation of the Moral Act."

35. Rhonheimer, "Intentional Actions," 292, 288.

36. Ibid., 306. Here Rhonheimer reiterates and develops some of what he says in "Intrinsically Evil Acts"; see especially 20–21 in the latter.

37. Rhonheimer, "Intentional Actions," 10, 35.

38. Rhonheimer, "Intrinsically Evil Acts," 24–25.

39. Porter, *Nature as Reason*, 129.

40. Ibid., 130.

41. Long, "Moral Theology," 467.

42. Rhonheimer, "Intrinsically Evil Acts," 14.

43. See Rhonheimer, *Natural Law*, 109–38. Porter's discussion led me to this example; see *Nature as Reason*, 190. See also Murphy, "Aquinas on the Object and Evaluation of the Moral Act," 239.

44. Rhonheimer, "Intentional Actions," 24.

45. Rhonheimer, "Intrinsically Evil Acts," 27. See Black, *Christian Moral Realism*. Black orchestrates a conversation among Grisez, Stanley Hauerwas, and Oliver O'Donovan that highlights points of possible convergence among these three thinkers. Rhonheimer would make a helpful addition to the conversation, but Black makes no reference to him.

46. Pinches, *Theology and Action*, 182.

47. Ibid., 33.

48. Rhonheimer, "Intrinsically Evil Acts," 30.

49. Aquinas, *Summa theologiae*, pt. I-II, q. 18, art. 9.

50. Ibid., pt. I-II, qq. 1 and 6.

51. Ibid., pt. I-II, q. 14, art. 4.

52. Pinches, *Theology and Action*, 105.

53. Westberg, "Good and Evil," 92. See Aquinas, *Summa theologiae*, pt. I-II, q. 18, arts. 8–9.

54. See Pinches, *Theology and Action*, 116–17.

55. Aquinas, *Summa theologiae*, pt. I-II, q. 7, art. 1.

56. Westberg, "Good and Evil," 92. See also Porter, *Moral Action*, 95–96.

57. See Aquinas, *Summa theologiae*, pt. I-II, q. 18, art. 6.

58. Westberg, "Good and Evil," 98.

59. I might act with multiple ends. Scholastics developed a distinction between the end of the act (*finis operis*) and the agent's end (*finis operantis*). For instance, I could wash the dishes in order to avoid an argument about politics that is taking shape at the Thanksgiving dinner table.

60. Aquinas, *Summa theologiae*, pt. I-II, q. 18, art. 7.

61. See ibid., pt. I-II, q. 20, arts. 1–2. See also Porter, *Moral Action*, 97–98; Pinches, *Theology and Action*, 120–29.

62. Aquinas, *Summa theologiae*, pt. I-II, q. 20, art. 1.

63. See Pinches, *Theology and Action*, 129–36.

64. Aquinas, *Summa theologiae*, pt. I-II, q. 20, art. 2.

65. Porter, "Moral Act." See also Westberg, "Good and Evil," 96.

66. Keenan, *Goodness and Rightness*, 3, 8, 14; see also 9–13.

67. Ibid., 15.

68. Ibid., 8.

69. Mahoney, *Making of Moral Theology*, 30.

70. For a treatment of structural violence, see Farmer, *Pathologies of Power*. Religiously informed accounts can be found in various liberation theologies.

71. Fleming, "Right to Reputation," 80.

72. Ibid., 81.

73. Miller, "Consumer Culture and Morality," 40. See also Miller, *Consuming Religion*.

74. Miller, "Consumer Culture and Morality," 43–44.

75. McFadyen, *Bound to Sin*, 36–37.

76. Feminist theologies of sin speak to this point. See, e.g., Goldstein, "Human Situation"; Serene Jones, *Feminist Theory and Christian Theology*.

77. McKenny, "Responsibility," 237.

78. See Curran, *Loyal Dissent*, 199.

79. Ibid., 242.

80. Ibid., 243–44.

81. McFadyen, *Bound to Sin*, 20.

82. Weaver, *Self Love and Christian Ethics*, 19–22.

83. Faith in autonomy would require us to emphasize their freedom to do otherwise (albeit with consequences) or admit considerations (like fear of being fired) that weaken their autonomy.

84. McFadyen, *Bound to Sin*, 179, 110.

85. McKenny, "Responsibility," 242.

86. Schweiker, *Responsibility and Christian Ethics*, 146. Schweiker is indebted to Harry Frankfurt; see Frankfurt, *Importance of What We Care About*. See also the essays by Michael E. Bratman, Gary Watson, T. M. Scanlon, and Richard Moran in Buss and Overton, *Contours of Agency*, chaps. 3, 5, 6, and 7, respectively.

87. McFadyen, *Bound to Sin*, 176.

88. Schweiker, "Radical Interpretation and Moral Responsibility," 96.

89. See McFadyen, *Bound to Sin*, 220.

.

TRUTHFULNESS BEFORE GOD AND NAMING MORAL ACTIONS

Truthfulness before God is a gift persons receive in their encounter with God in Jesus Christ. It is inescapably ingredient to God's self-gift, grasping and claiming the person in reconciling love. Truthfulness before God is also a task, the task of a lifetime, inasmuch as this gift exposes the person in all her falsehood—her unbelief vis-à-vis God, her concomitant evasion of herself, her irreverent alliances with other persons and the goods of creaturely life—and demands instead a free response of confession, gratitude, and charity.

Reflecting on truthfulness before God and its opposite, the sin of falsehood, extends the theological account of persons and actions initiated in the previous chapters. It helps us to understand the way sin preconditions human agency, why we evade the intimacy God wills to have with us, and how fidelity to God consists in "practicing the truth in love" (Eph 4:15). Each of the previous chapters alerts us to the importance of naming moral actions—specifically, naming them in a manner that refers them and the agent who performs them to God. Here we see that the moral work of naming our actions is properly a collaborative endeavor to discover what we can about the truth of our involvements with God and the goods of creaturely life. This endeavor depends crucially on the explanatory power and moral realism that theological language affords and the formative power of Christian community and worship.

THE SIN OF FALSEHOOD

Truthfulness before God is a gift—God offers this manner of life freely and graciously. We know it to be a gift because of what occurs in God's offering of it. God reveals and offers the divine self as one who elects to redeem us, simultaneously disclosing the full truth of who God is and who we are in relation to God. This twofold disclosure takes place in the person and work of Jesus Christ, in and through whom God addresses the world. Truthfulness before God is a task because our encounter with the truth exposes us in all our falsehood by a good word that demands and empowers a fitting reply. We may explicate the sin of falsehood in terms of unbelief, evasion, and irreverence, each of which finds its contrast in the gift of truthfulness, which in turn normatively governs the moral work of naming our actions.

The sin of falsehood affects the person totally—determining her relation with God, with herself, and with others and the world. We may name falsehood's aspect in relation to God as unbelief. Falsehood consists in unbelief precisely because it is the refusal to accept and thus to live by the good word God speaks decisively in Jesus Christ. What is it that we refuse to believe in our falsehood? The word God declares, Karl Barth notes, is that God has reconciled the world in Jesus Christ. This word is "basically in harmony with [the person] and it speaks to his innermost self."[1] Yet it unsettles us—indeed, it repels and scandalizes us as we are apart from Christ.

Following Barth, we may understand why this is so by considering Jesus Christ, the true witness, in his "pure form" and in the form he takes in relation to us who hear his prophetic word. Barth identifies the pure form of Jesus Christ in terms of the unparalleled freedom between him and God.[2] Jesus unreservedly elects God as his sole good and concretely enacts his freedom in a life of faithful service to God. He does so from neither fear of punishment nor hope of reward, but out of delight in God for God's own sake. God accepts and approves of Jesus concretely and unreservedly, using his service and crowning him Lord in total freedom: "God does not have to be the God of this man, but He can be and He wills to be" (383). Says Barth, "The conjunction or unity of true God free for man and true man free for God constitutes the existence of this One who is the true Witness. As free God and free man meet and are one in Him, He is the truth and declares the truth in relation to which every other man shows himself to be a liar" (ibid.).

Jesus manifests his pure form indirectly, in his historical self-declaration to and for us sinners, in the form of the man of Golgotha. The action in which God reconciles the world and justifies us is the passion of Jesus (389–90). Thus, the one who encounters us is the one crucified for our sins, the one who proclaims and effects the world's reconciliation to God in his suffering and death, the one whose resurrection displays by its gratuity the full extent of our sinfulness. Importantly, the setting in which Christ thus encounters us is the temporal sphere between the "already"—the decisive accomplishment of reconciliation—and the "not yet"—its eschatological consummation. Sin is deprived of "all right and power" yet "still has in this sphere of ours a theatre in which to act with all its destructive consequences" (393). In this sphere the Jesus who encounters us is "the One who is still harassed and forsaken, accused and condemned, despised and smitten" (ibid.). Therefore we cannot truthfully regard Christ's sacrificial death as a distant contingency of history, an occasion for God's self-disclosure that is separable from the content of God's revelation.

What can we learn from Barth's consideration of the two forms of Jesus as the true witness who is himself the truth? The total and sovereign freedom of God's word to humanity and its inseparability from Christ's passionate death signal the absolute normativity and comprehensive reach of God's claim on us. Encountering Jesus Christ means finding oneself in God's sovereign grasp, a grasp that leaves the person "no normative conception of goodness, truth, right, love, salvation, well-being, or peace, with which to encounter God, to consider Him, to accept or reject Him, to wrestle with Him, to grasp or evade Him, to take up His cause or to argue with Him. At this point [the person] is dealing with the wholly self-determining God who controls the concrete content of all conceptions and is therefore alone normative" (446–47).

As Barth says, the person is dealing with God's love, but only as *God's* love. In her thinking concerning God, her attitudes toward God, and her decisions she must orient herself by the rule and direction disclosed in God's revelation (ibid.). Klaus Demmer makes a similar point, saying that in Jesus, God "supplies the ultimately binding interpretative key that the Christian employs," which issues in "a radical transformation of the form of thinking."[3] To encounter him is to encounter the living God who subverts our expectations and conditions, who leaves us no court of appeal in which we might negotiate our relations with him. There is only the terror of God's gracious freedom meeting ours in a love that would save us by killing us (444).

In short, the truth God declares repels and scandalizes us because the truth to which Jesus Christ witnesses is identical with and inseparable from Jesus Christ himself. The sin of falsehood thus takes shape as unbelief vis-à-vis God in our various endeavors to deny the identity of Christ's witness and Christ himself. The sin of falsehood is not identical with an explicit rejection of or transient doubt concerning the proposition that Christ is Lord, although we will consider the issue of explicit faith later. In fact, falsehood easily operates in explicit professions of Christian faith (436–38). We may try to domesticate the truth, manage it, and mask a palatable untruth as truth. Specifically, the person tries to reinterpret, to transform the identity of Jesus Christ and the truth he witnesses—say, by distancing God's love from Christ's passion, by professing Christ as a symbol, or by subordinating God to or substituting God with a system of eternal truths and principles. In all these ways the Christian marshals a counterfeit of the truth, ironically seeking to distance herself from the God who encounters her in Jesus Christ by trying to close the distance between her and God—that is, to mitigate the sovereignty and narrow the scope of God's claim on her.

Fundamentally, the sin of falsehood consists in a manner of being before God, who reveals in Jesus Christ the truth of who he is and the truth about us and the world. It is this manner of being that accounts for the moral impropriety of particular sorts of falsehoods; insofar as they instantiate a denial of God, they reflect and contribute to the disruption of proper relation to God. Saint Augustine, for example, argues that lying violates our creaturely status as *imago dei*; rather than reflect God, whose self-disclosure occurs in God's word, our lying violates the relationship between self-disclosure and speech.[4] Lying is performatively contradictory, and its moral evil, for Augustine, consists primarily in its theological significance. Unbelief is essentially a living refusal of God's sovereign claim on us, a manner of life we enact in our attitudes and decisions. It is pervasive, operating well beyond the properly religious propositions we adopt and practices we engage.

Alistair McFadyen captures something of my point in his contention that contemporary Western secular society is marked by "pragmatic atheism." McFadyen argues that secularism is not necessarily or intrinsically atheistic, but "what characterizes the basic secularity of our society is not so much that there are publicly accepted arguments against the existence of God, positive reasons for disbelieving in God, but that there is a *de facto* exclusion of God from public rationality, reference and discussion." How so? "Reference to God is effectively absent from every discipline of interpretation, analysis, explanation and action, from the natural and social sciences to public, political discourse, community development work, management, administration and social action. God is operationally excluded from those social and cultural processes which structure and shape our basic intentionality in desire, thought, action; reference to God is taken in practice to make no difference to the interpretation, explanation and understanding of the world, no difference to acting and living in it."[5]

This is why, notwithstanding particular persons' professed belief in God, our culture shapes us as pragmatic atheists, performatively incorporating us into its atheism while posing no apparent contradiction to belief in God on some personal, motivational level. Our culture is one of unbelief inasmuch as "it assumes the *practical* irrelevance of God's existence to the disciplines of reflection and practice we all use as we interpret and act in the world," the very cultural processes that shape our self-understanding and form the springs of our agency. Yet, "if God is the most basic reality and explanation of the world, then it must be the case that the world cannot adequately be explained, understood, lived in, without reference to God in our fundamental means both of discernment and action."[6]

Pragmatic atheism extends the Barthian description of unbelief just offered. We may say it constitutes a *feature* of unbelief in the sense that pragmatic atheism arises from the unbeliever's refusal to orient her thinking, attitudes, and actions by

God's comprehensively normative word. As she denudes the challenge of Christ's passion, obfuscates Jesus Christ in symbols, and subordinates God to universal principles, the liar endeavors to corral or sequester God's practical relevance for truthfully understanding and living in the world. In this way personal falsehood creates an environment conducive to a culture of practical atheism. It is worthwhile also to regard pragmatic atheism as a *form* of unbelief, because doing so alerts us to the way unbelief is writ large in the social and cultural processes that situate and shape us. The supposed sufficiency of our means for understanding and acting in the world and their ostensive neutrality with regard to personal belief in God effectively conceal the sovereign and comprehensively normative character of God's word. Pragmatic atheism limits God's practical relevance to personal motivation, thereby shaping moral agents who may claim that their acting has to do with God, but who believe that the world in which they act can be adequately comprehended apart from God. Pragmatic atheism amounts to a concrete loss of God—by operating on the assumption that God makes no difference to an adequate and truthful understanding of the world and our lives, we fail to accept and thus to live by the word God addresses to us, since this word is constitutive of reality as God establishes and redeems it.

In the sin of falsehood the person's unbelief vis-à-vis God is intimately bound up with evasion of herself, precisely because she "fears the One who encounters [her] and the implications of this encounter" (345). As Demmer puts it, God's self-disclosure in Jesus "disconcerts" us and "turns the customary evaluations of goods upside down."[7] The implications of this encounter are many, but chief among them is the exposure of who we are apart from Christ. God's self-disclosure in Christ measures and judges us in our sin. We seek to hide from God, Barth says, "who here comes upon Man, the father upon His estranged child, the Lord upon His runaway servant, the eternally Holy One upon the transgressor, the one who wants to love but cannot live alone or without Him, and in all these things the omnipotent Creator upon the creature which He has called out of nothing into being" (444).

In our falsehood we attempt to evade the sinful selves Christ shows us to be. The dreadfulness of being exposed in such poverty, ingratitude, and folly prompts us to hide ourselves from God by hiding the truth from ourselves. Confronted by God's sovereign freedom as he manifests it in a word that declares that to gain our lives we must lose them, we learn that we are not our own. We are not free, but bound, and we cannot make ourselves free. God offers us freedom, but we balk at this offer because to be born again to freedom is to be born to self-determination, "i.e., to that which accrues to [each of us] as a responsible covenant-partner of the free and self-determining God, as His creature, as the one who is loved by Him. What is given [us] and required of [us] is the freedom of one who belongs to the free God and is freed by Him" (447). In falsehood we evade not only the self we are measured and judged to be in our sin, but also the self God calls us to be with its obligation and burden of freedom. By her falsehood, then, the person refuses the new self God makes of her in Christ and instead unwittingly conjures the shade of the person "who in Jesus Christ, and therefore in the eternal election and historical act of God, has been displaced and overcome and put to death"—namely, the person "of sin who, as [she] denies and rejects God, [her] fellows and finally [herself], can only be denied and rejected and judged and damned by God, and can thus exist only in logical self-destruction, being doomed ultimately to perish and be lost" (464).

According to Barth, the sin of falsehood draws condemnation. In refusing the word of truth, the person refuses pardon, changing it into condemnation. As she lies, the person makes herself lost before God, implicating herself in a false situation, effectively cursing herself with death and damnation. She is not yet damned, but, refusing to live by "the truth of his deliverance from guilt and slavery," the person desires instead "to live by and in the untruth into which [she] attempts to change the truth"; she thus places herself under the threat that God will grant her "a life by and in untruth as the portion which [she herself] has chosen, a life which as such can only be a lost life" (462). In this situation, says Barth, the person lacks a center, a meaningful source of being that she "has not to posit, which is posited already, which cannot be lost, but which is once for all to be respected" (470). She flitters from one image of reality to another in search of a source of meaning that would govern her self-understanding, thinking, and acting and thinks that her freedom consists in this capacity to adopt and abandon one image after another. But because these images are untruths masked as truth, because they do not accord with her objective human reality as it is wholly determined by God, they offer "no limit nor law," and she thus lives as a prisoner to her "inner caprice and external fate" (ibid.).

The person not only lacks a center of being, living by a false image of reality, she also lacks real coexistence with fellow humans and with creation in general. Falsehood corrupts coexistence into "empty proximity and even hostility" (470), which may express itself in a range of attitudes and relations with others—an instrumentalizing concupiscence, indifference, defensiveness, bitter resignation, and so on. The point to grasp here is that in the sin of falsehood the person's unbelief before God and evasion of herself make for irreverence toward creatures.

Irreverence is the modus operandi of falsehood in relation to others in the world of goods God gives. God created the world good and reconciled it to himself in Jesus Christ. But in her falsehood, the person "does not see or have or experience anything," either self or world, "as it is, but only as it is not" (472). According to

Barth, the person must live with this distorted image that she sets up by her false-hood, seeing things not as they are in themselves, but as they are for her. The distorted image controls, determines, limits, and characterizes her existence, forcing her to have and to experience the world and herself in the defaced, distorted, and corrupted form in which they represent themselves to her in her image. She exists in a subjective reality that is alien to and contradicts objective reality (469). In her falsehood the person erects an image of reality that then sets the terms on which she encounters and responds to the world, on which she experiences her very self. Seeing and believing herself and the world to be thus and so, she cannot but come to herself and the world in a deceived and deceiving manner. She thus locks herself into an alienated existence. The sin of falsehood therefore preconditions the springs of human agency, distorting and corrupting reason and will. Falsehood debilitates us as knowers and lovers who are summoned to free self-determination in obedience as God's covenant partners.

This much becomes clear when we consider the problem of human speech. Speaking and hearing ought to convey human reality to others for the purpose of fellowship (472–73). But when we willfully live in untruth, speech necessarily fails this purpose. Rather than reveal human reality as fallen and redeemed by God, our speaking and hearing traffic in error and misunderstanding. We ought not assign the limitations of speaking and hearing solely to human finitude. The point is that as one "becomes a liar in the encounter with Jesus Christ," one "becomes a liar at every point" (452). Unwilling to live by the central truth of her existence disclosed in Jesus Christ, the liar is also unwilling to live by the peripheral and secondary truths of her historical existence. She willfully flouts the purpose of human speech, manipulating these truths into untruths to buttress the primary lie by which she lives—namely, her "attempt not to allow to be true that which is true between God and [her]" (374).

Why describe this dynamic as irreverence? Because it springs from the person's refusal to live by God's sovereign claim, from her self-serving evasion of the truth. The sin of falsehood operates as irreverence because the person commits herself to a self-protective manner of life that fails to receive and respect the goodness of creation—including the goodness of her own creatureliness—as it exists in and is ordered by God. Flighty and floundering under the threat of condemnation, the person attempts to posit and protect a self, a persona unavoidably built on "consoling illusions."[8] Lacking a center and incapable of genuine coexistence with fellow creatures, she suspects and feels this self to be the sham it is. She compulsively protects and reinvents it by resisting and manipulating the claims her fellow creatures impose on her. Irreverence names the ensuing disordered relations to and with creatures. In her irreverence the person wounds the integrity creatures have in God, be it by neglect, callousness, indifference, or by acquisitive and inordinate regard. She cheapens the dignity of creation—say, by disregarding the dire environmental consequences of her lifestyle, by using a would-be friend to advance her career, or by soiling another's reputation for the sake of entertaining gossip. She desecrates the mystery of persons in scornful criticism of her child's aspirations, in dismissive impatience with the elderly, in presumptuous curiosity about her colleagues. She trivializes the significance of ordinary human practices like eating, having sex, and speaking, or she exalts them unduly. In these and other ways the person engages in a self-serving evasion of the truth insofar as she mitigates the claims on her that creaturely goods impose as divine gifts God gives to order and enrich our lives.

THE GIFT OF TRUTHFULNESS

The gift of truthfulness before God demands and enables confession, gratitude, and charity. Confession concedes and corrects falsehood's unbelief in a twofold manner. First, confession affirms who God has shown the divine self to be by acknowledging Christ as Lord. Second, confession acknowledges who we are apart from and who we become in Christ; that is, it is a practice of repentantly naming ourselves as sinners and our sins as such. These two aspects of confession are indissolubly bound, but let us reflect on each in turn. To confess Christ as Lord is to consent to the word God speaks, to believe it, and this not merely as a disinterested, disengaged assent. One who confesses Christ's lordship does so as one who freely endorses this word, who commits herself to it, who stakes her life in trust of it, and thus as one who freely submits to its implications. Consenting to Christ's lordship means giving oneself up to God's sovereign grasp, entrusting oneself to the revolution of encountering Christ. While unbelief, as we charted it along Barthian lines, means seeking to distance ourselves from God by closing the distance between us and God, confession means drawing near to God in fear of the Lord—that is, in humble recognition of God's sovereign and gratuitous decision to be the wholly other who draws intimately near to us. What I mean is that confession, as consent to God's word, essentially involves receiving that word as one who must be addressed, as one in dire need of hearing a message not of her own making.

To confess Christ as Lord is to avow the identity of Jesus Christ and the truth he witnesses, God's reconciliation of the world in him. Thus, confessing Christ as Lord and confessing our sinfulness go hand in hand. We know the latter truly only in light of the former.[9] Christ's grace liberates us from our self-protective maneuvers, from the ennui or caprice of our dispersed freedom, from the props with which we try to corral God, from the principles and causes we don to conceal ourselves from God's sight, and from our compulsive grasping at creaturely goods, our stale indifference to them, our petulant hostility. As grace accomplishes this we see in greater clarity and truth the manifold ways—from the pathetic to the vicious—that we alienate ourselves from God and neighbors. Importantly, our liberation transpires in encountering Jesus Christ—when we confess his lordship we appropriate his saving activity, and the salvation story we affirm as true for the world is the story we take on as our own. In this narrative context, some of our actions become newly intelligible as sins. Indeed, confessing our sins is a practice of mindfully naming our actions in reference to God so as to acknowledge God as the measure and norm of who we are and what we do.

Moreover, as Saint Augustine knew and beautifully displayed, confession is a performative instantiation of truthfulness. In Paul Griffiths's words, "It is a speech act that simultaneously presents and enacts the grammar of the faith with respect to the categories of grace and free will. It is only in saying what confession says that the one who confesses is rightly related to God."[10] Confession thus concedes and corrects unbelief—the living refusal to live by God's word. It is a performative response to God's word that invites the truth's "offensive action" against the untruths we manufacture, by which we place ourselves under Christ as the law of God, submitting to Christ's determinative power and comprehensive claim.[11] For this reason, confession corrects the practical irrelevance of God that is both a feature and a form of unbelief. It is an act (enabled and empowered by God's prior and gratuitous action) of adopting an identity-conferring commitment (i.e., becoming a disciple of Jesus Christ), such that our own integrity is staked on coming to know ourselves and the world in God, which is to say, in the truth. In other words, confession is that practice by which we testify that God makes an indispensable difference to truthful knowing and acting in the world.

If confession concedes and corrects falsehood's unbelief in relation to God, gratitude overcomes its aspect as self-evasion. Gratitude is incompatible with self-evasion inasmuch as it requires the one who is grateful to take up her identity as the recipient of a gift and, accordingly, as one who is not sufficient unto herself. Gratitude locates her in relation to her benefactor, as one beholden, not by strings attached to the gift (for then it would not be a gift), but by a debt.[12] A "debt of gratitude" refers to the objective reality that obtains between the gift giver and the recipient, such that truthful bearing toward the gift giver is cut to the measure of the particular relation in which the gift giver and recipient stand before one another and corresponds to the nature of the gift given. A child's debt of gratitude toward her parents, for example, is morally structured by the parent-child relation and the particular gifts given her therein. Gratitude enables the person's self-evasion to give way to self-respect and to freedom of conscience in relation to the judgments of others.[13]

Gratitude is the proper response to the good news that Christ is Lord and as such has reconciled us to God. Gratitude accords with the unmerited character of God's self-gift in Jesus Christ and befits the response of a creature to her creator, an estranged child to her welcoming and forgiving father. It displaces the wounded indignation and shame our exposure as sinners elicits. Indeed, since we know our sins as such in light of our redemption from them, gratitude fittingly accompanies and increases by confessing them. In grateful acceptance of God's pardon the person centers her understanding, thinking, and acting around recognition of the divine gift. She thereby takes up the demand for free self-determination given to and required of her by this gift. She assumes the new self God makes of her. Hence, concrete acts of remembering God's mercy are crucial for the formation of Christian discipleship. Gratitude to God in Jesus Christ fundamentally transforms the Christian's knowledge of herself and the world, rendering it more truthful inasmuch as the Christian comes to see herself and the world in the light of God's will to sanctify them for the sake of loving fellowship in and with God.

Gratitude is thus closely related to the charity that comes with truthfulness. By charity I mean simply our participation by grace in the life of God, who is love. Recall Barth's point that falsehood draws condemnation, that by her falsehood the liar makes herself lost from God. Charity, by contrast, is a sharing in divine love. While falsehood entails and effects irreverent and therefore false relations with others and with creaturely goods, charity denotes God's grace, which enables us to love others and all of creation truthfully, which is to say, as they exist in God.

Augustine described this proper love of creation by distinguishing "use" (*uti*) and "enjoyment" (*frui*) as modes of love, insisting that God alone is to be enjoyed and creaturely goods are to be used. His claim may unnerve us since it seems to commend an instrumentalizing love of creation that values particular goods only inasmuch as and for as long as they satisfy our acquisitive purposes. But this concupiscible love is precisely what Augustine means to reject in his distinction. Augustine understands that the problem of human love is that we love the wrong things, or the right ones in the wrong way. We cleave to finite goods as though they were infinite, looking to them for our center of being, and thus investing these perishable and imperfect goods with a purpose that they, as such, cannot bear. God alone is to be enjoyed—loved for God's own sake—because God alone is truly, inherently good; the goodness that inheres in creatures exists only because and to the extent that they participate in the being and goodness of God. For Augustine, then, what it means to love creatures well is to love them as they really are, with a love ordered in measure and content by a truthful apprehension of them in relation to God.[14]

Christian tradition designates charity as a virtue—that is, as a disposition to act—and names charity a theological virtue, one infused in us humans by God. For Thomas Aquinas, charity's primary object is God, and through charity one loves God and loves what God loves. Charity consists in union or friendship with God: "Charity reaches God as He is in Himself."[15] Given this share in God's own life, charity interiorly transforms the person.[16] Aquinas specifies charity in terms of an "order of love" that effectively ranks creaturely objects of love according to their respective degrees of participation in God and by indexing them to the human being's natural inclination to her own good. So, for example, I ought to love myself more than my neighbors, such that I ought never to sin and thereby jeopardize my own share in beatitude for their sake, yet I ought to subordinate my bodily good to the demands of neighbor love for the sake of promoting our common share in beatitude. We need not tarry with the details of Aquinas's ordering here, only appreciate that charity, as a virtue, transforms the springs of human agency. Charity orders reason, will, and passions in accordance with the objective characteristics of creation as it finds its origin and end in God.

Charity transforms the irreverence of falsehood because it rightly relates us to creation. It enables genuine coexistence with fellow human beings and other creatures. In charity the Christian honors and promotes the integrity of creation. Charity engages the person's will in loving solicitude for creatures, thereby overcoming callousness and indifference. It measures regard by chastening acquisitive impulses. As an architectonic virtue, charity informs and perfects other virtues, like temperance, justice, and prudence, that dispose us to be affected by and to act rightly and well in relation to creaturely goods. Charity practically governs the Christian's acting, habituating agents by forming them in fellowship with God. Importantly, the God loved in charity, and in whom creatures are loved, is the God who elected to become incarnate, who suffered and died to reconcile creation, and who gives his Spirit to sanctify it. Thus, charity impels us more deeply into the human moral world, enabling us to see and act in it with a more truthful apprehension of it and ourselves as belonging to God.

Truthfulness before God is inescapably ingredient to God's self-gift in Jesus Christ. It is part and parcel of the redeemed existence that participation in Christ yields. Encountering Christ, the true witness, we respond as the sinners we are with a falsehood that refuses to live by God's gracious word. We choose to live by and in an untruth that curtails God's practical relevance for our lives. Our study of unbelief highlighted the ways we conceal the concrete and comprehensive significance of Christ. This concealment is simultaneously a self-evasion. We flee the sinful selves Christ shows us to be and the new selves he calls us to be in free response to him. Unwittingly reviving the sinner Christ put to death, we live as ones lost to and in a false situation that corrupts our agency and thereby issues in irreverent relations with fellow creatures. The effects of falsehood are real and destructive. But they are gradually overcome by the grace of Christ as we are drawn into the truth. Truthfulness is a living acceptance of God's word. We enact truthfulness before God as we confess Christ's lordship, as we appropriate his saving activity as our own story. Confessing Christ's lordship we endorse and submit to God as the measure and norm for who we are and what we do; hence, we more truthfully understand our own actions and their significance in and for our God relation. We grow in ever-deeper awareness of God's gracious presence as determinative of our thinking, attitudes, and decisions. Gratitude for God's self-gift locates us in a concrete and particular relation with God, specifying the debt we owe God in freedom. Charity is that gracious share in God's life and love that transforms the very springs of our agency, disposing us to deliver on the debt with rightly ordered love of God and creation.

NAMING MORAL ACTIONS

We live and move and have our being in God as the particular creatures we are. Apart from God, we cannot truthfully understand ourselves, our actions, and the rich and varied world in which we live with others. Since truthfulness before God consists in a living acceptance of God's word, since it encompasses the breadth and depth of our existence, since it transforms the very springs of our agency, we would do well to reflect briefly on truthfulness in conduct before we turn to the matter of naming moral actions.

I argued in chapter 3 that we are created by God for intimacy with God. God is our highest good, the source and end of human freedom. As we exercise our freedom in choosing concrete actions, we negotiate our relation with God in ways that deepen or diminish the intimacy for which we are made and which is our good. In his study of Augustine on lying, Paul Griffiths notes that the person's desire for her own good "is duplicitous (and therefore also mendacious) when it is coupled with a mode of life that contradicts it. This is why Augustine says that nothing could be more of a lie than a desire contradicted—canceled out—by a mode of life that prevents its fulfillment."[17] Truthfulness before God is a living acceptance of God's self-gift, a manner of life we enact in all our thoughts, attitudes, and decisions. We respond to God in a world laden with divine gifts given for the sake of the divine self-promise, in a world of other persons, and therefore in an ineluctably moral world.

Our experience of and response to God's word, the divine self-gift, are mediated by our relations with others and the creaturely goods we encounter in the world. Hence, our intimate involvement in and with others and the world is always also an involvement with the God who gives it and loves it and loves us. "When a created good (speech, sex, material objects) is used for evil ends (lying, adultery, killing) the good in question is placed under the sign of contradiction"; such a performative contradiction "in part erases it, reduces it to nothing, but . . . also permits it to have effects not implied in its existence or intended by its creator."[18] We do not conduct ourselves truthfully—we do not live by and in the truth—if and to the extent that our actions do not correspond to the created moral order God establishes. That is to say, our actions are lies when they do not correspond with the reality of the world under God, including the reality of our created nature, corrupted and graciously redeemed in Christ.

Accordingly, we do not name human actions truthfully if we do not refer them to God and if we do not concretely locate them in the world God creates, redeems, and sustains. Naming our moral actions is the task of discovering what we can about the truth of our actions as involvements with God and the goods of creaturely life. This work is troubled by the misunderstandings of persons and acts that we noted at the outset of this book. Contemporary Western moral thinking remains bewitched by modern views of the moral agent as a maker of moral meanings, an isolated center of freedom acting in a world shorn of value apart from that which she creates by her choices. Morality thus appears as a separable component of human life, one realm among others, and right and wrong, good and evil consist solely in opinions and preferences. While postmodernism counters this moral anthropology, strong versions of it go beyond acknowledging a situated self and insist there is no such thing as a self; what we take to be the moral life is nothing other than the interplay of various discourses and constructs determining us. Either way, the moral life is construed in an unrealistic fashion, as having no ties to some objective moral order in the world.

Moreover, as the previous chapters argued, even the more robust moral anthropologies that contemporary Christian ethics offers misconstrue or inadequately render the relation of persons and their acts. Prominent strands of Roman Catholic ethics effectively distance the person from her acts in an understandable but costly attempt to correct earlier Catholic tradition's tendency to focus on acts at the expense of adequate attention to the persons who perform them. These recent Catholic ethics now exhibit an inordinate agnosticism about the significance of the person's actions for her God relation. Much of Protestant ethics is characteristically reticent to focus on moral actions insofar as this courts works righteousness. The surge of interest in virtue ethics among Protestants and Catholics alike enriches

Christian moral anthropology and assists us in the work of naming moral actions, but does not suffice for an adequate account of persons and actions since, as earlier chapters noted, virtue or vice action descriptions tell us much about agents but not enough about the world—the home of human actions.[19] Since truthfulness in conduct means acting in conformity with the reality of the world under God, naming our actions rightly and well is vitally important for understanding, as we can, how we negotiate our relation with God therein.

Moral Concepts and Moral Action

I once heard a program on National Public Radio that focused on a book about the Middle Eastern television station Al-Jazeera.[20] In the course of interviewing the book's author, the program's host—an American—seized on the author's mention of Al-Jazeera's practice of referring to suicide bombers as martyrs. She was particularly troubled by the way "martyr" connotes sanction of the suicide bomber's action. The author replied to the effect that "martyr" refers rather generically to anyone who dies in the course of fighting an enemy. The reply seems to beg the question implied by the host (who, we might note, did not seem terribly troubled by the author's notice of Western television news practices that, e.g., name U.S. military action in Iraq "liberation" rather than "invasion").

The implicit question, I take it, is whether the name "martyrdom" justifiably describes an action whereby one loses her life not at the hands of her enemies but in the course of deliberately killing them and/or innocent bystanders. Now, this question itself raises a host of others. Is the specific cause for which particular martyrs die just, and if not, are these people rightly called martyrs? How are religious warrants (mis)applied to justify martyrdom, and what role might religiously informed perspectives play in morally distinguishing some forms of martyrdom from others?[21] Does martyrdom include suicide in service to a cause? Does it refer to the sacrifice of one's own life by eschewing violent resistance of one's enemies? How does the suicide bomber's killing of bystanders compare with the killing of noncombatants in what military agents term "collateral damage"? Is Al-Jazeera's linguistic practice (or those of Western news stations) responsible? What obligations, if any, do news agencies have in exercising their powers of naming events and persons?

Many more such questions can be posed and plumbed. Rather than dwell on this case, however, I want to tease from it several points about naming moral actions: (1) Naming moral actions occurs in a rich, ineluctably moral world, one where human beings have things like enemies and causes, engage in varied forms of killing, suffer persecution and terrorism, and so forth. (2) Naming human actions always already involves us in evaluating them; we do not arrive at a complete neutral description of an action and then subsequently morally judge it. (3) Naming human actions proceeds analogically with reference (explicit or implicit) to allied sorts of actions and according to rules for usage entailed in the linguistic notions or descriptions we use. (4) Naming moral actions matters not only for understanding truthfully what we do, but for shaping ourselves as agents, and thus for acting truthfully. (5) Naming our actions rightly and well is a matter of responsibly apprehending and promoting the human and common good. Let us consider these points in turn with the help of Charles Pinches and others.

Pinches argues persuasively that a range of contemporary moral theories founder on a shared problem; they attempt to theorize about human actions apart from the home actions have in the human moral world. Consider, for example, the veritable X-Acto knife that is modern analytic action theory.[22] This philosophical school aims to identify what a human action is; "it presumes, simply, that beneath all the various ways one might *refer* to an action lies the *action itself* in its basic, stripped-down form."[23] Action theory manifests this presumption in its tendency to treat actions as events, a tendency clearly operating in formulaic expressions like "M breaking eggs at *t*." As Pinches points out, this approach extracts human actions from their home in the world by ignoring the narrative contexts that give human actions their intelligibility—the formula ignores, for example, whether M broke eggs in the middle of giving a lecture on Kant or in the course of making breakfast in his kitchen.[24] Some action theorists themselves take issue with the description of human actions as events. Jennifer Hornsby, for example, says that the orthodoxy on which much philosophy of mind or philosophical action theory is founded is an events-based conception of action that in fact leaves out the agent. Such a conception of action cannot account for the exercise of agency in omissions, nor does it convey why an action occurs.[25]

According to Pinches, other more properly ethical theories similarly run roughshod over the purposes, practices, and varied discourse of everyday human life. Pinches argues against what he calls principle monism, an ethical approach he discerns in rival theorists Joseph Fletcher (who championed situation ethics) and Paul Ramsey (whose ethics focused on Christian agape).[26] "Principle monism" refers to ethics that ground morality in a single principle that is purportedly constitutive of the moral life, like Kant's categorical imperative and Bentham's principle of utility. The difficulty with principle monism, according to Pinches, is that it coopts the vast and varied moral descriptions we use, ignoring arguably salient moral data because the principle does not identify it as such (e.g., Bentham's principle of utility looks solely to consequences to determine the rightness or wrongness of a course of action). Principle monism unnecessarily reworks and reduces our moral vocabulary. For example, considering the action of promise keeping under the principle of utility distorts the very meaning of "promise," since promises are not promises if their binding character is rendered as a conditional matter of usefulness.[27] Principle monism thus removes human actions from their home in our human moral world so as to make them accord with a supreme moral principle.

Pinches mostly takes aim at those whom he takes to be a third group of perpetrators of such "action extraction," the so-called proportionalists (revisionists) of recent Roman Catholic moral theology. His criticism of revisionists overlooks significant differences among them and bypasses their insights into persons and actions. But Pinches does attend to the relation among intentional action, the human moral world, and moral concepts. A number of revisionists, as we saw in previous chapters, criticize strands of Catholic ethics—notably the magisterium's—for identifying moral actions in the abstract, apart from the agent's intentions and the action's circumstances, and often on the basis of the physical movements that constitute the action. For example, self-stimulation (masturbation) is judged wrong apart from considering whether the agent performs this act for the sake of self-pleasuring or for sperm testing.[28] Revisionists argue that to name and morally evaluate an action we must consider the act in its totality. This requires an expanded notion of an action's object. Recall that the object of a moral action is that which makes it what it is—that which makes, say, this killing murder and that killing self-defense. Revisionists insist that we cannot identify the object apart from the agent's intention and the circumstances surrounding the act. The action plus intention and circumstances constitute an expanded object.

As we noted in chapter 4, Pinches faults revisionism for presuming a neutral premoral world as the field of human action and for rendering human actions as events by which agents intend to produce some balance—some proportion—of values. Revisionists do not understand "premoral" to mean "neutral" and likely would not recognize themselves in his description of their work. His argument, however, provides a helpful point of departure for reflection on naming moral actions. According to Pinches, the problem is not that proportionalism insists that intention crucially determines the object of an action, but that it treats human actions as neutral events that receive moral value from the agent's intention. Yet human action is intentional; it always occurs in an already moral world and necessarily consists in the agent's willing relation to the goods found therein.

In direct and vigorous contrast to these theories, Pinches turns to Thomas Aquinas's treatment of human action and argues that Aquinas rightly acknowledges that human actions are moral actions. Not everything a human being does is a human action—involuntary acts like gestation or tics are acts of man.[29] Human actions, however, involve reason and will, and therefore all human acts are moral acts. Pinches favors Aquinas's approach to human actions over against the contemporary theories noted above, because, unlike these theories, Aquinas's account acknowledges that human actions occur in the intentional, moral human world. Pinches sees this connection displayed in the species classifications Aquinas employs to treat human actions (e.g., "murder," "adultery," "almsgiving," "walking through fields"). Human action is teleological—that is, intimately involved with some real or seeming good(s). Aquinas's species classifications acknowledge as much because they name human actions according to their ends, the real or apparent goods at stake in them.[30]

Pinches suggests we consider washing one's hands. We are likely to think hand washing is more closely related to showering than, say, to dealing cards, even though the physical movements involved in hand washing and dealing cards are more alike than those in hand washing and showering. We think hand washing and showering are more closely related, says Pinches, because both concern the good of personal hygiene. This is not to say that all hand washing is good (Pilate's infamous hand washing was not) or equally good (hand washing acquires greater importance in the case of a surgeon scrubbing in). "Classification by end relates not just to what was done, but to why it was done. And to ask why something was done by someone is, in effect, to ask whether it was good that it was done, just as we assume that the one who acted had some good in mind, real or apparent."[31] For Aquinas some species classifications imply moral judgment, like murder or adultery, while others are indifferent, like walking through the fields.[32] I will say more below about naming an action and morally evaluating it. Here I want to stress that since all human actions are moral actions, every individual action—each particular instance of walking through the fields—will be either good or evil, and that goodness or evil will depend on factors like the circumstances of a specific walk through the fields as well as the object or ends pursued by the one walking. Nonetheless, species classifications like Aquinas's fix actions in the human moral world. "In a species description particularly as it informs us of the object of an act, we receive a description of the action not just in relation to a particular agent's purposes, but also in relation to the world—and by 'the world' we mean here not merely the 'natural' or physical world, but the intentional, human world in which it takes place."[33]

Pinches's criticism of modern moral theory and his reasons for preferring Aquinas's approach to human action show the first point I want to make in this section: The work of naming moral actions occurs in a rich and ineluctably moral world. Our naming is more adequate—more truthful—if it locates our particular actions in the intentional human world, if it captures the truth about our involvements with the goods of creaturely life.

Let me connect this first point to my second, that the work of naming human actions always already involves us in morally evaluating them. Naming or describing human actions not only occurs in the human moral world, it presumes this world. Moral notions, like all notions, have meaning and force as they are rooted in human life, a point Pinches illustrates with the following list: "'writing,' 'arguing,' 'theft,' 'courage,' 'love,' 'soap,' 'gun,' etc." To know anything about these things is to know something about how they fit in human life. Notice that Pinches's list includes actions, dispositions, and material objects. He points out that, while notions like "writing" and "arguing" refer directly to the world of human action, notions like "courage" and "soap" nonetheless presume this world, which is why we grasp the notion of "soap" better "by relating it to washing one's hands or taking a shower than by attending to its usual color, shape, or consistency."[34] There is no sharp, impermeable boundary between moral notions and nonmoral notions (e.g., murder and soap); in fact, the urge to construct one implies that the moral life is a separable component of human life, the very idea Pinches correctly opposes by invoking Aquinas's claim that all human actions are moral actions.

Since all human actions are moral actions, "it follows that the descriptions of human acts, their names together with any descriptive elaboration have moral import from the beginning. They signal that moral judgment applies and, in many cases, carry that judgment in their very name."[35] We do not (and ought not endeavor to) arrive at a complete neutral description of an action and then subsequently morally evaluate it. Moral judgment begins with our initial descriptions. Our initial descriptions generally will not suffice for morally judging an act; we need to consider mitigating factors, for instance. Moreover, a number of descriptions may be true of a specific action—say, that taking a chalice from a church is both an act of theft and an act of sacrilege. Some descriptions, however, are more morally significant than others. Take, for example, the action of Joe murdering Mary by cutting her throat. Joe's action is both a cutting and a murdering, but "murder" is the primary or most proper name since murdering is morally more important. Pinches insists we do not need a theory or criterion for knowing this. Since cutting and murdering are actions that find their homes in our human moral world, their relative moral seriousness is established therein.[36] Pinches illustrates this claim well with an imagined conversation.

"I'm feeling kind of guilty."

"Why?"

"I broke a promise."

"Oh? What did you do?"

"Well, I promised Jim I wouldn't kill him, but I broke my promise."
"What?! You killed Jim?!"[37]

The first speaker's choice to describe her action as promise breaking does not remove its more serious moral reality as a killing.

The first two points I have argued relate closely to my third, which is that naming moral actions proceeds analogically according to rules for usage that moral notions themselves entail. The work of naming moral actions consists in determining whether or not relevant action descriptions apply to specific deeds and the persons who do them. As we noted in chapter 2, this work—which is already a process of moral evaluation—proceeds analogically, comparing one kind of action (cybersex, say) to other sorts (like masturbation, viewing pornography, sexual intercourse with a third party, etc.) to determine whether or not it counts as an instantiation of a moral notion (like adultery).[38] The point of this process is to discover what we can about the moral truth of human actions, which is to say, the truth about ourselves and the lives we human beings fashion in this world. Importantly, even when reflecting on contested moral matters (whether euthanasia counts as murder, e.g.), we are not deciding so much as discovering the moral truth about an action. Disagreement is inevitable, given the complexity and diversity of us human beings and the world in which we live. Yet, as Jean Porter notes, moral disagreement assumes considerable consensus; disagreement concerning whether euthanasia is truthfully named "murder" assumes consensus about paradigmatic cases of killing, as well as shared (though not universal) assumptions about suffering, health, illness, and about moral life in general. The investigation of a specific human action or kind of human action, then, employs reliable though not infallible inherited moral wisdom, distilled in the array of (moral) notions that are a prerequisite for the investigation.

Tied as they are to human life, all notions—moral or not—"require that the person who rightly uses them has a practical grasp of the way of life of the group and has made it her own."[39] Put less abstractly, my sons learn various notions simultaneously with rules for using them and the shared human practices in which they are intelligible: "This is a spoon." "This is not a spoon, it is a bowl." "We use the spoon and the bowl to eat our oatmeal." "Oatmeal is for eating, not throwing at the wall." Notice that there is little if any point in naming the spoon and bowl apart from their place in the purposeful and shared human action of eating. There are rules or criteria for using notions correctly; these criteria arise in the intersubjective practices of particular linguistic communities.

The rules for using a notion correctly are tied to the notion's "formal element," that element "in virtue of which the various instantiations of the concept can be recognized for what they are, that is, instantiations of this concept."[40] Any notion tells us something about us human beings. "Table" seems a straightforward notion, yet Stanley Hauerwas observes that "the reason we have our notion of table is the need we have for tables that is embedded in our social conventions to sit, to eat on, or to place objects off the floor. . . . The formal element of our notions is but the recognition that we know them for some reason."[41] Moral notions are tied to human life in a twofold manner, Pinches says; moral notions "are not only *for us* to use as we interact with the world but also *about us* as we do so."[42] Moral notions convey information about human needs, aspirations, and so forth, because they reflect what we value and disparage. This is not to say that all moral notions include a definite moral judgment; they can be more or less complete in that regard. Pinches notes that "murder," for example, already includes the judgment that such an action is wrong, while "abandon" is more open (it is sometimes right to abandon a building, but not a baby).

As I stated above, the work of morally evaluating an action begins with our initial descriptions of it. These descriptions presume the human moral world. Using them correctly requires a practical grasp of our intentional human world; our notions are for us to use as we interact with the world since they arise from our wants, needs, aspirations, and conventions. Moral notions are also about us as we interact with the world, signaling what we value and disparage. Acknowledging all this brings me to my fourth point, that naming moral actions matters not only for understanding truthfully what we do, but for shaping ourselves, for acting truthfully. We apprehend ourselves and the world in which we live through the language we inherit and construct. We and the world have a creaturely integrity, a moral order, not entirely of our own making; we receive this world and we act in it and on it with the language we use to interpret it and ourselves. Thus, our practices of naming may be impoverished, insufficient to the complexity of the world and human life. We saw as much by considering how principle monism reworks and reduces action descriptions. Our practices of naming may simply lack contact with the world, as in analytic action theory. Or, as Oliver O'Donovan charges of revisionism, in our naming we may refuse the world that is given us in favor of some other world that we invent.[43] Since our naming shapes our capacities as agents, Pinches notes that "we may lose the capacity even to *do* certain things, to engage in the actions for which we have lost descriptions." Losing a robust sense of "sacrilege," for example, we may also dilute a notion like "consecration," so that it becomes increasingly difficult to engage in this practice.[44]

Naming human actions, then, is itself a practice of considerable power. Hence, my fifth point is that naming actions rightly and well is a matter of responsibly apprehending and promoting the human and common good; it is a matter of truthfulness. Naming human actions truthfully is a collaborative endeavor that depends crucially on the concrete communities that furnish, enliven, and sustain our moral vocabularies. As I have argued, we faithfully perform this task only by apprehending and loving the world in God, and only by referring ourselves and our actions to God. This is what it means generally to say that truthfulness before God normatively governs the moral work of naming actions. In order to specify this claim in a way that is mindful both of the sin of falsehood and the character of truthfulness as a gift, let us consider briefly a literary example.

Truthfully Describing Actions as a Share in God's Grace

Shusaku Endo's novel *Silence* tells the story of Sebastian Rodrigues, a Jesuit missionary to Japan in the mid-seventeenth century.[45] At this time Japanese rulers were systematically executing Christians. Realizing that the witness of Christian martyrs often inspired and strengthened the Christians' commitment to their faith, Japanese rulers began to torture Christians with the aim of making them apostatize. Getting priests to apostatize was considered particularly useful for crushing the spirit of the lay Christians. One method of torture was to hang Christians in the pit; they were bound (with one hand free to make the sign of apostasy) and hung upside down in a pit containing excrement, allowed to bleed slowly to death through a cut placed on the forehead.

Endo's novel opens with a rumor that Christavao Ferreira, Rodrigues's beloved former teacher and a long-time missionary in Japan, has apostatized. Rodrigues travels to Japan to learn whether the rumor is true, bringing with him an acute sense of his priestly identity (he believes the fate of the Japanese church rests in his hands) and a conception of martyrdom as a glorious share in Christ's suffering and death. Once in Japan, he is able to hide among some Christian peasants and minister to them. In the squalor, hunger, and tension of his hiding, Rodrigues sustains himself by meditating on the face of Christ as a lover would meditate on the face of his beloved. Eventually Japanese officials learn that the peasants among whom Rodrigues lives are Christians, and from his hiding place Rodrigues watches as two of them are martyred. Their martyrdom displays nothing of the glory he expected, only pain and misery, and Rodrigues wonders at the silence of God in the face of such suffering. Realizing the danger he has brought to the Christians who welcomed him, and fearing that they will hand him over to the Japanese officials to protect themselves, he sets out in search of another underground Christian community but is shortly betrayed to the officials by an apostate Christian.

Although Rodrigues's incarceration is initially uneventful and even permits him the opportunity to minister to other Christians in prison, he soon witnesses two other martyrdoms. The martyrdoms again elicit doubt and perplexity about the silence of God, though Rodrigues also knows moments of hope and joy in which he believes himself united in his suffering to Christ and to the martyrs he has seen. At long last the officials take Rodrigues to meet his dear mentor, Ferreira, who is in fact an apostate living under Japanese control. Ferreira tries to persuade Rodrigues to apostatize by telling him that the Christian faith the missionaries tried to sow in Japan cannot take root in its culture, that the god the Japanese Christians worship is not the Christian God but something else. The Japanese faith Rodrigues thinks he would defend in being martyred is false.

Following his meeting with Ferreira, Rodrigues is told to apostatize by trampling on a *fumie*, a plaque affixed with an image of Christ. An interpreter urges Rodrigues: "We're not telling you to trample in all sincerity. Won't you just go through with the formality of trampling? Just the formality! Then everything will be alright" (155). Rodrigues refuses and is taken to the magistrate's office in Nagasaki. There he is locked in a tiny, dark cell, the floor covered with urine. He thinks again on the face of Christ and struggles with the contempt he feels for his betrayer and his resentment at God's silence. From a distance a sound reaches him—the snoring of a guard. At first the sound causes him to laugh. Then Rodrigues is filled with rage that on this, the most important night of his life, he should be disturbed by such a vile sound. The guard, he thinks, "had not the slightest idea of the suffering that would be inflicted on others because of his conduct. It was this kind of fellow who had killed that man whose face was the best and most beautiful that ever one could dream of" (165).

Rodrigues bangs on the wall and complains to the interpreter who comes to him. Ferreira is there, too, and tells Rodrigues that the sound he hears is not snoring but the moaning of Christians hanging in the pit. Rodrigues is stunned by the realization that in his pride he believed he alone was sharing in the suffering of Christ. Ferreira proceeds to tell Rodrigues that he spent a cold, terrible night in that very cell listening to the Christians in the pit, told they would be released and tended to if only he apostatized. His fervent prayers for them went unanswered by God, and for this reason he finally apostatized.

He tells Rodrigues to do the same: "You are preoccupied with your own salvation. If you say that you will apostatize, those people will be taken out of the pit. They will be saved from suffering. And you refuse to do so. It's because you dread to betray the Church. You dread to be the dregs of the Church like me." A priest, says Ferreira, should imitate Christ, and "certainly Christ would have apostatized for them" (169). Leading Rodrigues from his cell, Ferreira says, "Now you are going to perform the most painful act of love that has ever been performed." The *fumie* is brought out. Rodrigues grasps it, filled with sadness, and gazes at the "ugly" face of Christ. The novel reaches its climax:

> "It is only a formality. What do formalities matter?" The interpreter urges him on excitedly. "Only go through with the exterior form of trampling."
> The priest raises his foot. In it he feels a dull, heavy pain. This is no mere formality. He will now trample on what he has considered the most beautiful thing in his life, on what he has believed most pure, on what is filled with the ideals and the dreams of man. How his foot aches! And then the Christ in bronze speaks to the priest: "Trample! Trample! I more than anyone know of the pain in your foot. Trample! It was to be trampled on by men that I was born into this world. It was to share men's pain that I carried my cross."
> The priest placed his foot on the *fumie*. Dawn broke. And far in the distance the cock crew. (171)

In the months and years that follow Rodrigues comes to believe that the struggle that led up to his trampling was not with the Japanese officials but with his own faith.

> I fell. But, Lord, you alone know that I did not renounce my faith. The clergy will ask themselves why I fell. Was it because the torture of the pit was unendurable? Yes. I could not endure the moaning of those peasants suspended in the pit. As Ferreira spoke to me his tempting words, I thought that if I apostatized those miserable peasants would be saved. Yes, that was it. And yet, in the last analysis, I wonder if all this talk about love is not, after all, just an excuse to justify my own weakness.
> I acknowledge this. I am not concealing my weakness.... I know that my Lord is different from the God that is preached in the churches. (175)

Endo tells us that Rodrigues "could not understand the tremendous onrush of joy that came over him" when he trampled (190). He loves the Lord "now in a different way from before. Everything that had taken place until now had been necessary to bring him to this love. 'Even now I am the last priest in this land. But Our Lord was not silent. Even if he had been silent, my life until this day would have spoken of him'" (191).

How are we to understand Rodrigues's action? Is his trampling an act of neighbor love? Rodrigues seems to conclude this, and certainly even a moment's reflection on the agony the Christians were suffering in the pit propels us toward agreement. But this conclusion, as Rodrigues himself acknowledges, is troubled by the possibility that "neighbor love" is a self-deceptive description. Moreover, it seems to require us to set aside the notion of Christian martyrdom as a participation—par excellence, if not glorious—in Christ's redeeming death. Furthermore, there is the matter of how Rodrigues's decision to trample enacts or betrays love for his other neighbors—other Christians in Japan who need to be sustained in their faith in a time of persecution, other Christians in the church around the world. Rodrigues realizes he will be maligned by these Christians, but tells himself that Christ alone knows he did not renounce his faith. Does that mean that his trampling is, as the Japanese officials suggest, merely a formality, that his faith is essentially unconnected to the external renunciation he performs? Just before he tramples Rodrigues rejects this, and rightly so, since the very notion of apostasy tells against it. Apostasy is a public rejection of faith, and Christians place their faith not in abstract ideals or universal principles but in Jesus of Nazareth, who freely submitted to execution rather than betray the will of his father. Yet it was the will of the father that his son be trampled upon so as to share in men's pain, which presses the question—Is Rodrigues's action a failure of faith or a kind of profession of it?

We need not repair back to the "formality" description to see that these two possibilities are not necessarily mutually exclusive. Rodrigues's trampling is an act of apostasy. Naming it as such is crucial for maintaining its ties to the human world, for recognizing that his trampling has a moral and spiritual significance that cannot be removed by whatever other descriptions Rodrigues or we might wish to apply to it. Importantly, Christ urges Rodrigues to trample, not in a way that suggests it does not count, but in a way that refers the trampling to his own identity as the one crucified for our sake. Granted, Rodrigues may have imagined Christ speaking as an illusion to justify his decision. Rodrigues certainly struggles with the lure of self-deception after he apostatizes. But the struggle itself prompts him to continually refer his action, his self-justifying descriptions of it, and himself back to Christ.

We would strain the artistry of Endo's novel by trying to read in it every aspect of the account of falsehood and truthfulness I offered at the outset of this chapter. But Rodrigues's tale does display its main features. Rodrigues's unbelief operates within his explicit faith in Jesus Christ. His struggle with God's silence prior to his apostasy suggests that he clings to some "normative conception of goodness, truth, right, love, salvation," and so forth, with which he tries to deal with God, a conception that God's silence calls into question and that the message Christ delivers from the fumie overthrows.[46] Rodrigues's apostasy is arguably a confession of Christ's lordship, one that is inclusive of naming his fall as such. He is made to deal with God's love as *his* love and accordingly comes to affirm the identity of the truth Christ witnesses and of Christ himself, the crucified one.

Rodrigues's self-understanding is centrally determined by his priesthood. Throughout the novel he reproaches himself for his weakness, cowardice, and resentment, all of which he finds unfitting in a priest; in this respect he may evade rather than face his sinfulness, insofar as his self-reproach signals indignation and shame regarding his exposure as a sinner. Certainly Rodrigues's priesthood is a means by which he takes up God's call to free obedience as a covenant partner, yet Rodrigues increasingly comes to feel that God's silence makes an absurdity of his life. The pain he feels in trampling on Christ's face is, I think, the pain of sacrificing the false aspects of his priestly identity, so as to take it up in a new way, as one weak and broken. Rodrigues's efforts to understand his apostasy illustrate the way grateful acceptance of God's gift requires us to take up the new self that God's unmerited love makes of us. This is why Rodrigues can say that even if God had not been silent his life would have spoken of God. The confusion Rodrigues feels about what love for neighbor requires along with his pride, contempt, and resentment all signal something of falsehood's disordered and disordering irreverence. Granting the ambiguity of his apostasy as an act of neighbor love, Rodrigues is drawn more deeply into God's life in a way that transforms his apprehension of and loving in the world.

What we may learn from Rodrigues's apostasy is that a fall from grace may be a fall into grace. This lesson specifies my claim that the gift of truthfulness before God normatively governs the work of naming moral actions. Insofar as our actions and our names for them are true, they are so because of the charity God creates in us by his grace. In this way they share in God's reconciliation of the world. Reckoning that in our falsehood our actions and our names for them are all too often lies, we hope and pray for the grace to recognize them as such in the faith that the God to whom we make ourselves painfully lost is the God who draws intimately near to us in reconciling love.

Naming Moral Actions Is a Moral Practice

In previous chapters I stressed that particular human actions are historical, particular, and provisional. Truthfully naming human actions requires us to acknowledge as much. We act in history, in a time always already established by and oriented to God's redeeming self-gift in Jesus Christ, short of the eschatological consummation of God's reconciliation of the world, and hence in a time when the force or power of sin disrupts proper relation to God and fellow creatures. Moreover, our actions belong to the personal histories we forge in response to God's self-offer.

Their meaning becomes intelligible in the narrative context of our respective lives as these participate in salvation history. Our actions are thus particular because they are *our* actions. They disclose something of who we are, have been, and are called to become in God. They speak of and transact our individual (though never isolated) relations with God in the concrete, particular circumstances of our lives. Our actions are provisional since the freedom we enact and embody in them and the history in which we exercise our freedom are unfinished. The provisionality of our specific actions both relativizes their meaning (since our conversion and its opposite remain real possibilities) and heightens it (since our actions bring about something new for our relations with God and others, something that matters and persists precisely because we fashion these relations with our lives). Accordingly, the names and evaluations we apply to our actions are provisional since the full meaning of any action is hidden in the counsel of God.

Although the truth about our actions is known finally and fully only by God, as creatures called to free self-determination in faithfulness as God's covenant partners, we are bound to discover what we can about the truth of our actions as involvements with God and creaturely goods. Since human action is intentional, what an agent intends to do must factor centrally in truthfully naming her actions. Yet she can be mistaken about what she does when she acts, if she deceives herself, if she is blind to some of her motives, and if she "has been raised on a false set of descriptions of the world, if [she] has been taught to speak a language that falls consistently short of reality."[47] Moreover, as I argued in the previous chapter, our actions involve us with a host of creaturely goods and values; however unwittingly we thus involve ourselves, these alliances reverberate in our multiple relations to ourselves, others, and God. The descriptions we give our own actions can fail to capture these aspects and effects. All this is to say that "what I did when I acted . . . is not entirely up to me to determine. It must be located within the ongoing language, life, and story of those with whom I live."[48]

The descriptions under which an agent acts and by which she tries to understand (or lie about) her actions arise in human community. Naming our actions is therefore an unavoidably collaborative endeavor. This is good news and bad news. The inescapably collaborative character of naming is good news since an agent's community furnishes her with an array of descriptions that can substantiate, flesh out, and correct those the agent is inclined to use. It is bad news since her community may offer impoverished and false descriptions, since her neighbors sometimes have something to gain by encouraging a false understanding of her actions. The same human community that enables her to receive and respond to creation through a shared language and life is the community that incorporates her thereby into an economy of sin. The shared human life that gives rise to our action descriptions both enables and distorts the practical skills we require to fashion and refer our lives to God. We are therefore not only personally responsible for discovering what we can about the truth of our actions, we share that responsibility with and for others.

In short, naming moral actions is itself a moral practice. Truthfulness before God normatively governs our naming; if we are to name our actions truthfully, our naming needs to reflect how they do or do not correspond with the reality of the world under God, including the reality of our created nature, corrupted by sin and redeemed in Christ. For this, we must subject our actions and ourselves to God's comprehensively normative claim on all our thoughts, attitudes, and decisions. Yet by our unbelief we endeavor to domesticate and curtail this claim; we thereby deny or sequester God's practical relevance in a pragmatic atheism that amounts to a concrete loss of God. Losing God, we lose ourselves, evading the sinful selves God shows us to be and the new selves God calls us to be in freedom. We adopt a self-protective manner of life that issues in irreverent, disordered relations with creation; we thus live in and by lies, in and by false descriptions of reality. That is to say, we live as liars.

The havoc and harm we wreak in our falsehood is real and painfully effective. But, as Barth tells us, "the reality of God and man in Jesus Christ is superior to the pseudo-reality to which we are delivered by our falsehood. Nor is it idle in respect of it, but on the offensive against it." The truth is identical with Jesus Christ, with the promised Spirit, and "therefore with the present reality of God and man in this time of ours."[49] The truth disrupts and thwarts our lying, unsettles and attacks us by its great and small manifestations and in the experiences of the good and the beautiful that God lavishes upon us; we may resume our efforts to conceal and corral the truth, but the truth that God reconciles the world limits and checks them.[50] We cannot claim full and final deliverance from falsehood as a liberation to which we are entitled, but we may and should hope and pray for the gift of truthfulness before God.

CONCLUSION

"A person who reflects on God's prevenient action in Jesus of Nazareth," says Demmer, will aim "to construct an intellectual world of mercy, which then reflects ethical teaching both in form and in content."[51] Inasmuch as the descriptions by which we live arise within such a world, the names we give our actions will be healing words. They will reflect and partake in God's reconciliation of the world. The names we give our actions will convey and promote whatever goodness inheres in our deeds as a share in the life and love of God, as rightly ordered involvements with God and creaturely goods. Our names will identify and lament whatever sinfulness our actions express and sustain. They will eschew self-despair and hypocrisy; they will resist hateful judgment on the one hand and irresponsible if well-meaning reticence on the other. We will name our sins in a compassionate charity that keeps before us the hope that a fall from grace may be a fall into grace. We learn to hear and to speak such healing words in the community God promises to sustain and sanctify by his Spirit, the church. Our prospects for naming our actions truthfully therefore depend crucially on the explanatory power and moral realism of its God talk, its theology, and on the formative power of its practices and worship, a point the next chapter will explore in light of our reconciliation in God.

NOTES

1. Barth, *Doctrine of Reconciliation*, 376.
2. Ibid., 379–83. In the following discussion, references to pages in this work are given parenthetically in the text.
3. Demmer, *Living the Truth*, 21–22.
4. Augustine, "Against Lying." See also Griffiths, *Lying*.
5. McFadyen, *Bound to Sin*, 9, 8. Similarly, Stanley Hauerwas observes that an especially pernicious contemporary form of unbelief is "not the unbelief that denies God in a highly articulate manner, but . . . an unbelief that considers such a denial not worth the effort since the affirmation makes no difference in the first place." *Vision and Virtue*, 113.
6. McFadyen, *Bound to Sin*, 8, 12.
7. Demmer, *Living the Truth*, 21.
8. The phrase is Iris Murdoch's; see her *Metaphysics as a Guide to Morals*.
9. See Alison, *Joy of Being Wrong*.
10. Griffiths, *Lying*, 91–92.
11. Barth, *Doctrine of Reconciliation*, 475.
12. An anonymous reviewer wondered if the language of "debt" implies that gratitude is an obligation rather than a free response to a gift. I retain the language, not because I think gratitude should (or even can) be exacted from someone, but because it captures the fact that ingratitude is generally held to be blameworthy or unfitting.
13. Demmer, *Living the Truth*, 76.
14. Augustine's uti/frui distinction, and much else in his corpus, does not appear patient of contrasting falsehood's irreverence with reverence for creatures, which is one of the reasons I think "charity" better captures how the gift of truthfulness transforms our relationship with fellow creatures. Yet I think the notion of reverence is not entirely at odds with an Augustinian account of love, since we might apply a strong sense of reverence as worship to God and a weak sense of reverence as duly respectful and charitable regard to creatures.

15. Aquinas, *Summa theologiae*, pt. II-II, q. 25; ibid., q. 23, art. 6.

16. For some recent work on Christian love, see Jeanrond, *Theology of Love*; Cates, *Aquinas on the Emotions*; Pieper, *Faith, Hope, Love*; Pope Benedict XVI, *Deus caritas est* (2006), Vatican website, www.vatican.va/holy_father/benedict_xvi/encyclicals/documents/hf_ben -xvi_enc_20051225_deus-caritas-est_en.html; Pope Benedict XVI, *Caritas in veritate* (2009), Vatican website, www.vatican.va/holy_father/benedict_xvi/encyclicals/documents/hf_ben -xvi_enc_20090629_caritas-in-veritate_en.html.

17. Griffiths, *Lying*, 87.

18. Ibid., 94.

19. See Pinches, *Theology and Action*, 109.

20. The book is *Inside Al-Jazeera: The Arab News Channel That Is Challenging the West*, by Hugh Miles. Terry Gross, "Inside Al-Jazeera, as It Plans an English Version," *Fresh Air*, March 14, 2005, www.npr.org/templates/story/story.php?storyId=4533916.

21. The literature on religion and violence is vast. The following are only a handful of resources: Cavanaugh, *Myth of Religious Violence*; Appleby, *Ambivalence of the Sacred*; Avalos, *Fighting Words*; Esposito, *Unholy War*; Juergensmeyer, *Terror*; Kimball, *When Religion Becomes Evil*; Lincoln, *Holy Terrors*; Schwartz, *Curse of Cain*; Sells, *Bridge Betrayed*.

22. See, e.g., Hyman and Steward, *Agency and Action*; Demmer, *Living the Truth*; Ginet, *On Action*; Davidson, *Essays on Actions and Events*.

23. Pinches, *Theology and Action*, 30.

24. Ibid., 19.

25. Hornsby, "Agency and Actions," 2, 9.

26. See Fletcher, *Situation Ethics*; Ramsey, "Case of Joseph Fletcher" and "Case of the Curious Exception." See also Ramsey, *Basic Christian Ethics*.

27. So-called rule utilitarianism purports to overcome this problem by specifying rules for action that are useful for society. Promises are to be kept because keeping promises serves human relations. Arguably, however, rule utilitarianism devolves into act utilitarianism, since the principle of utility requires us to consider whether breaking a promise might yield better consequences than keeping it and thus whether a particular act of promise breaking qualifies as an exception to the rule.

28. Richard McCormick offers this example to demonstrate his claim that intention tells us what an action is; see "Some Early Reactions to *Veritatis splendor*."

29. Aquinas, *Summa theologiae*, pt. I-II, q. 1.

30. Pinches, *Theology and Action*, 114, 138.

31. Ibid., 114; see also 137–38.

32. "It is possible to describe a human act in general terms, e.g., 'walking through the fields,' with nothing being implied in the description about whether it was good or bad for it to have been done," whereas other species classifications, like murder, already imply moral judgment; see Pinches, *Theology and Action*, 117.

33. Ibid., 102–5, quotation on 120.

34. Ibid., 154, 155.

35. Ibid., 91.

36. Ibid., 93; see also 135.
37. Ibid., 136.
38. See Porter, *Moral Action*, 21.
39. Pinches, *Theology and Action*, 149.
40. Porter, *Moral Action*, 49.
41. Hauerwas, *Vision and Virtue*, 15, 16.
42. Pinches, *Theology and Action*, 153.
43. O'Donovan, "Summons to Reality."
44. Pinches, *Theology and Action*, 160, 166.
45. In the following discussion, references to pages in this work are given parenthetically in the text.
46. Barth, *Doctrine of Reconciliation*, 467.
47. Pinches, *Theology and Action*, 2.
48. Ibid., 165.
49. Barth, *Doctrine of Reconciliation*, 477, 475.
50. Ibid., 476–77.
51. Demmer, *Living the Truth*, 23.

CHAPTER SIX

RECONCILIATION IN GOD AND CHRISTIAN LIFE

There has been a lot of talk about sin in this book—certainly more than one is likely to find in much of contemporary Christian ethics. There are risks associated with this insofar as talk of sin is regarded as coming at the expense of our appreciation of grace or an affirmation of creation's goodness. Rather than signal misanthropy or a moribund worldview, due recognition of sin's pervasive disruption follows from the grace-occasioned, worship-inducing, astonished awareness of creation's beauty and God's loving intention to reconcile all things, including each of us. We become aware of sin in the knowledge of grace, so that talk of sin can be one key in which grace plays. If a fall from grace can be a fall into grace, we can speak of the gravity of sin and gratuity of grace together. Talk of sin can function as a crucial resource in the personal and communal processes of healing ruptured relationships and righting our involvements with creaturely goods. It can also, of course, contribute to those very ruptures, wounds, and wrongs. The church is that faith-formed community where we learn to speak and to hear words of sin and grace together. As a pilgrim community that enjoys a taste of God's reconciling grace but is not yet fully reconciled, it can be a source of harm and scandal as well as healing and edification. These facts provide all the more reason why our understanding and practices of forgiveness and reconciliation need to be mindful of but not limited to determinations of moral culpability.

The reasons why and the way to speak of sin and grace together become clearer when we reflect on forgiveness and reconciliation. This chapter begins with two stories of reconciliation, one about a clearly, terribly wrong act and the other about a case that does not involve wrongdoing. We then turn to some recent scholarship on forgiveness in light of which these two stories appear both vexing and instructive. The chapter will argue that God's forgiveness permits and prods us to reinterpret moral wrongdoing in a way that creates new possibilities for moral agents. Forgiveness, however, is not yet reconciliation. Reconciliation encompasses forgiveness but also exceeds it. It does not require determinations of culpability or depend upon the satisfaction or removal of some perceived claim upon the offender, though it could include these. Reconciliation entails a communion that corrects and overcomes the disruption of proper relationship between persons.

The chapter then considers the importance of ecclesial contexts and practices for Christian life. A theology of reconciliation, enlivened and embodied in ecclesial life, provides crucial insights into the integrity and limits of Christian moral life as well as the discipline of Christian ethics. A theology of reconciliation relativizes Christian ethical distinctions and judgments while simultaneously securing them in an affirmation of God's reality as the author and end of creation and the source of freedom and value. This theology of reconciliation thereby makes our endeavors truthfully to understand our moral acting a penitent, shared practice in which we come to realize our involvements with sin as we grow in awareness that we are graciously drawn into mutual abiding in God and one another.

TWO STORIES OF RECONCILIATION

On October 2, 2006, in Nickel Mines, Pennsylvania, a gunman named Charles Roberts walked into a one-room Amish school intent on sexually assaulting and killing the female students. The teacher and one girl escaped early on. The gunman released the male students along with three adult women who were visiting and their small children. He bound the remaining ten girls. He phoned his wife and told her he would not be coming home. He said he could not forgive God for allowing their newborn daughter to die hours after her premature birth some nine years ago. He claimed that he had sexually molested two female relatives as an adolescent, though they denied it ever happened, and that he was tormented by the urge to molest young girls again.[1] Roberts said he hated himself and hated God. When police arrived he called 911 and ordered everyone off the property. He warned that he would begin shooting. Seconds later, he fired at all ten girls and once at the policemen storming the building, and then he shot and killed himself. Five girls died. The other five were seriously injured, though in varying degrees.

Within hours of the shooting, an Amish minister and several Amish men went to visit Roberts's wife and children to express their forgiveness, and another Amish man went to see Roberts's father.[2] Roberts's grandfather-in-law went to the home of two of the Amish victims and was received by the victims' father with a handshake. The father placed his arm around the grandfather "and said there was no grudge, only forgiveness, and that they held nothing against [the Roberts family]." These were the first of many visits between the Amish and Roberts's family. Several of the victims' families invited Roberts's wife and children to their daughters' funerals. At Roberts's funeral, half the attendees were Amish.[3]

By the evening of October 2, reporters already were commenting on the swift expressions of forgiveness offered by the Amish and their outreach to the Roberts family. In the following days their forgiveness became the focus of many news reports, editorials, and Internet discussions. Some of the response was negative.[4] A few wondered if the forgiveness by the Amish was irresponsible.[5] The majority of comments, however, were positive. These responses frequently reflected surprise or awe that victims' families and neighbors could forgive so promptly and graciously.

For their part the Amish were matter-of-fact about their forgiveness. They understand forgiveness to be scripturally commanded. In the Sermon on the Mount Jesus makes one's own forgiveness by God conditioned on whether one forgives others (Mt 6:14–15). The Amish take this injunction literally. Their understanding of forgiveness is especially grounded in the notion of *Gelassenheit*, "an ethic of yielding to one another, renouncing self-defense, and giving up the desire for justification or efforts at revenge."[6] Gelassenheit is practically depicted for the Amish in biblical parables such as the story of the prodigal son and examples set by Anabaptist martyrs. It is warranted by their faith that God providentially rules over creation. It is facilitated by their compassionate regard for others.[7] There was no question for the Amish that the only appropriate response to the events of October 2 was forgiveness. That is not to say that their forgiveness signaled an absence of grief or anger. Some members of the Nickel Mines community have sought professional help from counselors. They acknowledge that forgiveness is a struggle, a commitment that must be made anew each day.

Soon after the shooting, the Amish asked Herman Bontrager, an insurance company CEO who grew up Amish and now practices as a Mennonite near Nickel Mines, to serve as their spokesman. Bontrager identifies several features that are unique to Amish forgiveness. In addition to—perhaps because of—the belief that forgiveness is a religious duty, for the Amish forgiveness is immediate rather than forestalled until the victim is emotionally ready to forgive. Forgiveness in this regard is both a nonnegotiable expectation and a decision. Granted, forgiveness remains something to live into. The emotional dimension of forgiveness is directed and facilitated by practice. Moreover, as Bontrager notes, the practice of forgiveness is corporate or communal. "The community assumes the responsibility to forgive. One purpose of community is to 'share one another's burdens.' In an offense of this magnitude Amish would never expect the individual alone to extend instant forgiveness. The community took responsibility to practice forgiveness knowing that the individual victims were too crushed to do it."[8] The Amish understand that forgiveness is necessary for the community's survival and well-being and for the good of the individual members. The community thus upholds and reinforces the expectation that forgiveness is normative and unconditional, exercises that forgiveness in conjunction with—and perhaps initially on behalf of—the individual victim, and supports the victim in living into forgiveness. The communal or corporate character of Amish forgiveness is self-consciously a condition for and causal factor in the victim's exercise of his own agency in response to an offense he has suffered. Moreover, the communal character of Amish forgiveness polarizes it toward the greater fullness of reconciliation.

In a talk Bontrager gave just after the two-year anniversary of the shooting he shared the following:

> A couple months ago I entered the plain but warm kitchen/dining/living
> room of a young Amish family in Nickel Mines, Pennsylvania. Two healthy
> sons rose satisfied from the supper table and went straight to playful tussling.
> Across the room sat a woman with short, spiky hair, in slacks, obviously not
> Amish. She was holding Rosanna, totally disabled by shots to the head, the
> eight-year old daughter of Christ and Mary Liz. The woman was reading to
> her. Once a week she comes. She is the mother of Charles Roberts, the man
> who shot Rosanna and nine of her classmates, killing five. She gives care, and
> hopes for healing for her own wounded heart. Mary Liz and Christ, though
> weeping for themselves and for Rosanna, offer Mrs. Roberts hospitality, a
> space to mourn her son. Here, a simple country home, surrounded by lush
> fields of grain, is a haven for wounded hearts.
> Are there limits to forgiveness?[9]

This moving account is a story of reconciliation. It does not turn on assignations of blame or bother with questions such as whether only those directly injured are in a position to forgive. These determinations and questions have a proper place and usefulness, but we would be mistaken to allow them to suffice or dictate the terms for understanding forgiveness and reconciliation. Rosanna's family's hospitality toward Roberts's mother shows us what reconciliation looks like, at least insofar as we can have it in the wake of an evil deed that cannot in this life fully be set right. Rosanna's parents and siblings might easily and understandably find it difficult to couple their forgiveness with hospitality toward Mrs. Roberts. Mutual presence might feel too painful. But their hospitality creates space for forgiveness to blossom into reconciliation. Mrs. Roberts might easily and understandably be isolated in fear, guilt, and shame. But she opens herself to Rosanna and her family in order to give and receive care. Together they work for healing. Their mutual vulnerability toward each other permits a give-and-take in which each party can assist in the other's healing, which in turn contributes to their own.

Without wanting to gloss over the distinctiveness of the Amish way of life or ignore theological differences between their understanding of forgiveness and others considered here, it is important to refrain from regarding their example as exotic, so yoked to their way of life as to be inaccessible to, impracticable by, or not normative for other Christians. Granted, the Amish enjoy a degree of communal cohesion and support missing in many other contemporary Christian communities. But their forgiveness is nonetheless a process, an arduous journey to be lived into. They sincerely offered forgiveness in the aftermath of the shooting but reportedly found forgiveness a decision they needed to make again and again.[10] Bontrager asked several of the Nickel Mines Amish whether there are limits to forgiveness. Their first response was no. Upon reflection, they said that "the only limits they could think of are the human tendencies to harbor grudges, to desire vengeance, to get stuck in self-pity—all of which are either contrary to God's will or manifest some people's inability to develop coping mechanisms."[11] Such obstacles might be found in any human heart. The Amish, then, struggle in a universally human fashion, one that they would not hesitate to name as sin, and endeavor to live into and out of the grace promised to them in the gospel.

The school shooting in Nickel Mines is one story of reconciliation. A Mennonite offers a second, this one thankfully free of tragedy. John L. Ruth relates the following:

> In the last few weeks of my father's 101 years a visitor from Lancaster County
> stopped by his bed. It was Amos Hoover, legendary bibliophile, collector
> of Plain Mennonite lore, and founder of the Muddy Creek Farm Library.
> Instantly remembering that he had once visited the library in the Hoover
> home, my father confessed a fear that he might not have properly reshelved
> a book he had looked at there. Expecting to hear Amos say it didn't matter, I
> was struck to hear, instead, "Well, you're forgiven." The effect was strangely,
> humorously healing. My super-conscientious father hadn't been diminished
> but embraced.[12]

The first story involved an unambiguously wrong act, whereas this one concerns a small matter perhaps only Ruth's father would identify as wrong. Indeed, its force depends on an expectation that readers generally would think Ruth's father required a friendly correction ("There's nothing to forgive") rather than forgiveness. Appreciatively relaying a story like this might in fact vex those who worry that forgiveness offered too quickly, easily, or in situations where no wrong has occurred only erodes a commitment to justice, or even skews our perception of what justice requires. It might also trouble those who worry about the ways religious communities sometimes create scruples that pain people for no manifestly good reason.

Subsequent sections of this chapter will consider reproach and respect as indicating a concern for justice, something contained in earlier discussions of truthfulness and fidelity. The first chapter shared concerns over earlier Christian tradition's inflation of particular actions' capacity to bear the full meaning of sin. Undoubtedly, moral communities, and in a special way religious communities, can fuel shame and guilt and obstruct access to forgiveness and healing. Nevertheless, this story can teach us something about forgiveness and reconciliation—namely, that reconciliation exceeds and sometimes requires us to transcend concern over moral culpability in favor of mutual presence and acceptance. Reconciliation, I will argue, consists in a communion that corrects and overcomes the disruption of proper relation to God, ourselves, and others. Just as we emerge as individual sinners within an economy of relations that preconditions our agency, we are summoned, led, and empowered within an alternative community, the church, to know ourselves as ones forgiven who must and may likewise forgive.

FORGIVENESS AND RECONCILIATION

Forgiveness currently receives considerable scholarly attention in the humanities and social sciences. It has also become a veritable industry in popular culture, as self-help books and workshops proliferate. Much talk of forgiveness today is therapeutic, by which I mean that it focuses on empowering the victim emotionally to move beyond the injury or offense she suffers.[13] In other words, the bulk of recent popular and social scientific approaches to forgiveness focus on the benefits that accrue to victims when they forgive others. Less often considered are issues of accepting forgiveness, which though beneficial can also be difficult, or accounts of forgiveness centered around releasing the offender from the burden of her guilt.[14] Philosophical and theological treatments of forgiveness tend to explore a wider range of issues. Particularly important for philosophical treatments is whether we can square forgiveness with respect for moral standards and the dignity of victims. Philosophical treatments also typically endeavor to distinguish forgiveness from and relate it to allied concepts such as excuse, pardon, mercy, forgetting wrongdoing, and so forth.[15] Christian theological discussions of forgiveness address many of these matters, too, but typically forward accounts of forgiveness imbued, as we might expect and hope, by some understanding of God's forgiveness of humanity in Jesus Christ; these accounts lead to more complex understandings of the relation between offenders and victims.

At stake in forgiveness and reconciliation are basic questions regarding the meaning of moral actions, particularly wrongdoing, for a person's moral identity and for her relationships with others. Does forgiveness distance the agent from her wrong actions? How does forgiveness fit into our concern to speak of the gravity of sin and the gratuity of grace together? Given Christian faith that God has forgiven us once and for all in Jesus Christ, what is the import of this forgiveness for our understanding of human freedom's unfinished character and for the work of morally discriminating among concrete human actions? This section will review recent work on divine forgiveness, interpersonal forgiveness, and group forgiveness and draw from these discussions to forward an account of forgiveness and reconciliation.

Divine Forgiveness

Some philosophical and theological treatments of forgiveness devote what I take to be an inordinate amount of time to pondering whether divine forgiveness is compatible with traditional attributes of God. If God is perfect, for instance, how can God be injured so as to even be in a position to forgive?[16] While these arguments can nudge theologians toward greater conceptual clarity and precision, they risk misunderstanding divine forgiveness inasmuch as they try to square an account with a preexisting (and rather static and overwhelmingly transcendent) picture of God rather than the storied self-disclosure of a living God.

Scripture speaks of God's forgiveness in a variety of ways. In the First Testament God negates or forgets our sin (Is 43:35) or washes sin away (Ps 51:2). Imagine God hurling our sins with tremendous force across a vast distance until they sink into the dark oblivion of the ocean (Mi 7:19) or, in fatherly compassion, distancing us from our sins as far as the east is from the west (Ps 103:12–13). In the Second Testament Jesus proclaims God's forgiveness of sins, as for instance with the sinful woman who washes his feet (Lk 7:36–50), and "embodies" it in his death and resurrection.[17] Repentance and forgiveness of others are sometimes identified as preconditions for being forgiven by God (Mt 6:14–15 and 18:23–35), whereas other times God's forgiveness is presented as unconditional (Lk 15:11–32), about which I will say more in a moment.

Christian understandings of divine forgiveness draw crucially upon interpretations of Jesus's death and resurrection. Does this death and resurrection signal that God frees us from punishment for our sins because a substitutionary victim bears the penalty on our behalf? Does it mean that God's demand for justice has been satisfied, which then frees God to regard us as if we were innocent? If we can free ourselves from the grips of atonement theory, we can appreciate with Nigel

Biggar that "the paradigmatic context of forgiveness is neither feudal nor forensic, but friendship."[18] Jesus's death and resurrection reveal God's desire to give us a share in his life and constitute God's conquering opposition to what hinders or obstructs that share. God's forgiveness is not principally or strictly the cancellation of a debt—though one of its consequences is that it frees us from sin's intrinsic punishment of living in estrangement from God—nor does it involve God's regarding us as something we are not. God's forgiveness is the gift of himself, a divine initiative to draw us into closer relation to him. It justifies us by inaugurating a new possibility for us in relation to God; sanctification is the ongoing realization of this possibility as, over time, grace counteracts the disorienting, debilitating, and disintegrating effects of sin.

Scripture sometimes speaks of divine forgiveness as unconditional, and surely the overall picture is one of profligate mercy. Importantly, the gratuity of God's forgiveness, extended to us as ones who do not deserve it, does not mean that God loves us *despite* our sinfulness, that God makes us unlovable creatures lovable. There is nothing begrudging or niggling about God's forgiveness.[19] It manifests that God already loves us *in* our sinfulness. There is nothing about us that requires or deserves forgiveness, and yet God not only endowed us with intrinsic worth, God longs to enter into the mess we are and have made so as to draw us out of it.[20] God compassionately responds to our sinfulness and delights in showing us mercy (Mi 7:18). Our having been lost is part of the joy God takes in welcoming us home. When like the prodigal son we squander our inheritance from God, when we awaken to find ourselves lonely and hungry in a life of dissipation (Lk 15:13), God comes to meet us while we are still far away. God rejoices in our return and invites others to share in this delight. God's readiness to forgive is central to who God is, a hallmark of the divine character. Our God chooses to "welcome sinners and eat with them" (Lk 15:2).

In the Gospel of Matthew God's forgiveness seems conditional, particularly in the parable of the unforgiving servant (Mt 18:23–35). The parable suggests that God's forgiveness of us is conditioned on whether we will forgive, a conviction operative in the Amish understanding of forgiveness. The overall witness of scripture is that God offers forgiveness in Jesus gratuitously and unconditionally. Our acceptance or appropriation of this forgiveness, however, requires us to forgive others. As the Nickel Mines Amish exemplified, we sometimes need to live into forgiveness of others. The notion that God's forgiveness is conditioned on whether we forgive others tells us something about the character of divine forgiveness, that we cannot be drawn into a deeper share of God's life if our hearts are set against our brothers and sisters. Forgiving them is part of being forgiven precisely because being forgiven means being given a new future to live, the terms of which are not dictated by sin's multidimensional estrangement. Similarly, repentance is not a prerequisite for the divine offer of forgiveness, which God has already made irrevocably and unconditionally in Jesus Christ. Repentance is necessary, however, as an ingredient of human acceptance of God's forgiveness. By our repentance we open ourselves to God's forgiveness, which in turn enables greater repentance on our part.[21]

What of those scriptural images of God forgetting our sins or removing sin from us as far as the east is from the west? Does divine forgiveness make a new future for us precisely by treating us as if we were innocent of sin? As if our sins never happened? Such language metaphorically renders the fact that one's identity resides in God's regard and the freedom this regard creates in our own history before and with God. I do not mean that God regards us as if we were innocent. Nor do I mean that God overlooks our sins, much less undoes them. "It is not the case at all that forgiveness is to do with our slates being wiped clean so that we can be fitted back into a pre-existing model of creation. On the contrary: forgiveness is our access to being created in the first place: it is the undoing of a temporary hitch on our way into becoming sharers in God's life."[22] Forgiveness undoes *us*, making us new creatures by changing the meaning of our sin(s) so that what was estrangement and enmity, disorientation and debilitation, disorder and disintegration becomes the site of God's self-giving nearness to us, God's reconciling share in his own life.

Interpersonal Forgiveness

The picture of interpersonal forgiveness one finds in recent philosophical and theological literature is rather chastened. Like the therapeutic approaches of many popular and social scientific sources, philosophical treatments concede that forgiving an offender can benefit the victim; however, one is more likely to find greater debate regarding whether some offenses or persons are unforgivable (a question set aside in the therapeutic endeavor to render forgiveness as "moving on"), moral defenses of resentment, and more stringent conditions placed upon offenders if forgiveness of them is to qualify as morally commendable. Philosophical accounts of forgiveness also devote considerable attention to what forgiveness is not. Charles Griswold, for example, argues that forgiveness collapses into condonation, rationalization, or excuse without certain conditions being met. Delineating forgiveness in relation to such allied concepts is an exercise in specifying criteria for moral responsibility and for applying moral blame. If it is clear that a particular grievance involves a morally blameworthy offense reliably imputed to a given offender, we enter the territory of forgiveness. Other conditions need to be met if the victim's altered response to the offense is really to be a (morally commendable) instance of forgiveness; these conditions chiefly center on the offender's taking of responsibility, contrition, sympathetic outreach to the victim, and sincere attempts to change for the better.

If the victim chooses to forgive, this choice consists in holding the offender responsible while also relinquishing resentment and revenge and seeing the offender and herself in a new light.

> Re-framing does not come to the view that the wrong-doer is not to be considered as being the wrong-doer, to "washing away" the fact of her having done wrong. . . . So it must involve something like distinguishing that "part" of the self responsible for the injury from the "whole person." Now, the wrong-doer will very probably be seen "in a new light" not solely or even primarily on the basis of the "whole person" as already evinced, in part through the offender's narrative, but also on the basis of her projects for reform of self. "Reframing" and forgiving are in this sense forward looking.[23]

Griswold's description of forgiveness is helpful inasmuch as it insists that forgiveness involves associating persons with their wrongdoing while reframing that wrongdoing to prevent its tyranny over the future. It displays concerns to avoid cheap or otherwise irresponsible forgiveness and to see that the dignity of victims is respected through appropriate behaviors by the offender. Nevertheless, approaches like Griswold's narrowly understand that which requires forgiveness and involve individualistic and constrictive accounts of responsibility and forgiveness.

The stories of reconciliation offered above are instructive precisely because they vex the more calculating approaches just discussed. In the first story, the Amish are unconcerned with worries about third-party forgiveness, implicitly reject the idea that an offense could be unforgivable, and demonstrate forgiveness toward an unrepentant offender. The second story does not even evidently involve wrongdoing but rather the fear that a mistake was made. Without clear determinations of culpable wrongdoing that directly connect victims to their offenders, it is unclear whether, on the terms of the preceding, forgiveness even applies. After all, Roberts's family members are not offenders. Yet Amish forgiveness is directed at them, too. What distinguishes these stories from the approach to interpersonal forgiveness characteristic of recent philosophical work is the compassionate initiative of the victim.

Recent theological scholarship on forgiveness tends to display this characteristic, too, which of course reflects God's compassionate initiative toward offenders and leads to more nuanced perspectives on the relation between victims and offenders. Miroslav Volf's account of forgiveness accents the victim's initiative without making forgiveness all about her emotional release.[24] The starting point for forgiveness is the victim's readiness to make a space in which she apprehends the offender's basic humanity and comes to will reconciliation. Volf insists that the offender must truthfully own up to her wrongdoing. He thinks punishment of wrongdoing is compatible with forgiveness and a desire to be reconciled. Following the offender's taking of responsibility and possible punishment and restitution, the victim can forgive. This forgiveness can stop short of embrace. Geiko Müller-Fahrenholz also accents the victim's initiative. He describes interpersonal forgiveness through the German concept *Entblössung*, which he translates as "denuding oneself," to identify the process of entering into the painful shame associated with having perpetrated or undergone a grave wrong. For both perpetrator and victim *Entblössung* involves a kind of disarmament, laying down defenses and opening oneself to the pain of this evil. "When forgiving does happen it leads to the profound recognition that the pain of the other is also my pain. There is a mutuality of defenceless openness which enables each side to recognize in the other a human being in need of help. Forgiving is more than an encounter; it is an exchange of pain. The result is a deepened understanding of the other and of oneself."[25]

Is there a Christian duty to forgive? Gregory Jones says that since we are made in God's image, and readiness to forgive is a divine attribute, we ought to forgive.[26] More modestly, Anthony Bash says there is not a moral duty to forgive but rather to do all one can in order to make forgiveness possible.[27] Truthfulness before God certainly rules out cheap forgiveness, but as we will see it also prohibits us from making too much of comparative moral judgments regarding the moral worth of persons or particular offenses. Fidelity to God requires at least that a maximum effort be made to forgive or accept forgiveness. Whether and how a person endeavors to forgive others and to seek forgiveness bears on her relationship with God. James Alison puts his finger on why this is so. According to Alison, the Christian must stop seeing herself as primarily "a victim and secondarily a forgiver, but someone who is primarily forgiven, and for that reason capable of being a forgiving victim for another, without grasping onto that, or being defined by it. . . . Without [this] we will not . . . understand the salvation which we are receiving from Christ."[28]

Forgiveness and Political Life

Across a range of disciplines and professional fields, interest is growing in prospects for forgiveness in political life or following significant wrongdoing by groups or institutions. Usually the wrongdoing under consideration is particularly complex and heinous, like genocide. Here I can only briefly review the main issues this growing field of study and practice tackles.

Bash poses the primary questions: "Can groups forgive or be forgiven? ... Can individuals forgive groups? In other words, are groups 'forgivable' (that is, able-to-be-forgiven) by individuals? ... To what extent are individuals personally responsible for the actions they do on behalf of groups?"[29] If we can answer any of these questions affirmatively, what might facilitate forgiveness while also meeting basic demands for justice and contributing to conditions necessary for a better future? A related question concerns whether third parties may forgive or accept forgiveness on behalf of victims and perpetrators; this question is particularly important with regard to forgiveness in political and social life since the primary or original victims and perpetrators may be dead or unavailable to participate in the process of expressing repentance and offering forgiveness. Moreover, since victims and perpetrators are in these cases multiple, some members of the group of victims may refuse to forgive, and some of the perpetrators may feel no remorse or repentance and may spurn proffered forgiveness. Third-party forgiveness is also likely to affect political or group forgiveness because political communities and corporations operate with representatives or proxies whose individual agency is complexly related to the moral identity and agency that may properly be attributed to the group.[30]

A number of scholars argue against the possibility of group responsibility, repentance, and forgiveness.[31] Christof Gestrich thinks the idea of collective responsibility is untenable given modernity's individualism and secularization. Bash argues that responsibility is often obscured within groups and institutions so that it becomes difficult if not impossible to identify a wrongdoer and, hence, to forgive. He exemplifies Gestrich's point, but in doing so simply fails to draw upon sufficiently complex accounts of responsibility and structural violence. Bash further contends that forgiveness refers to interpersonal efforts to restore relations between individuals; groups operate differently, though they can undertake efforts akin to forgiveness, such as offering apologies or expressing regret.[32] Griswold argues that political apologies do not rest on repentance because they do not involve sentiment. They are speech acts aimed at acceptance and with a view to possible legal, economic, and strategic consequences.[33]

Others argue for the possibility of corporate responsibility, repentance, and forgiveness. For example, Carl Reinhold Bråkenhielm argues for a "multidimensional" account of forgiveness and discerns similar features at work in both interpersonal and political forgiveness, such as the "degree of remission of punishment sought or awarded" and the "degree of desire for fellowship or community in a moral and personal sense."[34] Donald Shriver grants that maintaining a sense of collective responsibility through communal memory is necessary if current and future generations are to avoid repeating the mistakes of the past.[35] Müller-Fahrenholz argues that without repentant confession, forgiveness is not possible;

even if some form of restitution is made, such efforts are insufficient, for only a repentant confession instantiates the honest acknowledgment of wrongdoing that victims and perpetrators require if healing is to occur.[36]

The same sorts of concerns about respect for moral standards and integrity that mark treatments of interpersonal forgiveness arise with regard to corporate forgiveness. When a government, for instance, grants amnesty to perpetrators in exchange for their testimony (as happened in the South African Truth and Reconciliation Commission [TRC]), does this amnesty amount to a violation of justice? Are some cases of corporate wrongdoing so massive and evil as to be unforgivable? In a post-Holocaust world we rightly worry about cheap forgiveness. And yet, as the South African TRC exemplified, forgiveness in some cases amounts to a survival strategy rather than a betrayal of victims and moral standards. Forgiveness was a pragmatic response in the wake of apartheid, when the sort of punishment and reparations that would have been requisite for strict justice simply were not possible. More positively, Müller-Fahrenholz says that *"forgiveness goes beyond justice.* While legal systems and procedures provide societies with reliable structures of punishment and protection, forgiveness strives to heal the grief and re-establish the deepest qualities of humanity."[37]

Truthfulness plays a vital role for such healing. Truth telling establishes accountability. It lays a foundation on which to build future relations. It not only provides a shared record of wrongdoing, it can illuminate legacies (of pain, conflict, strength, and hope) that underlie and inform a group's cultural identity and patterns of relating. Truth telling constitutes a form of justice that can help to heal sociopolitical harms, even when full restitution to victims is not possible. Griswold and Müller-Fahrenholz link truthfulness to political or group memory. Truthfulness enables participants in the forgiveness process to confront themselves and one another. Says Griswold, "Remembering is supposed to be compatible with the possibility of redefining identity in such a way that peaceful cooperation between the parties—call it 'reconciliation'—is possible."[38] The redefinition Griswold has in mind is not a denial or downplaying of the past, particularly the wrongdoing in question, but a way of reframing it that makes possible a new future.

Related to discussions of forgiveness and politics are discussions and practical approaches that fall under the name "restorative justice." In its statement about crime and criminal justice the United States Conference of Catholic Bishops expresses well the paradoxical quality of restorative justice: "We cannot and will not tolerate behavior that threatens lives and violates the rights of others. We believe in responsibility, accountability, and legitimate punishment. Those who harm others or damage property must be held accountable for the hurt they have caused. The community has a right to establish and enforce laws to protect people and to advance the common good." Nonetheless, the bishops insist we must "not give up on those who violate these laws. We believe that both victims and offenders are children of God. Despite their very different claims on society, their lives and dignity should be protected and respected. We seek justice, not vengeance."[39]

Advocates of restorative justice recognize that crime harms many people beyond the primary victim, such as family and friends of the victim and the perpetrator, nearby homeowners with falling property values and rising levels of anxiety about their personal safety, and so forth. Restorative justice certainly aims at repairing the relationship between offenders and their primary victims, but it also looks to repair the wider harm that crime causes and, where possible, to rehabilitate offenders and restore them to a positive, functioning role in society. Restorative justice assumes that persons are interdependent and that when one person harms another, they both are diminished—albeit in different ways—and the common good is likewise adversely affected. While restorative justice faces some of the same obstacles as larger-scale approaches to political or corporate wrongdoing, it both signifies shifts in moral imagination and fosters them by casting criminal wrongdoing in a different light and by placing goals of personal and communal healing on the horizon.

Political forgiveness and restorative justice serve very practical ends; their advocates focus on creating conditions necessary for the future survival and well-being of afflicted communities. Similar impulses operated in Nickel Mines following the school shooting. Christian faith prompts hope that substantive progress can be made in forgiving sociopolitical wrongdoing and transforming structural violence in the direction of more just social arrangements. This hope is also a chastened one, soberly and penitently aware that full justice and full reconciliation are not possible in this world. As a pilgrim people we have the task to enact forgiveness and foster reconciliation in our communal, institutional, and sociopolitical life as part of the response we make to God, who is present and active in these spheres of human life, calling us into more intimate contact with him and one another. As we carry out this task, however, we must remain mindful that our responsibility is limited or chastened, lest our practical efforts to create conditions for our collective well-being become twisted by self-interest or aggrandizement, personal agendas, prejudice, or simple presumption.

Reconciliation

Reconciliation as I am defining it exceeds forgiveness.[40] If forgiveness makes a new future possible, reconciliation is a process of realizing that new future's promise through our incorporation into an alternative economy of relations that transforms our possibilities as moral agents. Reconciliation overcomes and corrects the alienation from God and others that wrongdoing may and sin does express and instantiate. It can very well include determinations of moral culpability, punishment, and restitution, but we can speak meaningfully of and partake in reconciliation apart from all this, in cases where no wrongdoing has occurred or when determinations of culpability and prospects for punishment and restitution are muddled or limited. Reconciliation is an embrace of mutual presence and acceptance that overcomes sinful alienation, which we suffer in ways not reducible to moral culpability.

We turn now to the problem of forgiving oneself. Self-forgiveness brings together a number of concerns regarding the import of particular wrong actions for a person's moral identity and relationships with God and others, the relationship between forgiveness and respect for victims and moral standards, and the relationship between being forgiven by God and being reconciled to him.

FORGIVING ONESELF

There are good moral reasons to greet talk of self-forgiveness warily. As one moral philosopher notes, "One recognizes how dangerous it would be if it were felt to be a virtue. For it would then be all too easy to slip into the habit of condoning the injury which one inflicts on others."[41] Forgiving yourself can seem "a self-indulgent cheat, an attempt to feel good about yourself that betrays a failure of responsibility and a lack of self-respect."[42] However, the possibility of cheap and morally irresponsible self-forgiveness ought not deter us from recognizing that it can be good. It is an important condition for reconciliation with (though not forgiveness from) neighbors we injure. Moreover, self-forgiveness is independently good, both in cases where we injure ourselves and in cases where our neighbor refuses or is unable to forgive us. A neighbor may forgive us, but our lack of self-forgiveness will impede the reconciliation we might both desire; I develop the claim that reconciliation exceeds forgiveness later.

Self-forgiveness need not wait on forgiveness from the other. Indeed, as Margaret Holmgren argues, self-forgiveness helpfully precedes our efforts to seek forgiveness from others because it can shore up respect for them and for ourselves and safeguards against abusive dynamics between the injured party and the offender.[43] Moreover, when forgiveness from the other is lacking, because she is dead, unaware of, or otherwise unable to forgive our trespass, self-forgiveness is important for the offender's present and future prospects as a responsible moral agent and flourishing human being. Christian faith offers grounds for affirming self-forgiveness as good, even independently so. Indeed, responsibly forgiving oneself is morally obligatory.

Defenses of self-forgiveness in contemporary psychology and moral philosophy frequently link self-forgiveness to self-respect. They generally insist that self-forgiveness expresses self-respect inasmuch as it entails taking responsibility for a morally wrong action and refusing to regard that action as entirely morally determinative of one's identity and worth. Self-respect both provides the principal warrant to forgive oneself and is the fruit of self-forgiveness. My own argument for self-forgiveness is sympathetic to these approaches. The problem is that they don't do justice to human self-relation or locate the self in a recognizable moral world. Christian moral anthropology positions us better to understand self-forgiveness in relation to one's agential history, relational prospects, and moral communities.

Self-Forgiveness and Self-Respect

Simply "doing wrong isn't sufficient to call for forgiveness. For if one doesn't call it wrong, or isn't bothered by it, or is bothered but gets over it, the need to forgive oneself doesn't arise. Self-reproach is required."[44] And this self-reproach must have a kind of staying power; it is the kind not easily set aside or rationalized away. Moreover, self-forgiveness concerns far more than wrongdoing. We may reproach ourselves for being the sort of person who would do such things, in which case self-forgiveness encompasses issues of character and not only action. We may reproach ourselves for what we failed to do, for what we desire, for our apparently involuntary responses to people who repulse us but whom we should love or to things that excite us though we ought to find them repellant. Finally, we "can do, want, be what is not wrong and still understandably condemn" ourselves.[45] I might blame myself bitterly for an inability to care for an aging parent in my own home, for relinquishing a child under safe haven laws even though I believe it was the right decision, for accidentally killing someone, or for keeping a secret that is not mine to share but nonetheless could alleviate the hurt of a loved one. Some of these examples point to experiences where, one could argue, self-reproach is unwarranted. And in such cases perhaps what is needed is not, strictly speaking, self-forgiveness, but an adjustment to the expectations that lead me to reproach myself for things that aren't wrong or can't be helped. Such corrections are part of the process of reconciliation, as we learn what we reasonably and charitably may expect and fittingly accept about ourselves and others.

Whether I reproach myself for my wrongdoing, for my character or dispositions, for my omissions, or for things that are not wrong or cannot be helped, my agency is in each case implicated in the object of my self-reproach. But for talk of self-forgiveness to apply, my agency must be doubly implicated. My self-reproach must be more than attitudinal. It must be an active self-reproach, a way of relating to and acting upon myself. A person becomes a candidate for self-forgiveness when her self-reproach "is not self-limiting," when it is self-punishing, self-cursing, when it is a wound she nurses, a state of being to which she delivers herself, when its scope and intensity and durability interfere with normal functioning—when, in short, it becomes corrosive.[46]

Self-Forgiveness and Responsibility Work

Margaret Holmgren makes a strong case for self-forgiveness as an independent, positive good. She insists that genuine self-forgiveness is necessary for self-respect, as well as respect for the victim and for moral obligations generally. Holmgren describes genuine self-forgiveness as a process of responding to one's own wrongdoing, of overcoming negative feelings like guilt and self-contempt in order to reach an "appropriate attitude" toward oneself, an internal self-acceptance. According to Holmgren a wrongdoer must first recover some self-respect in order to acknowledge her intrinsic worth in spite of her wrongdoing. She thereby acknowledges a difference between who she is and what she has done. Nonetheless, she must avoid self-deception by taking responsibility for her wrongdoing and appreciating the harm she has visited upon the victim. She must allow herself to experience feelings connected to her offense. "Her feelings serve to connect her with the reality of what she has done, the value of the victim, and the importance of her moral obligations."[47]

The offender must then address the attitudes, behavioral patterns, and character defects that underlie her wrongdoing. Holmgren insists that this step is necessary both to reduce the likelihood that she will commit the same act again and as a matter of respect for the victim and for morality. The offender next must discern how best to make amends to her victim and perhaps to others connected to him. This may or may not include an apology and some sort of restitution; this step toward self-forgiveness admits of creativity. Here, too, self-respect plays a role, by limiting the forms or extent of restitution the victim legitimately may ask for. Self-forgiveness cannot come at the cost of submitting to degrading or unduly punitive requests by the victim.

After she makes amends, says Holmgren, the wrongdoer's guilt, self-resentment, and self-contempt have served their purpose of getting her to address the wrong. She can now relinquish the focus on her past wrongful behavior, which was necessary as she worked through the process of addressing her wrong, and look at herself with love, respect, and compassion. By seeing herself as a vulnerable human being subject to various needs, pressures, and confusions, she can come to understand why she did what she did. She can have the humility to recognize that neither she nor any human being is immune from making wrong choices. And she can honor herself as a valuable person, which she remains in spite of her wrong-doing. At this point the offender has reached a state of genuine self-forgiveness. Her self-forgiveness is genuine as she is not deceiving herself about any significant aspect of her wrongdoing nor evading any of the tasks she needs to perform to amend the wrong.[48]

Self-Respect and Self-Reproach

Robin Dillon puts some helpful questions to Holmgren. If self-respect both positions me to forgive myself appropriately and is the fruit of self-forgiveness, "it would seem that the journey is almost over with the first step. But how might that step be taken?"[49] Moreover, if the "responsibility work" Holmgren delineates dissolves my self-reproach, what work is left for self-forgiveness to do? If self-reproach remains, what precisely does self-forgiveness do to resolve it? Why call that work "self-forgiveness" and not something else, like "self-acceptance"? Is the aim of self-forgiveness really to recover a sense of my intrinsic worth? Can't this remain intact even as I acknowledge and reproach myself for a significant transgression? What if my transgression is such that even after my responsibility work, feelings of self-reproach are warranted? "To overcome the attitudes would be to renounce the judgment and the standards that entail it. But when those standards are central to one's normative self-identity . . . renouncing them would be a failure to respect oneself and a sacrifice of moral integrity, which would give one additional grounds for self-condemnation. Trying to forgive oneself would be self-defeating" (57–58). In other words, "it seems that self-forgiveness either must be earned through fully taking responsibility, in which case it looks to be superfluous, or is not so earned, in which case it looks to be not self-respecting. How is it, then, that self-forgiveness does morally significant work without sacrificing self-respect?" (58).

Dillon agrees with Holmgren that self-forgiveness addresses damaged self-respect, but what kind of self-respect? Not necessarily the sort that consists in a sense of intrinsic worth, what Dillon calls "recognition self-respect."[50] Indeed, "recognition of one's dignity as a person is compatible with the negative self-appraisal that structures self-reproach" (70). The sort of damaged self-respect that underlies self-reproach is what Dillon calls "evaluative self-respect." This form of self-respect concerns one's merit and consists in assessments of whether one is living congruently with one's normative self-conception. A normative self-conception is an idea one holds regarding who one wants to be or thinks one should be along with a judgment of whether one is approximating or betraying this norm. A normative self-conception contains "both moral and nonmoral ideals we aspire to and standards we hold ourselves to." It "forms one part of our moral self-identity; the other part is our presentation to ourselves of how we stand in light of it. Our view of ourselves, that is, is always double; we see ourselves both as we think we are and as we would have ourselves be" (67).[51] Importantly, self-reproach can be morally valuable and consonant with a recognition of our intrinsic worth. It can be a sign of our being good despite having done wrong. When "self-reproach involves correct judgments vis-à-vis warranted standards," it manifests what Dillon calls recognition self-respect and "sustained commitment to the values and standards of one's normative self-conception, as well as an honest appraisal of oneself that refuses to compromise for the sake of comfort" (78).

Like Holmgren, Dillon insists that responsibility work is requisite for genuine or morally honest self-forgiveness.[52] So, then, what morally important and distinctive work does self-forgiveness do? "Repentance and atonement deal responsibly with *the wrong*. But after that's over, there remains the task of dealing responsibly with *oneself*, and that is the task of self-forgiveness. Important questions remain to be settled: how shall I think of myself now, how shall I go on from here? For someone properly concerned with self-respect the hardest work is settling such questions without betraying oneself" (79).[53] For Dillon, then, self-forgiveness is principally about how to see oneself in the wake of moral failure. She insists there is no "underlying reality" to the self that settles such questions. Rather, divergent appraisals of oneself vie for dominance. The difficulty of self-forgiveness, says Dillon, is that "there are strong reasons for, and strong pressures toward, different ways of seeing" (80). One did, after all, do or fail to do or feel in ways that violated one's normative self-conception, and one is the sort of person who could commit such acts or omissions or be so disposed.[54]

In the simplest cases of self-forgiveness, responsibility work fully justifies replacing self-reproach with evaluative self-respect. By virtue of one's responsibility work, one transcends the past and is again a person of merit vis-à-vis one's normative self-conception. Self-forgiveness here assumes that "the self was not transfigured or indelibly stained" by what one did, or perhaps assumes that responsibility work expunges one's moral record. But Dillon argues that "it is more respectful of our reality as beings whose lives have a history and whose characters are inevitably shaped by it to say that self-forgiveness does not erase the past but only alters its power or meaning for us" (80).

Harder cases of self-forgiveness are those in which responsibility work does not fully justify a person's replacing self-reproach with evaluative self-respect, perhaps because her moral failure is so grievous that it cannot be made right, because her wrongdoing does reflect or instantiate badness, or perhaps because the responsibility work does not improve her deeply flawed character. One possibility Dillon grants is that the person has done something unforgivable and must live as one unforgiven, in which case she may possess some meager recognition self-respect in forever withholding evaluative self-respect. Dillon devotes more attention to the possibility of overcoming self-reproach and reaching self-respect. How do we do so when responsibility work is insufficient to our moral failure? Self-forgiveness remains a matter of how to see ourselves, but in harder cases our self-appraisal is more chastened and ambivalent. Says Dillon, "For most of us most of the time, there is more to the story about the self than condemnation tells. True, I am the one who did something awful and is still capable of doing it, I am one whose character is deeply flawed; but I am other than this as well. . . . To forgive myself would be to see me as I am, not as I only imagine myself to be, to tell a richer story about myself, one that is more honest for being richer" (81).

Self-forgiveness puts "the negative judgments in their proper place," placing them within a more holistic evaluation of oneself (82). Moreover, since I am not only the object of my condemnation but the one condemning, I can choose to evaluate myself differently both because a broader view of myself provides reasons to do so and because I may thereby improve myself morally. "Self-forgiveness may involve a conscious choice to be more generous, merciful, optimistic, less harsh, demanding, obsessed with justice. Nor need this involve self-betrayal. . . . To try to forgive oneself for the sake of improving one's character is to de-center standards that underwrite condemnation and to privilege other dimensions of one's self-conception, perhaps even to improve the conception itself" (ibid).

A final possibility, says Dillon, is that we do not overcome self-reproach but simply lessen it and live with it. Warranted self-reproach is a valuable testament to our normative commitments, reminding us what we care about and thereby decreasing the chance of moral recidivism (78). Ongoing self-reproach can also serve the demands of retributive justice. According to Dillon, "one can both value oneself enough to get on with one's life and yet rightly carry a burden of guilt and shame to one's grave. . . . To go on like this can be to have forgiven oneself" (83).[55] Forgiving oneself isn't ultimately about the presence or absence of self-reproach but about its power; when we can temper self-reproach so that it no longer oppresses and debilitates us, we can come to a self-respect that entails a "low sense of merit" that is not only appropriate but virtuous for its honesty and humility (83).

Assessing the Arguments

Holmgren's and Dillon's treatments of self-forgiveness are representative of the literature in several respects. They share a concern to distinguish morally good self-forgiveness from cheap and dishonest forms, and for this they look to responsibility work. Both consider self-reproach a sign and symptom of damaged self-respect, by which they mean that moral failure calls into question the offender's sense of her own value. The literature varies in terms of how badly this sense of value must be damaged for self-forgiveness to apply. As Jean Hampton describes it, the state to which self-forgiveness applies consists in feeling "cloaked in evil," "morally hideous, unclean, infected," and in believing "there is nothing good or decent" in oneself.[56] Jeffrie Murphy considers this description a bit extreme for anyone less than a moral monster. Still, he retains Hampton's language of "moral self-hatred," which he defines as an experience of shame on top of one's guilt.[57] Despite variances, some self-reproach is required that is both resistant to ameliora- tion and corrosive. In sum, the literature treats the occasion of self-forgiveness as a state of self-reproach predicated on damaged self-respect.

For Holmgren, we forgive ourselves when we relinquish self-reproach, and it is good to do so if we have done our responsibility work. Self-respect is the warrant for, measure, and telos of self-forgiveness. By making amends and addressing the factors that led us to offend, we may recover self-respect. While Holmgren could clarify the interrelation of self-reproach, self-respect, and self-forgiveness, it is safe to say that she understands forgiving oneself as the recovery of self-respect, justi- fied and facilitated by responsibility work.

For Dillon, self-forgiveness is also, in all but the hardest cases, the replacement of self-reproach with self-respect, specifically the evaluative sort whereby I esteem myself as coming "up to scratch."[58] But Dillon also alerts us to the potential lim- its of responsibility work and the possibility of forgiving oneself while retaining some measure of warranted self-reproach. Self-forgiveness and self-reproach are not utterly incompatible, and in fact self-respect might require both. As noted, self- forgiveness isn't finally about the presence or absence of self-reproach but about its power. Self-forgiveness results from a broad but honest self-appraisal that legiti- mately seeks and considers reasons to justify forgiving oneself. The terminus and telos of self-forgiveness is not the banishment of self-reproach but the recovery of self-respect. The kind (recognition, evaluative) and degree of self-respect depends on our normative self-conception and our violation of it.[59]

Dillon's and Holmgren's arguments show well that self-forgiveness entails fun- damental ethical questions regarding the import of particular actions for moral identity and integrity and the moral psychological conditions for agency. They are helpful stimuli for Christian moral reflection on self-forgiveness. Their pri- mary deficiency, in my judgment, is an inadequate depiction of the self who would forgive herself. Self-respect is an impoverished moral reference point for self- forgiveness. There is more to the occasion of self-forgiveness than damaged self-re- spect captures; there is more to warrant self-forgiveness than self-respect; and there is more good that self-forgiveness may realize than the recovery of self-respect.

Self-Forgiveness in Christian Perspective

To speak about self-forgiveness—or self-respect and self-reproach, for that matter—is to grant the fact of self-relation, that selfhood is both who we are and something we have, a way of being that we forge and fashion, conceptualize and evaluate and act upon. Nevertheless, most studies of self-forgiveness do not develop accounts of self-relation. As a consequence, important aspects of forgiving oneself go unnoticed. Dillon does forward a rich and valuable description of self-respect as a "complex of multilayered and interpenetrating phenomena" of cognition, valuation, affect, motivation, interaction, and so forth.[60] But Dillon never recognizes that the self necessarily experiences, interprets, and evaluates herself in relation to others or describes the self as inhabiting any sort of world. Yet the person only comes to herself as she responds to others and the world. She becomes aware of herself, understands herself, and fundamentally determines herself in and through her encounters with and responses to them. The person takes up and negotiates who she is in and through these encounters and responds in the full and embodied range of her understanding, valuing, and acting.

In all this she also responds to God, the origin and end of her life, the creator and sustainer of her being. The person's relationship to God is intimately interwoven in her relation to her self. To recall Saint Augustine, God is "more inward than my most inward part."[61] The connection between the person's self-relation and relation with God means that her self-determination, in its particulars and as a whole, is always also a negotiation of her relationship with God, a response to God's self-offer, such that the person experiences the gain or loss of God in her self-relation.

What's more, human self-relation has an inescapably embodied and worldly character. We of course experience ourselves and others as being and having bodies. The material world mediates our multiple relationships and provides basic experiences of value, such as pleasure and pain. This world is home to a vast array of more complex goods, many realized in relationships with others, that contribute to human well-being or flourishing. Our experience of and response to God and others are mediated by the objective goods and values that constitute our lives. So our encounter with and engagement in this world is always also an encounter and engagement with the God who gives it and loves it and loves us.

With this notion of human self-relation in mind, let us consider the occasion or state that self-forgiveness addresses.

THE OCCASION OF SELF-FORGIVENESS

Sometimes we say things like, "If I did such and such, I don't think I could live with myself," or, when considering the punishment another deserves for her wrongdoing, "She's going to have to live with herself," surmising that such a prospect is worse than many others we could devise. Such expressions point to an important feature of the state or occasion that self-forgiveness addresses. We not only experience negative feelings and judgments about ourselves, we experience ourselves as being the sorts of persons to whom such feelings and judgments apply. In my own person, in the depths of my self-relation, I experience the disarray, conflict, and confusion, the bitterness or selfishness or wantonness that my moral failure reflects. In worse cases I experience myself as corrupt, as ruined, and knowing it was wrought by my own hands I feel enmity within myself. That enmity is infectious and comes to operate, often unacknowledged, in behaviors toward myself, like failures of self-care or an inclination to risky behavior.

Dillon points out that the self is the object of condemnation and the judge who delivers that verdict. But the self is also another victim, a casualty, because we injure ourselves in and by our moral failure. The wider literature on forgiveness tends to treat self-forgiveness as a puzzle, even an impossibility, because self-forgiveness supposedly doesn't involve a victim. But this is wrong. By our moral failure we deprive ourselves of real human goods, like the peace that comes from being trustworthy, the joy of being generous and kind, the freedom that comes with being honest. We deprive ourselves of relational possibilities as well, things like greater intimacy and mutual support, a good reputation, the respect of someone we admire. We make trade-offs, exchanging, say, magnanimity for the momentary satisfaction we take in a well-executed malicious comeback, and the myriad other ways we spend our wages for what is not bread, for what fails to satisfy (Is 55:2). We diminish our relationships and ourselves in turn. We wreak havoc and harm in and by our actions and then experience the fallout in our own person. We shape our character in vicious ways and then live the reality of our compulsiveness, our intemperance, our vindictiveness.

The occasion of self-forgiveness is, then, a state of damage, but the injuries extend well beyond self-respect. In fact, the occasion or state that self-forgiveness would address is a particularly painful instantiation or appearance of what is in fact an encompassing condition—sin. As chapter 2 argued, sin is the disruption of proper relation with God. Sin involves an estrangement or alienation from God, a disruption of our self-relation, and estrangement from our neighbors and the world. The occasion of self-forgiveness is always a manifestation of sin—though not necessarily our own. Sin also affects the way we respond to such disruption, inclining us to mismanage or exacerbate it rather than repair or heal it. Without denying that we can engage in responsibility work to good effect, it remains the case that we cannot eradicate sin through our own efforts.

The occasion of self-forgiveness is one wherein we reckon with our sinfulness in relation to the one who is the good, the guarantor of our lives. As we labor under the burden of self-reproach, we negotiate our relationship with God, who would forgive and reconcile us. We discern whether and how we might have the courage to place ourselves before him, to allow him to show us to ourselves, to go where he would lead us.

And so we arrive at a new insight into self-reproach, that it is a form of attending to ourselves whereby we may in fact evade ourselves. Painful as our judgment is, we may prefer it to abandoning ourselves to God's mercy. Self-reproach can be a prop, something to hold onto, a set of reasons we furnish to ourselves to forestall movement into the unknown, an odd consolation whereby we mete out punishment to ourselves as though we could beat others, including God, to the punch. Withholding forgiveness from ourselves can be a way to bide time, to avoid dealing with questions about ourselves and the future. It provides a measure of surety and control at a time when, having injured ourselves, we may not be able to trust ourselves to do what is best.

We do not really understand self-reproach apart from fear. In the wake of grave moral failure we certainly fear its immediate consequences or repercussions. More fundamentally we fear for ourselves and for the future. These fears may be crystallized around a particular dread or horror that what we have done or been is irrevocable.[62] In our freedom we have wrought destruction. Because we determine ourselves in and through the exercise of our freedom there is an eternal quality to our failure. It cannot ever be undone. We cannot ever return to being people who would never do such a thing. We fear what that mark on our permanent record will mean henceforth. We realize that, perhaps rather unwittingly, we have made ourselves into people who cannot live freely and authentically with others. We may feel incorrigibly like a fraud. Eventually we may feel as though we have damaged relationships that didn't even exist at the time of our wrongdoing; for instance, a new parent might worry that a preparenthood indiscretion has forever deprived her of the opportunity to be the sort of person she wishes to be for her children. The point I want to make is that all this suffering over the irrevocability of our past failures is really fear over the future. Experiencing, painfully, that our freedom really does accomplish something that cannot be undone, we feel the burden of our freedom, which is as yet unfinished. What may we make of ourselves now?

In such a state belief in God's forgiveness may not console us. For the real terror lies in knowing that to accept God's forgiveness, really to entrust ourselves to it, will mean being stripped of all our props, of all our works and all appeal to merit. It will mean exchanging the burden of our self-reproach for the yoke of

God's tenderness, which in our confusion appears even more terrible, because in his tenderness he invites us to be ourselves before him, and what could be more awful than that? What we do not realize, or know but don't believe, is that, though we fear what is in the depths of our being, though we are afraid to face ourselves squarely and devoid of all props, we will not encounter the monstrous visage we imagine. We will not discover anything that can hurt us. There is only our poverty, only our need for God's healing, only the wound that was already there.

In sum, the occasion of self-forgiveness includes the pain of our own judgment, our reproachful self-appraisal, the pain of our estrangement (alienation not only from ourselves but from others, from concrete goods, from God who is the good), and the pain of our poverty. To choose, as Dillon suggests, to look at ourselves differently—through a more generous, compassionate hermeneutic lens—can alleviate some of the pain of this situation. Still, the fact and experience of our being wounded remains and requires healing.

What Self-Forgiveness Seeks

The telos of Christian self-forgiveness is reconciliation with God, with others, and with oneself. While it includes and is facilitated by efforts like the responsibility work Holmgren so clearly delineates—taking responsibility for moral failure, making amends where possible, working to identify and address factors that lead one to offend—and while it includes moments of choice about how to see oneself, the path of self-forgiveness is, in my judgment, not quite as fixed as Holmgren and Dillon imagine. Self-forgiveness consists in a process of continual self-interpretation that at various times will involve ongoing stages of self-reproach, moral confusion, and acceptance. The proper question is not what work self-forgiveness does so much as what it seeks and how this telos is actualized in our narratives, relationships, and projects.

Self-forgiveness is a process of transfiguring self-reproach into a repentance that actively seeks reconciliation. To reproach is to blame, judge, condemn. To repent is to cultivate a change of heart. As a self-interpretive process it is also necessarily a process of self-disposal, of continually entrusting oneself to the merciful judgment of God, continually receiving oneself anew from God's loving care. Full reconciliation is not possible in this life. Some remorse or contrition regarding particular moral failures is therefore appropriate in fitting measure. When is it fitting? When it is not excessive or self-preoccupied or corrosive or evasive, when it opens us in compassion and humility, when it makes us more forgiving of others.

Forgiveness is not reconciliation but is a necessary condition for it. Withholding forgiveness from ourselves prevents us from moving into reconciliation with God. God wants to heal us, each of us in our particularity. But God accomplishes this by challenging us to confront ourselves, by inviting us ever more deeply into an intimate relationship, one in which we are freed to be truly ourselves. God's forgiveness makes our self-forgiveness more about slaying our normative self-conception, escaping its shadow, than fulfilling it through our efforts. We often will experience progress in forgiving ourselves after the fact, in moments when we accept our painful judgments about ourselves and then set them aside, moments when we realize some repair or healing has taken place in our relationships. Gradually we learn that to enter into our poverty, to place ourselves in need before God, is to draw close to the one who is life in its abundance.

We are therefore obliged to forgive ourselves, first and foremost, in response to God's forgiveness to us. Self-forgiveness is also obligatory for the sake of responsibly assuming and exercising our freedom in concert with God's reconciling work. Self-forgiveness is further warranted and obligatory on account of our value, but this value finds its source in the God who made us and who cherishes us, not in the good works we accrue.

Our obligation to forgive ourselves includes a duty to seek assistance from others, which brings me to the relation between forgiveness and moral communities, particularly the church.

RECONCILIATION AND THE CHURCH

The literature on self-forgiveness often ignores or underestimates the role our moral communities play.[63] Yet how we see or evaluate ourselves—reproachfully, forgivingly   is socially mediated. The standards or values according to which we appraise ourselves are learned, endorsed, interpreted, and reinforced in communities. Decisions about how to see ourselves, then, cannot be isolated from feedback we receive telling us who others think we are and how we measure up or fall short. Our experience of ourselves is profoundly shaped by the standards, values, and appraising eyes of others. Put differently, we humans are creatures capable of seeing ourselves as we are seen by others. How important it is, then, to place ourselves in communities that will show us to ourselves honestly and charitably.

Indeed, our moral communities may obstruct or facilitate self-forgiveness as well as interpersonal and corporate forgiveness. My family's fondness for teasing me about some indiscretion, for instance, may keep self-reproach alive when I otherwise would have resolved it, while my friends may shape my moral commitments in ways that inhibit any self-reproach concerning, say, my conspicuous consumption. Moral communities can facilitate forgiveness by endorsing and encouraging it as good, through practices of charitably reckoning with faults, by supplying insights into why I or my group or institution might have erred as we did, by acknowledging our responsibility work, and by drawing us into the future life of the community as it unfolds. Our moral communities largely determine our prospects for forgiving appropriately and effectively.

The church is where we learn to live as people who are forgiven and where we are commissioned to forgive others. We learn to live as ones forgiven through the formative word we encounter in the church and through character-forming practices like the sacraments. The story of what God has done in Jesus Christ— announced by Jesus himself when he read Isaiah's prophecy in the temple and declared to his listeners that it was fulfilled in their hearing (Lk 4:16–21), and inaugurated in his birth, ministry, death, and resurrection—reveals to us both the fact that we are forgiven and our need of forgiveness.[64] The shape of our forgiveness and our need of it reaches vertically, horizontally, and reflexively, such that our reconciliation in God necessarily involves our inner transfiguration and the transformation of our relationships with others and the world. Put differently, we are reconciled in and as the people of God, the body of Christ, the church. "Salvation, then, is best understood not as being accepted no matter what we have done, but rather as our material embodiment in the habits and practices of a people that makes possible a way of life that is otherwise impossible. That is why we are not saved in spite of our sin, but we are saved precisely through practices of confession, forgiveness and reconciliation, which make Christian happiness possible."[65]

In the church we receive the healing gift of God's Spirit. We are incorporated and enlisted as members of his body, commissioned to live in witness to the saving work of Christ. Christ establishes the church as a sign and sacrament of this reconciliation, entrusting "the ministry of reconciliation" to the church (2 Cor 5:19). The church carries out its mission through its proclamation and interpretation of scripture, sacraments, prayer, preaching, pastoral action, and witness, dialogue, political intervention, and catechesis.[66]

Of course, the church, like any human community, can also obstruct forgiveness, wreak havoc and harm against persons and creation, and participate in structural violence. So the church is that community that mediates God's forgiveness at the same time that it stands in need of that forgiveness.

We live in a world mis-structured by the vicious processes of recrimination, scapegoating and stigmatization from which Jesus came to deliver the human race, and to the extent that we fail to understand the scope and dynamics of forgiveness, we remain bound. Churches as institutions and communities embedded in particular contexts share in that mis-structuring, with the result that the mediation of forgiveness frequently goes wrong—sometimes appallingly wrong—as those who claim to *possess* the freedom for which Christ has set us free (Gal. 5:2) not only celebrate their un-freedom but impose intolerable burdens and indignities upon others. . . . Intertwined as they are with human dependence and vulnerability, the "means of grace" by which forgiveness is communicated are always ambiguous and potentially oppressive. They are all too easily co-opted into anxious, restrictive or exploitative human projects, thereby becoming alienated from the life-giving dynamic which they represent.[67]

The church's own complicity in sin and need for forgiveness should not surprise us, though some instantiations of that sinfulness, like the sexual abuse of minors by clergy and the institutional cover-up of such abuse, seriously wound us as individuals and as a community and rightly scandalize people inside and outside the church. As Pope John Paul II says, "The church, if she is to be reconciling, must begin by being a church, in order ever more effectively to proclaim and propose reconciliation to the world, must become ever more genuinely a community of disciples of Christ . . . united in the commitment to be continually converted to the Lord and to live as new people in the spirit and practice of reconciliation."[68]

Apart from the fulfillment of God's reconciling work, the church will remain a pilgrim community and hence must resolutely be a penitential one. Practices of confession, forgiveness, and reconciliation are therefore essential for the church's integrity. In addition to persistent reliance on practices of confession, forgiveness, and reconciliation the church must commit itself to organizational arrangements and postures that promote the identification of and restorative responses to alienating features of the church and ecclesial complicity in wrongdoing. These arrangements and postures include empowering laypersons in ecclesial administration and pastoral leadership opportunities, making commitments to institutional transparency, welcoming and listening to those who speak from marginalized positions, and showing a readiness to entertain criticism from inside and outside the church. The church gives us a foretaste of the Kingdom of God, but it is not identical with that Kingdom. Failures to appreciate this in ecclesial self-understanding and practice lead not only to eventual disillusionment but also to alienating and even violent treatment of those deemed fallen, dissident, or foreign. As the church undertakes practices of confession and forgiveness, this pilgrim people must seek continuously for arrangements and postures that promote fidelity, truthfulness, and reconciliation.

RECONCILIATION AND CHRISTIAN ETHICS

Despite variances in particular explications of God's forgiveness, common to Christian accounts is an insistence on human solidarity in sin, the gratuity and salvific import of God's forgiveness of sin, and its close connection to sanctification or moral regeneration. This basic account challenges, even relativizes ethical distinctions between good and bad persons, better and worse deeds. Like the obedient elder brother to the prodigal son (Lk 15:11–32), or the laborers who have worked all day for the same wage now accorded to latecomers (Mt 20:1–16), we sometimes cling to comparative moral judgments and respond poorly to the challenge divine forgiveness makes, that we become a people in whom "mercy and truth are met together, righteousness and peace have kissed each other" (Ps 85).

The parable of the prodigal son describes both the readiness of God's forgiveness and the resentment it can meet on the part of those who otherwise are faithful to him.

> Then Jesus said, "There was a man who had two sons. The younger of them said to his father, 'Father, give me the share of the property that will belong to me.' So he divided his property between them. A few days later the younger son gathered all he had and travelled to a distant country, and there he squandered his property in dissolute living. When he had spent everything, a severe famine took place throughout that country, and he began to be in need. So he went and hired himself out to one of the citizens of that country, who sent him to his field to feed the pigs. He would gladly have filled himself with the pods that the pigs were eating; and no one gave him anything. But when he came to himself he said, 'How many of my father's hired hands have bread enough and to spare, but here I am dying of hunger! I will get up and go to my father, and I will say to him, "Father, I have sinned against heaven and before you; I am no longer worthy to be called your son; treat me like one of your hired hands."' So he set off and went to his father. But while he was still far off, his father saw him and was filled with compassion; he ran and put his arms around him and kissed him. Then the son said to him, 'Father, I have sinned against heaven and before you; I am no longer worthy to be called your son.' But the father said to his slaves, 'Quickly, bring out a robe—the best one—and put it on him; put a ring on his finger and sandals on his feet. And get the fatted calf and kill it, and let us eat and celebrate; for this son of mine was dead and is alive again; he was lost and is found.' And they began to celebrate. Now his elder son was in the field; and when he came and approached

189

the house, he heard music and dancing. He called one of the slaves and asked what was going on. He replied, 'Your brother has come, and your father has killed the fatted calf, because he has got him back safe and sound.' Then he became angry and refused to go in. His father came out and began to plead with him. But he answered his father, 'Listen! For all these years I have been working like a slave for you, and I have never disobeyed your command; yet you have never given me even a young goat so that I might celebrate with my friends. But when this son of yours came back, who has devoured your property with prostitutes, you killed the fatted calf for him!' Then the father said to him, 'Son, you are always with me, and all that is mine is yours. But we had to celebrate and rejoice, because this brother of yours was dead and has come to life; he was lost and has been found.' (Lk 15:11–32)

Both sons tie their father's love to an estimation of their respective worth in his eyes. Each considers himself as a slave of the father rather than a son; for the prodigal son the status of slave is something to be hoped for given his expectation that the sonship he squandered will not be bestowed upon him again. He is restored to relationship with his father, but this renewed bond acknowledges the prior breach, for the son is welcomed and loved precisely as one who was lost and is found, was dead and has come to life. For him, reconciliation will require accepting a new identity, that of one forgiven.

The eldest likens his faithfulness as a son to slavery, suggesting an obedience tinged with resentment or motivated by hope for reward, or simply a failure to grasp how children may fittingly presume to ask their parents for what they desire (Lk 11:9). Both sons have thought too little of their father's love and too little of themselves in relation to their father. Moreover, the prodigal son's elder brother resents the lavish welcome his father gives his wayward brother. He believes that his faithfulness has earned him benefits that have been withheld. The elder brother clings to comparative judgments that, even in the midst of welcoming home a brother thought lost forever, would establish a hierarchy of favor and entitlement. The elder brother makes the mistake of thinking that his father's forgiveness and joy come at his expense. He separates himself from his brother by referring to him as "this son of yours." The father's gentle but emphatic correction ("this brother of yours") indicates that he rejoices both that his son is restored to him and that his eldest has his brother back. The father's forgiveness intends to extend to reconciliation of the brothers, a sign that divine forgiveness encompasses us all in God's plan for full and final reconciliation in eternal life.

The parable of the vineyard laborers challenges our sense of desert even more.

For the kingdom of heaven is like a landowner who went out early in the morning to hire labourers for his vineyard. After agreeing with the labourers for the usual daily wage, he sent them into his vineyard. When he went out about nine o'clock, he saw others standing idle in the market-place; and he said to them, "You also go into the vineyard, and I will pay you whatever is right." So they went. When he went out again about noon and about three o'clock, he did the same. And about five o'clock he went out and found others standing around; and he said to them, "Why are you standing here idle all day?" They said to him, "Because no one has hired us." He said to them, "You also go into the vineyard." When evening came, the owner of the vineyard said to his manager, "Call the labourers and give them their pay, beginning with the last and then going to the first." When those hired about five o'clock came, each of them received the usual daily wage. And when they received it, they grumbled against the landowner, saying, "These last worked only one hour, and you have made them equal to us who have borne the burden of the day and the scorching heat." But he replied to one of them, "Friend, I am doing you no wrong; did you not agree with me for the usual daily wage? Take what belongs to you and go; I choose to give to this last the same as I give to you. Am I not allowed to do what I choose with what belongs to me? Or are you envious because I am generous?" So the last will be first, and the first will be last. (Mt 20:1–16)

This is a story about God's initiative and our response. It depicts God as one who seeks out the idle, those unemployed and waiting for someone to hire them. Not only does God go in search of them, God's generosity increases in proportion to the time they have spent waiting for work. God employs those whom others passed by or did not need, giving to those who even late in the day stood waiting in the marketplace a share equal to the one given to those who were hired first. They may not have borne the day's full burden of laboring in the vineyard in scorching heat, but perhaps their labor was simply different, the labor of waiting, of hoping, of offering oneself and finding no takers. Such a possibility is entirely overlooked by the indignant folks who labored all day in the vineyard. They envy those who came at five o'clock for receiving a full day's wage for a fraction of the day's work without considering their own enviable position, having been hired early on while others had to wait and hope for employment as their chances grew more and more slim. God's gracious generosity fills a void we help to create when we pass others by or do not seize opportunities to engage them, when we fail to consider the situation of others with empathy or compassion, a void made as well by our sheer finitude.

191

This parable falls between the story of the rich young man (Mt 19:16–26) and that of the mother of Zebedee's sons, who lobbied to ensure her sons would be seated next to Jesus in his kingdom (Mt 20:20–28). Coming after the rich young man, who kept the commandments but could not forsake the many possessions that claimed his heart, this story plays off of and reiterates Jesus's previous insistence that the first will be last and the last first (Mt 19:30). It emphasizes that discipleship demands singleness of heart, detachment from our typical valuation of treasure and our typical sense of desert. Coming before the mother of Zebedee's sons, the parable reinforces that laboring for God's ends requires us to die to ourselves so that we might respond to others with the same sort of generous self-giving depicted by the vineyard owner and eschewed by the rich young man. Because in Christ God transvalues all our values, we must also be ready to sacrifice our moral self-estimation, our normative self-conception. It is God who determines the worth of our labors, God whose regard founds our identity.

Christian faith in God's forgiveness bears crucially on moral judgment. Comparative moral judgments regarding good and bad persons or better and worse actions function in a number of ways. They may soothe a troubled conscience by appraising our relative merit vis-à-vis another's viciousness, indulge a sense of injury or self-pity, bolster dividing lines between ourselves and others, and become whips with which we punish ourselves. These problematic operations should not blind us to the fact that comparative moral judgments and ethical distinctions have their proper place. They are the stock-in-trade of ethics. They help us to reflect critically on experiences of offense in order to determine whether our sense of injury is justified, misplaced, exaggerated, or wanting. They help us to calibrate our reproach or outrage on another's behalf. They involve us in reflection on why we believe particular actions, relations, and institutional practices or configurations miss the mark, what goods or values are realized, violated, or offset, and what roles and responsibilities pertain to the matter at hand.

Comparative distinctions draw us into and are the fruit of practical moral reasoning through analogies. These distinctions matter personally, relationally, and institutionally. Personally they belong to the formation and exercise of our conscience, the discovery and refinement of our cares and identity-conferring commitments. They matter relationally because they bear on our mutual expectations of one another, provide conditions for or obstacles to sympathy for others, index our corporate identity to shared values and commitments, establish and maintain boundaries for inclusion, exclusion, or status within social groups, and so forth. They matter institutionally because they inform and are influenced by policies and protocol, institutional culture, and corporate responsibility. We cannot do without moral judgments, and our moral judgments are inevitably comparative since they traffic in analogies. Making moral judgments is part of the responsible, faithful, and truthful exercise of our freedom.

While a theology of reconciliation relativizes moral judgments such that a thorn in the flesh is a site for God's power to operate (2 Cor 12:7–10) and a fall from grace may be a fall into grace, Christian faith that God is reconciling all things unto himself secures our moral judgments in an affirmation of God's reality as the author and end of creation and the source of freedom and value. In other words, our moral judgments are contextualized by salvation history and accordingly are particular and provisional but without becoming merely subjective or relative. This is because of the explanatory power and moral realism of theology.

Theology's Explanatory Power and Moral Realism

As chapter 5 argued, drawing on the work of Alistair McFadyen, our culture is pragmatically atheist insofar as "it assumes the *practical* irrelevance of God's existence to the disciplines of reflection and practice we all use as we interpret and act in the world." Yet "if God is the most basic reality and explanation of the world, then it must be the case that the world cannot adequately be explained, understood, lived in, without reference to God in our fundamental means both of discernment and action."[69] Theological claims, when they are true, have explanatory power precisely because they describe reality in relation to God. God is intimately present in and involved with his creation; therefore, talk about God "may not permissibly be carried on in abstraction from the world, nor, therefore, from worldly forms of self-understanding." Rather, the task of Christian theology "is to understand both God and reality from the perspective of God's concrete presence and activity in the world, and in relation to our concretely lived experiences of being in the world."[70]

Theological ethics is a form of moral realism. "Moral realism" names those ethics that affirm that the good and the right are grounded in reality rather than merely being products of social consensus or personal preference. Theological ethics is a form of moral realism because it affirms God as the ultimate source of morality. Some versions of theological ethics might emphasize that moral knowledge is revealed to us by God in history and sacred scripture, while others might emphasize that moral knowledge may be gleaned by reflecting critically on features of God's creation, particularly human needs, experiences, and capacities. In contrast to cultural relativism or moral subjectivism, morally realist ethics understand that moral claims can be shown true or false. One way their veracity is shown is dialectically, as they expose and overcome deficiencies in alternative positions and as they practically orient and inform moral agents and communities.

Accordingly, when formulating and assessing moral judgments Christian ethics must ask what account of the acting person grounds them and what understanding of the world, the field of human action, they presume. Truthful moral judgments must be rooted in truthful accounts of the acting person and the world, formulated and investigated with a view to discerning God's intimate and active presence in creatures and a creation that have their own integrity as such. Theology therefore works with other disciplines to explain concrete realities, to discern God's active presence at work in the world and the practical difference this makes for us. Forgiveness, for example, is not solely a psychosocial phenomenon. Nontheological disciplines like psychology, sociology, political science, or anthropology can articulate "neither the deepest realities of the pathology (that which is to be forgiven) nor of the forgiveness appropriate to it. Both are, at bottom, theological realities."[71] And yet we run the risk of speaking abstractly about these realities and allowing our theological reflection to operate at a distance from and perhaps in contradiction to reality. Christian ethics must therefore sustain a tensive, productive relationship between the given, natural (albeit interpretively mediated) touchstones of moral reflection—those human needs, experiences, and capacities that cross cultures and time—and the moral wisdom revealed in scripture and tradition.

William Schweiker has developed an approach to theological ethics that he calls "hermeneutical realism."[72] Hermeneutical realism is a version of moral realism that endeavors to take seriously the fact that human beings are creatures whose moral consciousness awakens in a world endowed with value, who necessarily interpret themselves and the world through complex and overlapping systems of language, belief, and cares. Christian faith provides a hermeneutic for interpreting the human experience of value or good and for understanding and directing our lives as subjects and agents who both discover goods in a given world and experience themselves as creators and interpreters of value.

With regard to the acting person and the world, Christian faith names God as the condition for experiencing both the goods given in creation—things like life, kinship, sexual pleasure, and friendship—and the values we realize in our actions and relations, things like peace and justice. God is the author and end of creation and the source of freedom and value. Because God is the ground of my own being as an acting person, the ground of the field of action I inhabit, my very self-relation is also an intimate involvement with God. Moreover, "God" is not simply a designation for which nontheistic terms could substitute without remainder, but rather the name of the I Am Who Am who reveals himself to have freely chosen to be Emmanuel, God for and with us. Understanding *this* God to be the ground of our being, to be actively present in the world and inviting us into a deeper share in his life, we learn that we are creatures made to receive this share and to give ourselves in return.

Faith in God's freely given and forgiving love is efficacious, transforming the way we regard ourselves and hence reconstituting our very prospects as agents. The first epistle of John captures the practical difference faith makes—namely, that we can experience in our very self-relation and in our relations with others the gain of God: "By this we know that we abide in him and he in us, because he has given us of his Spirit. And we have seen and do testify that the Father has sent his Son as the Saviour of the world. God abides in those who confess that Jesus is the Son of God, and they abide in God. So we have known and believe the love that God has for us. God is love, and those who abide in love abide in God, and God abides in them" (1 Jn 4:13–16).

CONCLUSION

Contemporary Christian ethics tends to minimize or ignore the importance of particular moral actions for the person's relationship with God. This volume has offered an account of the acting person that endeavors better to understand how, by our acting, we involve ourselves with God—our first and final good—and the material and social goods that make up the proximate end of human life. Rubrics of intimacy with God, fidelity to God, truthfulness before God, and reconciliation in God exceed without eclipsing matters of moral culpability. Taken together they render the person as a creature who lives and moves and has her being in God, a sinner whose very springs of agency are preconditioned by sin, an agent whose actions redound upon her and thereby impact the concrete possibilities and limitations for her relationships, and a new creature forgiven in Christ and being converted by the grace of him who reconciles all things unto himself (Col 1:20).

NOTES

1. "Amish Mourn Slain Girls," *San Jose Mercury News*, October 6, 2006.
2. Bontrager, "Limits of Forgiveness," 4.
3. Ruth, *Forgiveness*, 42, 47.
4. Cristina Odone, "Why Do the Amish Ignore Reality?" *Observer* (London), October 8, 2006.
5. John Podhoretz, "Hating a Child Killer," *National Review*, October 5, 2006; Jeff Jacoby, "Undeserved Forgiveness," *Boston Globe*, October 8, 2006.

6. Kraybill, Nolt, and Weaver-Zercher, *Amish Grace*, 101.

7. Several Amish remarked that Roberts must have been ill or in tremendous pain to have acted as he did.

8. Bontrager, "Limits of Forgiveness," 7.

9. Ibid., 13.

10. See, e.g., Kraybill, Nolt, and Weaver-Zercher, *Amish Grace*, 132; Ruth, *Forgiveness*, 97.

11. Bontrager, "Limits of Forgiveness," 10.

12. Ruth, *Forgiveness*, 141–42.

13. See, e.g., Luskin, *Forgive for Good*; Enright, *Forgiveness Is a Choice*.

14. Couenhoven, "Forgiveness and Restoration."

15. Haber, *Forgiveness*.

16. Minas, "God and Forgiveness."

17. See L. Gregory Jones, *Embodying Forgiveness*.

18. Biggar, "Forgiveness in the Twentieth Century," 181.

19. See Volf, *Free of Charge*. Volf argues that the gratuity of God's forgiveness does not mean that it makes no demands upon us by way of response. See also Jankélévitch, *Forgiveness*.

20. Alison, *On Being Liked*.

21. Jones, *Embodying Forgiveness*, 16.

22. Alison, *On Being Liked*, 44.

23. Griswold, *Forgiveness*, 57.

24. Volf, *Exclusion and Embrace*.

25. Müller-Fahrenholz, *Art of Forgiveness*, 26.

26. Jones, *Embodying Forgiveness*, chaps. 4 and 5.

27. Bash, *Forgiveness and Christian Ethics*, 105.

28. Alison, *On Being Liked*, 38.

29. Bash, *Forgiveness and Christian Ethics*, 111.

30. Griswold takes issue with the terminology of "third-party" forgiveness; see *Forgiveness*, 141.

31. Gestrich, *Return of Splendor in the World*. See also Haber, *Forgiveness*.

32. Bash, *Forgiveness and Christian Ethics*, 140.

33. Griswold, *Forgiveness*, 135–46. Griswold states that forgiveness involves sentiment and therefore does not aptly describe the acceptance of a political apology, though political apologies may affect the sentiments of victims.

34. Bråkenhielm, *Forgiveness*, 54–55.

35. Shriver, "Is There Forgiveness in Politics?"

36. Müller-Fahrenholz, *Art of Forgiveness*, 28–29.

37. Ibid., ix.

38. Griswold, *Forgiveness*, 190–91.

39. United States Conference of Catholic Bishops, "Responsibility, Rehabilitation, and Restoration: A Catholic Perspective on Crime and Criminal Justice," under "Justice, Peace and Human Development," November 15, 2000, www.usccb.org/sdwp/criminal.shtml. See also two essays from Enright and North, *Exploring Forgiveness*: Dickey, "Forgiveness and Crime," and Couper, "Forgiveness in the Community."

40. Griswold reverses their significance, defining forgiveness as the more comprehensive restoration of victim and offender. Reconciliation is possible, he thinks, in minimal forms of noninterference (interpersonal and political) and cooperation (political) without forgiveness; see *Forgiveness*, 193.
41. Horsbrugh, "Forgiveness," 275.
42. Dillon, "Self-Forgiveness and Self-Respect," 53.
43. Holmgren, "Self-Forgiveness and Responsible Moral Agency." Nancy Snow says that self-forgiveness is a "second-best alternative to interpersonal self-forgiveness." It is second best because it falls short of full forgiveness or reconciliation between the offender and victim. Snow generally ignores the possibility that self-forgiveness might be good even when the victim forgives us, except to allow it as a possibility when our wrongdoing is so serious that we cannot fully atone for it; see "Self-Forgiveness," 75. See also the response to Snow: Mills, "On Self-Forgiveness and Moral Self-Representation."
44. Dillon, "Self-Forgiveness and Self-Respect," 58.
45. Ibid., 59.
46. Ibid., 61. Snow argues that self-forgiveness is good because it "restores our capability to carry on as functioning agent"; "Self-Forgiveness," 75.
47. Holmgren, "Self-Forgiveness and Responsible Moral Agency," 77.
48. Ibid., 79.
49. Dillon, "Self-Forgiveness and Self-Respect," 56. In the following discussion, references to pages in this work are given parenthetically in the text.
50. Dillon specifies recognition self-respect into three types. Interpersonal recognition self-respect affirms our equality with everyone given the intrinsic worth of all persons. Agentic recognition self-respect takes seriously one's responsibility "to manifest one's dignity as a person" and, accordingly, to regard "certain forms of thinking, feeling, acting as befitting her as a person and others as degrading or shameful." Finally, personal recognition self-respect relates to a particular, personal conception of life to which one holds oneself, but perhaps not others, accountable (66).
51. Dillon identifies a third form of self-respect, basal self-respect, as "a mode of perception and so interpretation" that is "intrinsic and unconditional, and so unlike merit, but more intimate and less inferential than Kantian dignity." "Secure basal self-respect involves an implicit confidence in the rightness of one's being; but weak or distorted basal valuing is fundamental insecurity about one's worth or a tacit view of oneself as not good enough or as nothing that reverberates throughout one's self-experiences and life" (68).
52. "Self-respecting self-forgiveness requires both that one not overlook or reinterpret the wrong in one's actions and self and thus betray one's values, and also that one overcome the modes of attitude, thought, behavior, attention, and desire that carry the verdict of one's values" (77).
53. "Transformative self-forgiveness is overcoming a self-reproachful stance to reach a self-respecting one"—in other words, not love, compassion, or peace with oneself, which do not rest on an appropriate understanding of self-reproach, but tempt us to bypass responsibility work and preclude the possibility of a warranted, ongoing self-reproach. Dillon does not

give a sufficient defense for this position. The outcome of transformative self-forgiveness is that recognition self-respect is intact and functioning properly (in its three forms) and that evaluative self-respect is "appropriate" (75). Mills also treats self-forgiveness as a matter of reconciling conflicting moral self-representations; see "On Self-Forgiveness and Moral Self-Representation," 405.

54. It is unclear why one's normative self-conception should have such force. Simply changing a normative self-conception for one's own comfort is a cheat, and discounting one's violation of it is a form of self-betrayal or failure of moral integrity. But Dillon's description of a normative self-conception makes it seem unmoored in anything except one's own endorsement of it.

55. Snow also suggests that in cases where one cannot atone fully, self-forgiveness allows oneself to carry on agentially while living with "unreconciled repentance." Again, it is "but a second-best alternative to interpersonal forgiveness." Snow, "Self-Forgiveness," 80.

56. Quoted in Murphy, "Jean Hampton on Immorality," 217.

57. Ibid., 218.

58. Dillon, "Self-Forgiveness and Self-Respect," 66.

59. Our recovery of self-respect also depends on what Dillon calls "basal self-respect" and "preservative self-forgiveness." Recall that basal self-respect is, like recognition self-respect, an affirmation of our intrinsic worth, but more "primordial and implicit." It structures recognition and evaluative self-respect and shapes our experience of ourselves. Basal self-respect explains why one could interpret certain happenings as confirming that one is defective in spite of evidence to the contrary. Preservative self-forgiveness is a character trait or disposition toward self-forgiveness, a ready tolerance for one's fallibility along with the belief that doing, wanting, and being in ways that are wrong do not mean that one isn't a good person. If we have preservative self-forgiveness we are less vulnerable to the sort of corrosive self-reproach that indicates damage to our evaluative self-respect. See ibid., 68 and 72–74, respectively.

60. Ibid., 65.

61. Augustine, *Confessions*, 43.

62. Groups can undergo similar experiences in the wake of corporate wrongdoing.

63. Griswold's volume does include his brief discussion of self-forgiveness and a larger exploration of forgiveness in political life.

64. For a collection of essays on narrative theology, see Hauerwas and Jones, *Why Narrative?* and, in particular, Michael Root's essay therein (pp. 263–78), "The Narrative Structure of Soteriology."

65. Hauerwas, "Salvation Even in Sin," 74.

66. John Paul II, "Reconciliation and Penance," nos. 11–12.

67. Christopher Jones, "Loosing and Binding," 51–52.

68. John Paul II, "Reconciliation and Penance," no. 9.

69. McFadyen, *Bound to Sin*, 8, 12.

70. Ibid., 44.

71. McFadyen, introduction, 7.

72. Schweiker, *Responsibility and Christian Ethics*.

BIBLIOGRAPHY

Alison, James. *Faith beyond Resentment: Fragments Catholic and Gay.* New York: Crossroad, 2001.

———. *The Joy of Being Wrong: Original Sin through Easter Eyes.* New York: Crossroad, 1998.

———. *On Being Liked.* New York: Crossroad, 2003.

Althaus, Catherine. "Human Embryo Transfer and the Theology of the Body." In *The Ethics of Embryo Adoption and the Catholic Tradition: Moral Arguments, Economic Reality, Social Analysis,* edited by Sarah-Vaughan Brakman and Darlene Fozard Weaver, 43–67. Dordrecht: Springer Netherlands, 2007.

Andolsen, Barbara. "Agape in Feminist Ethics." *Journal of Religious Ethics* 9, no. 1 (1981): 69–83.

Annas, Julia. *The Morality of Happiness.* New York: Oxford University Press, 1993.

Anscombe, G. E. M. "Modern Moral Philosophy." *Philosophy* 33 (1958): 1–19.

Appleby, Scott R. *The Ambivalence of the Sacred: Religion, Violence, and Reconciliation.* Lanham, MD: Rowman & Littlefield, 2000.

Aquinas, Thomas. *Summa theologiae.* Translated by Fathers of the English Dominican Province. New York: Benziger Brothers, 1947.

Augustine. "Against Lying." In *Saint Augustine: Treatises on Various Subjects,* vol. 14 of *Fathers of the Church,* edited by R. J. Deferrai, 125–79. Washington, DC: Catholic University of America Press, 1965.

———. *City of God.* Translated by Henry Bettenson. London: Penguin Books, 1987.

———. *Confessions.* Translated by Henry Chadwick. New York: Oxford University Press, 1991.

Avalos, Hector. *Fighting Words: The Origins of Religious Violence.* Amherst, NY: Prometheus Books, 2005.

Barth, Karl. *The Doctrine of Reconciliation.* Vol. 4 of *Church Dogmatics,* pt. 3, 1st half. Edinburgh: T. & T. Clark, 1961.

Bash, Anthony. *Forgiveness and Christian Ethics.* Cambridge: Cambridge University Press, 2007.

Bieler, Ludwig. *The Irish Penitentials.* Dublin: Dublin Institute for Advanced Studies, 1963.

Biggar, Nigel. "Forgiveness in the Twentieth Century." In McFadyen and Sarot, *Forgiveness and Truth,* 181–217.

Black, Rufus. *Christian Moral Realism: Natural Law, Narrative, Virtue and the Gospel.* Oxford: Oxford University Press, 2000.

Böckle, Franz. *Fundamental Moral Theology.* Translated by N. D. Smith. New York: Pueblo, 1980.

———. *Law and Conscience.* Translated by M. James Donnelly. New York: Sheed and Ward, 1966.

Bonhoeffer, Dietrich. *The Cost of Discipleship*. New York: Macmillan, 1966.

Bontrager, Herman. "The Limits of Forgiveness." In *Forgiveness: Selected Papers from the Forty-first Annual Conference of the Villanova University Theology Institute*, edited by Darlene Fozard Weaver, 1–13. Villanova, PA: Villanova University Press, 2010.

Bråkenhielm, Carl Reinhold. *Forgiveness*. Translated by Thor Hall. Minneapolis: Fortress, 1993.

Brakman, Sarah-Vaughan, and Darlene Fozard Weaver, eds. *The Ethics of Embryo Adoption and the Catholic Tradition: Moral Arguments, Economic Reality, Social Analysis*. Dordrecht: Springer Netherlands, 2007.

Buss, Sarah, and Lee Overton, eds. *Contours of Agency*. Cambridge, MA: Massachusetts Institute of Technology Press, 2002.

Cahill, Lisa Sowle. "Accent on the Masculine." In Wilkins, *Considering "Veritatis splendor*," 53–60.

———. *Sex, Gender and Christian Ethics*. Cambridge: Cambridge University Press, 1996.

———. *Theological Bioethics: Participation, Justice, and Change*. Washington, DC: Georgetown University Press, 2005.

Cates, Diana Fritz. *Aquinas on the Emotions: A Religious-Ethical Inquiry*. Washington, DC: Georgetown University Press, 2009.

Cavanaugh, William T. *The Myth of Religious Violence: Secular Ideology and the Roots of Modern Conflict*. New York: Oxford University Press, 2009.

Congar, Yves. "Theologians and the Magisterium in the West: From the Gregorian Reform to the Council of Trent." *Chicago Studies* 17, no. 2 (1978): 210–24.

Connery, John R. "Morality of Consequences: A Critical Appraisal." In Curran and McCormick, *Moral Norms and Catholic Tradition*, 244–66.

Couenhoven, Jesse. "Forgiveness and Restoration: A Theological Exploration." *Journal of Religion* 90, no. 2 (2010): 148–70.

Couper, David. "Forgiveness in the Community: Views from an Episcopal Priest and Former Chief of Police." In Enright and North, *Exploring Forgiveness*, 121–30.

Crisp, Roger, ed. *How Should One Live? Essays on the Virtues*. Oxford: Oxford University Press, 1998.

Curran, Charles E. *Catholic Moral Theology in the United States: A History*. Washington, DC: Georgetown University Press, 2008.

———. *The Catholic Moral Tradition Today: A Synthesis*. Washington, DC: Georgetown University Press, 1999.

———. *Directions in Catholic Social Ethics*. Notre Dame: University of Notre Dame, 1985.

———. *Directions in Fundamental Moral Theology*. Notre Dame: University of Notre Dame, 1985.

———. *Invincible Ignorance of the Natural Law According to Saint Alphonsus*. Rome: Academia Alfonsiana, 1961.

———. *Loyal Dissent: Memoir of a Catholic Theologian*. Washington, DC: Georgetown University Press, 2006.

———. "*Veritatis splendor*: A Revisionist Perspective," in *Veritatis Splendor: American Responses*, edited by Michael E. Allsopp and John J. O'Keefe, 224–43. Kansas City, MO: Sheed & Ward, 1995.

Curran, Charles E., and Richard A. McCormick, eds. *Moral Norms and Catholic Tradition.* Readings in Moral Theology 1. Mahwah, NJ: Paulist, 1979.

Dante. *Inferno.* Translated with commentary by Charles S. Singleton. Princeton, NJ: Princeton University Press, 1989.

Davidson, Donald. *Essays on Actions and Events.* New York: Oxford University Press, 2001.

Demmer, Klaus. *Living the Truth: A Theory of Action.* Cambridge: Cambridge University Press, 2004.

———. *Shaping the Moral Life: An Approach to Moral Theology.* Washington, DC: Georgetown University Press, 2000.

Dickey, Walter J. "Forgiveness and Crime: The Possibilities of Restorative Justice." In Enright and North, *Exploring Forgiveness*, 106–20.

Dillon, Robin S. "Self-Forgiveness and Self-Respect." *Ethics* 112, no. 1 (2001): 53–83.

Dych, William V. *Karl Rahner.* New York: Continuum, 1992.

Ellison, Marvin M. "Common Decency: A New Christian Sexual Ethics." In *Sexuality and the Sacred: Sources for Theological Reflection,* edited by James B. Nelson and Sandra P. Longfellow. Louisville, KY: Westminster / John Knox, 1994.

Endo, Shusaku. *Silence.* Translated by William Johnson. New York: Taplinger, 1980.

Enright, Robert D. *Forgiveness Is a Choice: A Step by Step Process for Resolving Anger and Restoring Hope.* Washington, DC: APA Life Tools, 2001.

Enright, Robert D., and Joanna North, eds. *Exploring Forgiveness.* Madison: University of Wisconsin Press, 1998.

Esposito, John L. *Unholy War: Terror in the Name of Islam.* New York: Oxford University Press, 2002.

Farley, Margaret. *Just Love: A Framework for Christian Sexual Ethics.* New York: Continuum, 2006.

———. *Personal Commitments: Beginning, Keeping, Changing.* New York: HarperSanFrancisco, 1986.

Farmer, Paul. *Pathologies of Power: Health, Human Rights, and the New War on the Poor.* Berkeley: University of California Press, 2003.

Finnis, John. *Fundamentals of Ethics.* Washington, DC: Georgetown University Press, 1983.

Flannery, Austin, ed. *Vatican Council II: The Conciliar and Post Conciliar Documents.* New rev. ed. Northport, NY: Costello, 1992.

Fleming, Julia. *Defending Probabilism: The Moral Theology of Juan Caramuel.* Washington, DC: Georgetown University Press, 2006.

———. "The Right to Reputation and the Preferential Option for the Poor." *Journal of the Society of Christian Ethics* 24, no. 1 (2004): 73–87.

Fletcher, Joseph. *Situation Ethics: The New Morality.* Philadelphia: Westminster Press, 1966.

Foot, Philippa. *Virtues and Vices.* Oxford: Blackwell, 1978.

Frankfurt, Harry. *The Importance of What We Care About.* Cambridge: Cambridge University Press, 1988.

Fuchs, Josef. "The Absoluteness of Behavioral Moral Norms." In *Personal Responsibility and Christian Morality,* 115–52. Washington, DC: Georgetown University Press, 1983.

———. *Christian Morality: The Word Becomes Flesh.* Washington, DC: Georgetown University Press, 1987.

————. "Das Probleme Todsünde." *Stimmen der Zeit* 212 (February 1994): 75–86.

————. "Good Acts and Good Persons." In Wilkins, *Considering "Veritatis splendor,"* 21–26.

Gaffney, James. "The Pope on Proportionalism." In *Veritatis Splendor: American Responses,* edited by Michael E. Allsopp and John J. O'Keefe, 60–71. Kansas City, MO: Sheed & Ward, 1995.

Gallagher, John. *Time Past, Time Future: An Historical Study of Catholic Moral Theology.* New York: Paulist, 1990.

George, Robert P. *Natural Law and Moral Inquiry.* Washington, DC: Georgetown University Press, 1998.

Gestrich, Christof. *The Return of Splendor in the World: The Christian Doctrine of Sin and Forgiveness.* Translated by Donald Bloesch. Grand Rapids, MI: Wm. B. Eerdmans, 1997.

Gilleman, Gerard. *The Primacy of Charity in Moral Theology.* Westminster, MD: Newman Press, 1959.

Gilligan, Carol. *In a Different Voice: Psychological Theory and Women's Development.* 6th ed. Cambridge, MA: Harvard University Press, 1993.

Ginet, Carl. *On Action.* New York: Cambridge University Press, 1990.

Goldstein, Valerie Saiving. "The Human Situation: A Feminine View." *Journal of Religion* 40 (1960): 100–112.

Graham, Mark E. "Rethinking Morality's Relationship to Salvation: Josef Fuchs, S.J., on Moral Goodness." *Theological Studies* 64, no. 4 (2003): 750–72.

Grey, Mary. "Falling into Freedom: Searching for New Interpretations of Sin in a Secular Society." *Scottish Journal of Theology* 47, no. 2 (1994): 223–43.

Griffiths, Paul J. *Lying: An Augustinian Theology of Duplicity.* Grand Rapids, MI: Brazos, 2004.

Grisez, Germain. *Christian Moral Principles.* Chicago: Franciscan Herald, 1983.

Grisez, Germain, and Russell Shaw. *Fulfillment in Christ: A Summary of Christian Moral Principles.* Notre Dame: University of Notre Dame Press, 1991.

Griswold, Charles L. *Forgiveness: A Philosophical Exploration.* Cambridge: Cambridge University Press, 2007.

Gudorf, Christine E. *Body, Sex, and Pleasure: Reconstructing Christian Sexual Ethics.* Cleveland: Pilgrim, 1994.

Gustafson, James M. *Protestant and Roman Catholic Ethics: Prospects for Rapprochement.* Chicago: University of Chicago Press, 1978.

Haber, Joram Graf. *Forgiveness.* Savage, MD: Rowman & Littlefield, 1991.

Hall, Amy Laura. *Conceiving Parenthood: American Protestantism and the Spirit of Reproduction.* Grand Rapids, MI: William B. Eerdmans, 2008.

Häring, Bernard. *The Law of Christ.* 3 vols. Translated by Edwin G. Kasper. Westminster, MD: Newman Press, 1966.

————. "A Theological Evaluation." In *The Morality of Abortion: Legal and Historical Perspectives,* edited by John T. Noonan Jr., 123–45. Cambridge, MA: Harvard University Press, 1970.

Harrington, Daniel J., and James F. Keenan. *Jesus and Virtue Ethics: Building Bridges between New Testament Studies and Moral Theology.* Lanham, MD: Sheed & Ward, 2002.

Hauerwas, Stanley. "Going Forward by Looking Back." In *Sanctify Them in the Truth: Holiness Exemplified*, 93–103. Nashville: Abingdon, 1998.

———. *The Peaceable Kingdom: A Primer in Christian Ethics*. Notre Dame: University of Notre Dame Press, 1983.

———. "Salvation Even in Sin: Learning to Speak Truthfully about Ourselves." In *Sanctify Them in the Truth: Holiness Exemplified*, 61–74. Nashville: Abingdon, 1998.

———. "The Significance of Vision: Toward an Aesthetic Ethic," in *Vision and Virtue*, 30–47.

———. "Toward an Ethics of Character," in *Vision and Virtue*, 48–67.

———. *Vision and Virtue*. Notre Dame: Fides / Claretian, 1974.

Hauerwas, Stanley, and L. Gregory Jones, eds. *Why Narrative?* Eugene, OR: Wipf & Stock, 1997.

Hauerwas, Stanley, and Charles Pinches. *Christians among the Virtues: Theological Conversations with Ancient and Modern Ethics*. Notre Dame: University of Notre Dame Press, 1997.

Hollenbach, David. "Human Rights and Women's Rights: Initiatives and Interventions in the Name of Universality." In *A Just and True Love: Feminism at the Frontiers of Theological Ethics; Essays in Honor of Margaret A. Farley*, edited by Maura A. Ryan and Brian F. Linnane, 47–74. Notre Dame: University of Notre Dame Press, 2007.

Holmgren, Margaret. "Self-Forgiveness and Responsible Moral Agency." *Journal of Value Inquiry* 32 (1988): 75–91.

Hoose, Bernard. "Circumstances, Intentions and Intrinsically Evil Acts." In Selling and Jans, *Splendor of Accuracy*, 153–68.

———. *Proportionalism: The American Debate and Its European Roots*. Washington, DC: Georgetown University Press, 1987.

Hornsby, Jennifer. "Agency and Actions." In Hyman and Steward, *Agency and Action*, 1–23.

Horsbrugh, H. J. N. "Forgiveness." *Canadian Journal of Philosophy* 4, no. 2 (1974): 269–82.

Hursthouse, Rosalind. *On Virtue Ethics*. Oxford: Oxford University Press, 1999.

Hyman, John, and Helen Steward, eds. *Agency and Action*. Cambridge: Cambridge University Press, 2004.

Jankélévitch, Vladimir. *Forgiveness*. Translated by Andrew Kelley. Chicago: University of Chicago Press, 2005.

Janssens, Louis. "Ontic Evil and Moral Evil." In Curran and McCormick, *Moral Norms and Catholic Tradition*, 40–93.

———. "Theology and Proportionality: Thoughts about the Encyclical *Veritatis splendor*." In Selling and Jans, *Splendor of Accuracy*, 99–113.

Jeanrond, Werner. *Theology of Love*. London: T. & T. Clark International, 2010.

John Paul II. *Veritatis splendor*. Boston: St. Paul Books and Media, 1993.

Johnson, Elizabeth. *She Who Is: The Mystery of God in Feminist Theological Discourse*. New York: Crossroad, 2002.

Johnstone, Brian V. "The Revisionist Project in Roman Catholic Moral Theology." *Studies in Christian Ethics* 5, no. 2 (1992): 18–31.

Jones, Christopher. "Loosing and Binding: The Liturgical Mediation of Forgiveness." In McFadyen and Sarot, *Forgiveness and Truth*, 31–52.

Jones, L. Gregory. *Embodying Forgiveness: A Theological Analysis.* Grand Rapids, MI: W. B. Eerdmans, 1995.

Jones, Serene. *Feminist Theory and Christian Theology: Cartographies of Grace.* Minneapolis: Augsburg Fortress, 2000.

Juergensmeyer, Mark. *Terror in the Mind of God: The Global Rise of Religious Violence.* 3rd ed. Berkeley: University of California Press, 2003.

Kaczor, Christopher. *Proportionalism and the Natural Law Tradition.* Washington, DC: Catholic University of America Press, 2002.

Kalbian, Aline H. "Where Have All the Proportionalists Gone?" *Journal of Religious Ethics* 30, no. 1 (2002): 3–22.

Keenan, James F. "Can a Wrong Action Be Good? The Development of Theological Opinion on Erroneous Conscience." *Église et théologie* 24 (1993): 205–19.

———. *Goodness and Rightness in Thomas Aquinas's "Summa theologiae."* Washington, DC: Georgetown University Press, 1992.

———. *Moral Wisdom: Lessons and Texts from the Catholic Tradition.* Lanham, MD: Sheed & Ward, 2004.

———. "Spirituality and Morality: What's the Difference?" In *Method and Catholic Moral Theology: The Ongoing Reconstruction,* edited by Todd A. Salzman, 87–102. Omaha: Creighton University Press, 1999.

———. "Thomas Aquinas's Concept of Sin." *Heythrop Journal* 25 (1994): 401–20.

———. "Virtue Ethics." In *Christian Ethics: An Introduction,* edited by Bernard Hoose, 84–94. Collegeville, MN: Liturgical, 1998.

Kelly, Geffrey B. *Karl Rahner: Theologian of the Graced Search for Meaning.* Making of Modern Theology. Minneapolis: Augsburg Fortress, 1992.

Kelsey, David H. "Whatever Happened to the Doctrine of Sin?" *Theology Today* 50 (1993): 169–78.

Kilby, Karen. *Karl Rahner: Theology and Philosophy.* New York: Routledge, 2004.

Kimball, Charles. *When Religion Becomes Evil.* San Francisco: HarperSanFrancisco, 2002.

Klemm, David E., and William Schweiker. *Religion and the Human Future: An Essay on Theological Humanism.* Oxford: Blackwell, 2009.

Klubertanz, George P. *St. Thomas Aquinas on Analogy: A Textual Analysis and Systematic Synthesis.* Chicago: Loyola University Press, 1960.

Kopfensteiner, Thomas R. "The Theory of the Fundamental Option." In *Christian Ethics: An Introduction,* edited by Bernard Hoose, 123–34. Collegeville, MN: Liturgical, 1998.

Kotva, Joseph. *The Christian Case for Virtue Ethics.* Washington, DC: Georgetown University Press, 1996.

Kraybill, Donald B., Steven M. Nolt, and David L. Weaver-Zercher. *Amish Grace: How Forgiveness Transcended Tragedy.* San Francisco: John Wiley & Sons, 2007.

LaCugna, Catherine. "God in Communion with Us." In *Freeing Theology: The Essentials of Theology in Feminist Perspective,* edited by Catherine LaCugna, 83–115. San Francisco: HarperSanFrancisco, 1993.

Lincoln, Bruce. *Holy Terrors: Thinking about Religion after September 11.* Chicago: University of Chicago Press, 2003.

Long, Duane Stephen. "Moral Theology." In *Oxford Handbook of Systematic Theology*, edited by John Webster, Kathryn Tanner, and Iain Torrance, 456–75. Oxford: Oxford University Press, 2007.

Losinger, Anton. *The Anthropological Turn: The Human Orientation of the Theology of Karl Rahner.* Translated by Daniel O. Dahlstrom. Moral Philosophy and Moral Theology 2. New York: Fordham University Press, 2000.

Lottin, Dom Odon. *Principes de morale.* 2 vols. Louvain: Éditions de l'Abbaye de Mont César, 1947.

Loughlin, Gerard. *Telling God's Story: Bible, Church, and Narrative Theology.* Cambridge: Cambridge University Press, 1996.

Luskin, Frederic. *Forgive for Good: A Proven Prescription for Health and Happiness.* New York: HarperCollins, 2002.

Luther, Martin. "The Freedom of a Christian." Translated by W. A. Lambert. In vol. 31 of *Luther's Works*, edited by Harold J. Grimm, 364–71. Philadelphia: Fortress Press, 1957.

MacIntyre, Alasdair. *After Virtue.* 2nd ed. London: Duckworth, 1985.

———. *Three Rival Versions of Moral Enquiry: Encyclopaedia, Genealogy, and Tradition.* South Bend, IN: University of Notre Dame, 1990.

Mahoney, John. *The Making of Moral Theology.* Oxford: Oxford University Press, 1989.

Mannion, Gerard, Richard Gaillardetz, Jan Kerkhofs, and Kenneth Wilson, eds. *Readings in Church Authority: Gifts and Challenges for Contemporary Catholicism.* Aldershot: Ashgate, 2003.

McCormick, Richard A. "A Commentary on the Commentaries." In *Doing Evil to Achieve Good*, edited by Richard A. McCormick and Paul Ramsey, 193–267. Chicago: Loyola University Press, 1978.

———. "Killing the Patient." In Wilkins, *Considering "Veritatis splendor,"* 14–20.

———. "Some Early Reactions to *Veritatis splendor*." In *John Paul II and Moral Theology*, Readings in Moral Theology 10, edited by Charles E. Curran and Richard A. McCormick, 5–34. New York: Paulist, 1998.

McFadyen, Alistair. *Bound to Sin: Abuse, Holocaust and the Christian Doctrine of Sin.* Cambridge: Cambridge University Press, 2000.

———. Introduction to McFadyen and Sarot, *Forgiveness and Truth*, 1–14.

McFadyen, Alistair, and Marcel Sarot, eds. *Forgiveness and Truth: Explorations in Contemporary Theology.* New York: T. & T. Clark, 2001.

McKenny, Gerald P. "Responsibility." In Meilaender and Werpehowski, *Oxford Handbook of Theological Ethics*, 237–53.

McKim, D. K., ed. *The Cambridge Companion to Martin Luther.* Cambridge: Cambridge University Press, 2003.

Meilaender, Gilbert, and William Werpehowski, eds. *The Oxford Handbook of Theological Ethics.* Oxford: Oxford University Press, 2005.

Metz, Johann Baptist. *Faith in History and Society: Toward a Practical Fundamental Theology.* Translated by David Smith. New York: Seabury, 1979.

Miller, Vincent. "Consumer Culture and Morality: A Hidden Challenge." In *God and Mammon*, vol. 40 of *Proceedings of the Villanova University Theology Institute*, edited by Darlene Fozard Weaver, 37–54. Villanova, PA: Villanova University Press, 2007.

———. *Consuming Religion: Christian Faith and Practice in a Consumer Culture.* New York: Continuum, 2005.

Mills, Jon K. "On Self-Forgiveness and Moral Self-Representation." *Journal of Value Inquiry* 29 (1995): 405–6.

Minas, Anne C. "God and Forgiveness." *Philosophical Quarterly* 25, no. 99 (1975): 138–50.

Monti, Joseph. *Arguing about Sex: The Rhetoric of Christian Sexual Morality.* Albany: State University of New York Press, 1995.

Müller-Fahrenholz, Geiko. *The Art of Forgiveness: Theological Reflections on Healing and Reconciliation.* Geneva: WCC, 1997.

Murdoch, Iris. *Metaphysics as a Guide to Morals.* New York: Allen Lane, 1993.

Murphy, Jeffrie G. "Jean Hampton on Immorality, Self-Hatred, and Self-Forgiveness." *Philosophical Studies* 89, nos. 2–3 (1998): 215–36.

Murphy, William F., Jr. "Aquinas on the Object and Evaluation of the Moral Act: Rhonheimer's Approach and Some Recent Interlocutors." *Josephinum Journal of Theology* 15, no. 2 (2008): 205–42.

Nelson, James B. "Love, Power, and Justice in Sexual Ethics." In *Christian Ethics: Problems and Prospects*, edited by Lisa Sowle Cahill and James F. Childress. Cleveland: Pilgrim, 1996.

Niebuhr, H. Richard. "Man the Sinner." *Journal of Religion* 15 (1935): 272–80.

———. *The Responsible Self: An Essay in Christian Moral Philosophy.* San Francisco: Harper San Francisco, 1963.

Noddings, Nel. *Caring: A Feminine Approach to Ethics and Moral Education.* Berkeley: University of California Press, 1984.

Nussbaum, Martha. *Frontiers of Justice: Disability, Nationality, Species Membership.* Cambridge, MA: Harvard University Press, 2006.

———. *Women and Human Development: The Capabilities Approach.* Cambridge: Cambridge University Press, 2001.

Nussbaum, Martha, and Amartya Sen. *The Quality of Life.* Oxford: Clarendon, 1993.

O'Donovan, Oliver. "A Summons to Reality." In Wilkins, *Considering "Veritatis splendor,"* 41–45.

Odozor, Paulinus Ikechukwu. *Moral Theology in an Age of Renewal: A Study of the Catholic Tradition since Vatican II.* Notre Dame: University of Notre Dame Press, 2003.

O'Keefe, Mark. *Becoming Good, Becoming Holy: On the Relationship of Christian Ethics and Spirituality.* New York: Paulist, 1995.

———. "Social Sin and the Fundamental Option." *Irish Theological Quarterly* 58, no. 2 (1992): 85–94.

Ottati, Douglas. *Jesus Christ and Christian Vision.* Louisville, KY: Westminster / John Knox, 1996.

Outka, Gene, and Paul Ramsey, eds. *Norm and Context in Christian Ethics.* New York: Scribner, 1968.

Park, Andrew Sung. *The Wounded Heart of God: The Asian Concept of Han and the Christian Doctrine of Sin.* Nashville: Abingdon, 1993.

Parsons, Susan Frank, ed. *The Cambridge Companion to Feminist Theology.* Cambridge: Cambridge University Press, 2002.

———. *Feminism and Christian Ethics.* Cambridge: Cambridge University Press, 1996.

Pascal, Blaise. *Provincial Letters*. Translated by J. Krailsheimer. London: Penguin, 1995.

Patrick, Anne E. *Liberating Conscience: Feminist Explorations in Catholic Moral Theology*. New York: Continuum, 1996.

Pieper, Josef. *Faith, Hope, Love*. San Francisco: Ignatius, 1997.

Pinches, Charles R. *Theology and Action: After Theory in Christian Ethics*. Grand Rapids, MI: William B. Eerdmans, 2002.

Plaskow, Judith. *Sex, Sin and Grace: Women's Experience and the Theologies of Reinhold Niebuhr and Paul Tillich*. Lanham, MD: University Press of America, 1980.

Porter, Jean. "'Direct' and 'Indirect' in Grisez's Moral Theory." *Theological Studies* 57 (1996): 611–32.

———. "The Moral Act in *Veritatis splendor* and Aquinas's *Summa theologiae*: A Comparative Analysis." In *The Historical Development of Fundamental Moral Theology in the United States*, Readings in Moral Theology 11, edited by Charles E. Curran and Richard A. McCormick, 219–41. New York: Paulist, 1999.

———. *Moral Action and Christian Ethics*. Cambridge: Cambridge University Press, 1995.

———. *Nature as Reason: A Thomistic Theory of Natural Law*. Grand Rapids, MI: Eerdmans, 2005.

———. "Salvific Love and Charity: A Comparison of the Thought of Karl Rahner and Thomas Aquinas." In *The Love Commandments: Essays in Christian Ethics and Moral Philosophy*, edited by Edmund N. Santurri and William Werpehowski, 240–60. Washington, DC: Georgetown University Press, 1992.

———. "Virtue." In Meilaender and Werpehowski, *Oxford Handbook of Theological Ethics*, 205–19.

———. "Virtue and Sin: The Connection of Virtues and the Case of the Flawed Saint." *Journal of Religion* 75 (1995): 521–39.

———. "The Virtue of Justice (IIa IIae, qq. 58–122)." In *The Ethics of Aquinas*, edited by Stephen Pope, 272–86. Washington, DC: Georgetown University Press, 1983.

Rahner, Karl. *Foundations of Christian Faith: An Introduction to the Idea of Christianity*. Translated by William V. Dych. New York: Crossroad, 1993.

———. *Hearer of the Word*. New York: Continuum, 1994.

———. "Theology of Freedom." In *Theological Investigations*, vol. 6, 178–96. Baltimore: Helicon, 1969.

Ramsey, Paul. *Basic Christian Ethics*. Louisville, KY: Westminster / John Knox, 1993.

———. "The Case of Joseph Fletcher and Joseph Fletcher's Cases." In Outka and Ramsey, *Norm and Context in Christian Ethics*, 145–225.

———. "The Case of the Curious Exception." In Outka and Ramsey, *Norm and Context in Christian Ethics*, 67–135.

Rauschenbusch, Walter. *A Theology for the Social Gospel*. New York: Macmillan, 1917.

Rhonheimer, Martin. "Intentional Actions and the Meaning of Object: A Reply to Richard McCormick." *Thomist* 59, no. 2 (1995): 279–311.

———. "'Intrinsically Evil Acts' and the Moral Viewpoint: Clarifying a Central Teaching of *Veritatis Splendor*." *Thomist* 58, no. 1 (1994): 1–39.

———. *Natural Law and Practical Reason: A Thomist View of Moral Autonomy*. New York: Fordham University Press, 2000.

Roberts, Christopher C. *Creation and Covenant: The Significance of Sexual Difference in the Moral Theology of Marriage.* New York: T. & T. Clark International, 2007.

Robinson, Marilynne. *Gilead.* New York: Farrar, Straus, & Giroux, 2004.

Rogers, Eugene F. *Sexuality and the Christian Body: Their Way into the Triune God.* Oxford: Blackwell, 1999.

Rudy, Kathy. *Sex and the Church: Gender, Homosexuality, and the Transformation of Christian Ethics.* Boston: Beacon, 1997.

Ruth, John L. *Forgiveness: A Legacy of the West Nickel Mines Amish School.* Scottdale, PA: Herald, 2007.

Ryan, Maura. *Ethics and Economics of Assisted Reproduction: The Cost of Longing.* Washington, DC: Georgetown University Press, 2003.

Salzman, Todd A., and Michael G. Lawler. *The Sexual Person: Toward a Renewed Catholic Anthropology.* Washington, DC: Georgetown University Press, 2008.

Schüller, Bruno. "Direct/Indirect Killing." In Curran and McCormick, *Moral Norms and Catholic Tradition,* 138–57.

Schwartz, Regina. *The Curse of Cain: The Violent Legacy of Monotheism.* Chicago: University of Chicago Press, 1997.

Schweiker, William. "One World, Many Moralities." In *Power, Value, and Conviction,* 21–32.

———. *Power, Value, and Conviction: Theological Ethics in the Postmodern Age.* Cleveland: Pilgrim, 1998.

———. "Radical Interpretation and Moral Responsibility." In *Power, Value, and Conviction,* 91–110.

———. *Responsibility and Christian Ethics.* Cambridge: Cambridge University Press, 1995.

Selling, Joseph A. "The Context and the Arguments of *Veritatis splendor.*" In Selling and Jans, *Splendor of Accuracy,* 11–70.

Selling, Joseph A., and Jans Jans, eds. *Splendor of Accuracy: An Examination of the Assertions Made by "Veritatis splendor."* Grand Rapids, MI: William B. Eerdmans, 1994.

Sells, Michael. *The Bridge Betrayed: Religion and Genocide in Bosnia.* Berkeley: University of California Press, 1998.

Shriver, Donald W. "Is There Forgiveness in Politics? Germany, Vietnam, and America." In Enright and North, *Exploring Forgiveness,* 131–49.

Snow, Nancy E. "Self-Forgiveness." *Journal of Value Inquiry* 27 (1993): 75–80.

Tessman, Lisa. *Burdened Virtues: Virtue Ethics for Liberatory Struggles.* New York: Oxford University Press, 2005.

Vacek, Edward Collins. *Love, Human and Divine: The Heart of Christian Ethics.* Washington, DC: Georgetown University Press, 1996.

———. "Proportionalism: One View of the Debate." *Theological Studies* 46 (1985): 287–314.

Volf, Miroslav. *Exclusion and Embrace: A Theological Exploration of Identity, Otherness, and Reconciliation.* Nashville: Abingdon, 1996.

———. *Free of Charge: Giving and Forgiving in a Culture Stripped of Grace.* Grand Rapids, MI: Zondervan, 2005.

Walter, James. "The Foundation and Formulation of Norms." In *Moral Theology: Challenges for the Future,* edited by Charles E. Curran, 125–54. Mahwah, NJ: Paulist, 1990.

Weaver, Darlene Fozard. "Death." In Meilaender and Werpehowski, *Oxford Handbook of Theological Ethics*, 254–70.

———. "Intimacy with God and Self-Relation in the World: The Fundamental Option and Categorical Activity." In *New Wine, New Wineskins: A Next Generation Reflects on Key Issues in Catholic Moral Theology*, edited by William C. Mattison, 143–63. Oxford: Sheed & Ward, 2005.

———. *Self Love and Christian Ethics.* Cambridge: Cambridge University Press, 2002.

———. "Taking Sin Seriously." *Journal of Religious Ethics* 31, no. 1 (2003): 45–74.

Westberg, Daniel. "Good and Evil in Human Acts (Ia–IIae, qq. 18–21)." In *The Ethics of Aquinas*, edited by Stephen J. Pope, 90–102. Washington, DC: Georgetown University Press, 2002.

Wilkins, John, ed. *Considering "Veritatis splendor."* Cleveland: Pilgrim, 1994.

Wogaman, J. Philip. *Christian Ethics: A Historical Introduction.* Louisville, KY: Westminster / John Knox, 1993.

Wojtyla, Karol. *The Acting Person.* Translated by Andrzej Potocki. Edited by Anna-Teresa Tymieniecka. Dordrecht: D. Reidel, 1979.

INDEX

action theory, 145

Aeterni patris, 12

agency, 1, 2, 8, 15, 18, 20, 27, 32, 36, 38, 40, 49, 51, 53, 57, 65, 71, 80, 81, 87, 90, 93, 95, 99, 104, 110, 111–21, 131, 141, 142, 143, 145, 161, 166, 172, 175, 176, 177, 181, 198

agnosticism about moral acts, 2, 8, 23, 26, 27–28, 40, 41, 42–45, 50, 65, 71, 93, 99, 143

Alighieri, Dante, 55–57, 58

Alison, James, 171

Anscombe, G. E. M., 19

Augustine, Saint, 52, 53–54, 66, 118, 134, 139, 140, 142, 158n14, 182

Barth, Karl, 15, 132–33, 134, 135–36, 138, 140, 157

Bash, Anthony, 171–72

basic goods theory, 24, 25–26, 104–5

Bentham, Jeremy, 145

Biggar, Nigel, 168

Böckle, Franz, 41, 42, 60n16, 70, 78

Bonhoeffer, Dietrich, 14–15

Bontrager, Herman, 163–64, 165

Boyle, Joseph, M., 24

Bråkenhielm, Carl Reinhold, 172

Cahill, Lisa, 16, 21, 102

Calvin, John, 82

canon law, 12, 35

Catholic ethics, 7, 8, 9, 14, 15, 22–23, 31, 33, 34, 48, 49, 68, 79, 143, 146

    act-centered vs. person-centered, 1, 9–23, 31, 93, 143, 147, 166

    manualist 1, 11–12, 23, 34, 42, 101

    penitential handbooks of, 9–10, 23, 35

    revisionist, 2, 13, 18, 23, 24, 26, 68–79, 86, 87, 88, 89, 90n2, 90n15, 91n15, 92n31, 92n42, 98, 99, 101–7, 109, 111–12, 146, 150

    traditionalist, 2, 13, 18, 24, 26, 92n42, 98, 102–3, 104, 106, 111–12

character, 6, 18, 20, 21, 36, 50, 80, 96–97, 98, 122, 168, 176, 177, 179–80, 187

charity, 3, 13, 51, 74, 77, 97, 110, 138, 140, 141, 142, 158

choice, 21, 25, 26, 35, 41, 50, 51, 53, 68, 69, 70–73, 74, 75–78, 80, 87, 89, 90, 93, 101, 103, 106, 107, 109, 111, 113, 114, 116, 121, 122, 124, 142, 143, 178

church, 3, 8, 17, 131, 158, 161, 162, 186, 187

circumstances, 19, 26, 39, 69, 74, 76–77, 102, 107, 114, 146

community, 6, 12, 19, 20, 21, 22, 38, 47–48, 90, 94, 95, 106, 120, 126, 151, 156–57, 158, 164, 166, 176, 186–87

comparative moral judgments, 167, 171, 189, 190, 193–94

confession, 172–73, 187, 188 of Christ, 3, 7, 131, 138–39, 142 of sins, 9–11, 12, 50, 59, 93, 131, 138–39, 140

conscience, 10, 12, 20, 37, 38, 91n15, 192

consequences, 26, 75, 76, 101, 103, 104, 116, 145

contraception, 18, 23–24. See also *Humanae vitae*

conversion, 40, 53, 71, 113, 156, 188, 195

covenant, 93, 94, 95, 97, 122, 137, 155

culpability, 2, 13, 27, 32, 33, 34, 39, 40–45, 49–50, 52, 55, 59, 65, 112, 116, 117, 161, 164, 166, 169, 170, 175, 195

Curran, Charles E., 12, 35–41, 42, 43, 44, 49, 51, 59, 60n16, 92n42

Demmer, Klaus, 70, 133, 135, 157

Dillon, Robin, 178–82, 183, 185, 197nn50–53, 198n54, 198n59

dispositions, 16, 23, 31, 49, 53, 54, 55, 58, 77, 80, 96–97, 141, 148, 176

211

intrinsically evil acts, 23, 24, 26, 39, 75, 77, 91n15, 101–2, 103
irreverence, 2, 121, 131, 132, 136–38, 140, 141, 142, 155, 157

Janssens, Louis, 99, 100
John Paul II, Pope, 23, 24, 26, 44, 60n9, 61n16, 68, 69, 71–73, 74–76, 77, 78–79, 88, 89, 91n15, 92n31, 101, 102, 188, 189
Jones, Gregory, 171
justice, 7, 16–17, 20, 21, 26, 31, 88, 141
forgiveness and, 164, 166, 172, 173
restorative, 173–74

Kaczor, Christopher, 99, 101
Kant, Immanuel, 19, 145
Keenan, James, 11, 19–20, 40, 41, 42, 45, 50–51, 60n16, 77, 110, 111
Kholberg, Lawrence, 20
Knauer, Peter, 24
Kopfensteiner, Thomas, 72
Kotva, Joseph, 19

law, 1–12, 13, 31, 41, 42, 44, 97, 139
Leo XIII, Pope, 12
Lumen gentium, 13
Luther, Martin, 14

MacIntyre, Alasdair, 19, 20, 21
magisterium, 11, 14, 28n12, 75, 146
Mahoney, John, 9, 10, 35
Maréchal, Joseph, 70
Maritain, Jacques, 69
McCormick, Richard, 25, 76–77, 100, 101–2
McFadyen, Alistair, 31, 32, 33, 48, 51–52, 117, 118–19, 134–35, 193
McKenny, Gerald, 23, 115–18
Miller, Vincent, 113–14
Müller-Fahrenholz, Geiko, 171, 172–73
moral act, 2, 7, 25, 26, 40–47, 49, 55, 58, 59, 68–73, 74–79, 88, 96–97, 98–111, 145, 146, 195
as historical, particular, provisional, 2, 34, 56–58, 65, 73, 78, 88–89, 121, 155–56
as intentional, 103–9, 146, 147, 150, 156
as right or wrong, 18, 19, 24–25, 26, 38,

39, 40, 41, 42–45, 49, 87, 99, 100, 108, 111, 145
moral concepts, 46–49, 56, 102, 103, 144–50, 156
moral realism, 131, 158, 193–94
moral subjectivism, 2, 44, 65, 103, 143
motivation, 50, 51, 55, 86, 110, 118, 134, 135, 182, 190
motive, 14, 39, 41, 42, 44, 69, 74, 77–78, 87, 98, 101, 109, 111, 156
Murphy, Jeffrie, 181

naming, 1, 3, 8, 59–60, 108, 122, 125, 126, 131, 132, 139, 142–50, 156–57, 158
narrative, 2, 7, 19, 20, 21, 31, 49, 67, 80–81, 106, 139, 145, 156
natural law, 7, 24, 25, 35, 36–37, 38, 106
Niebuhr, H. Richard, 35, 53
Niebuhr, Reinhold, 15
Noddings, Nel, 20, 21
norms and principles, 20, 24, 26, 37, 38, 39, 42, 88, 89, 101–2, 103, 104, 125

object (of moral act), 39, 74, 76–78, 96, 98, 101, 107–10, 146, 147
O'Donovan, Oliver, 150
Odozor, Paulinus, 100
Optatum totius, 13

pastoral care, 9, 11, 27, 61n21, 37, 40, 45, 59, 126
Paul VI, Pope, 23–24
Paul, Saint, 5, 7, 27, 53, 97–98, 112
physicalism, 16, 59, 74, 75–76
Pinches, Charles, 63n62, 76, 102, 106, 107, 145–47, 148–49, 150
Porter, Jean, 22, 62n41, 62n46, 103, 104–5, 149
pragmatic atheism, 134–35, 157, 193
premoral values, 24–25, 33, 39, 41, 44, 72, 99–101, 102, 106, 109, 111, 146
principle monism, 145–46
probabilism, 12
proportionalism, 38, 75, 90n2, 90n15. *See also* Catholic ethics, revisionist
proportionate reason, 25, 26, 39, 100–101, 111